The Nature of Political Philosophy

The Nature of Political Philosophy

And Other Studies and Commentaries

James V. Schall, SJ

Edited by
William McCormick, SJ

Foreword by José Maria J. Yulo

The Catholic University of America Press
Washington, D.C.

The paper used in this publication meets the minimum requirements of
American National Standards for Information Science—Permanence of Paper
for Printed Library Materials, ANSI Z39.48-1984.

∞

Cataloging-in-Publication Data available from the Library of Congress
ISBN: 978-0-8132-3575-2
eISBN: 978-0-8132-3576-9

Anyone who wishes to judge impartially of the legitimacy of the prospects of the great design of modern man to erect the City of Man on what appear to him to be the ruins of the City of God must familiarize himself with the teachings, and especially the political teachings, of the Catholic Church, which is certainly the most powerful antagonist of that modern design.

—Leo Strauss, *What Is Political Philosophy? And Other Studies*

If happiness is an activity in accordance with virtue, it is reasonable that it should be in accordance with the highest virtue; and this will be that of the best thing in us. Whether it be reason or something else that is this element which is thought to be our natural ruler and guide and to take thought of things noble and divine, whether it be also itself divine or only the most divine element in us, the activity of this in accordance with its proper virtue will be perfect happiness. That this activity be contemplative, we have already said.

—Aristotle, *Ethics*, 1177a12–19

The question I am posing here is *not* to know, in general, what to do when everything else is said. It needs to be precisely: what to do when it is God who has said everything he has to say. And here, this "everything" signifies nothing less than everything that is (creation), or everything else God himself is.

—Rémi Brague, *On the God of the Christians*

It is our duty to act virtuously and wisely. . . . We must beware of the danger, which is now becoming greater than it ever was before, of trying to escape "into anti-social dreams." One cannot but agree with this sober and manly conclusion.

—Leo Strauss, "Appraisal of Yves Simon's *The Philosophy of Democratic Government*," in *What Is Political Philosophy? And Other Studies*

Instead of divine consolation, they (modern philosophers) want changes that will redeem suffering by removing it: not by redemption through suffering, but redemption from suffering is their watchword; not expectation of divine assistance, but the humanization of man by man is their goal.

—Joseph Ratzinger, *Dogma und Verkündigung*, quoted in *Co-Workers of the Truth*

I mean a human character; the divine, as the saying goes, is an exception to the rule. You should realize that if anyone is saved and becomes what he ought to be under our present constitution, he has been saved—you might rightly say— by divine dispensation.

—Plato, *Republic*, 492e

Table of Contents

Foreword

Fr. James Schall, SJ, was known for saying that one could get an education—even while at college. The same could have been said for acquiring an education even while at lunch, at least in his company. Meeting Fr. Schall for lunch was always quite an experience. He would come down from his room at the retired Jesuits' center in Los Gatos, the same place he had entered the order when it was a novitiate many decades ago. No doubt he was pulling himself away from his constant writing and correspondence. He would exit the elevator and immediately hand me a manila envelope filled with a recent, or sometimes past, article, saying, "Here's some more propaganda."

This always struck me as being in keeping with Fr. Schall's reputation as an "American Chesterton," using wordplay in order to illumine through the realization of contradiction and paradox. Schall taught government at Georgetown for thirty-five years. He was as knowledgeable on current global events and politics as would be expected from someone with his academic pedigree. In addition, what completed his body of learning was a thorough grounding in political philosophy. Schall knew well what separated this from political science as first seen with Machiavelli: the emphasis on searching for the best possible regime. Though he was a most eminent professor of politics, he was not in the least a politician.

Propaganda, the practice of moving people to action by any means, and often for political gain, was never Schall's charge. If you were being handed something by him, it was not only not propaganda; these writings served rather to make people think before they began to act.

Next, Fr. Schall would make it a point to introduce his luncheon guest to practically every member of the Jesuit Center's staff. This practice was especially pronounced in the lunch room itself, where he would address each worker by name and make sure his guest made the acquaintance.

Power—the subject and object of Machiavelli's *The Prince*, as well as the end that propaganda served in politics—seemed to be eluded by the priest. He was a respected and renowned academic whose career spanned stints at not only Georgetown University, but the Pontifical Gregorian University in Rome as well. The esteemed cultural capital Schall possessed did not translate into viewing humanity in the abstract, something into which the academically erudite, separated by such capital from the greater whole of their communities, may frequently lapse. To Fr. James Schall, each individual was a human being, deserving of acknowledgment, courtesy, and kindness.

After introductions, there was the usual query, "José, do you want a beer?" This was the official beginning of lunch with Schall and its attendant contemplative conversations. Two subjects stand out as topics he would return to repeatedly over the years.

The first of these began as, of all things, a mild reminder for me to think a bit harder. During a past email exchange, I'd noted how remarkable were the thoughts of Marcus Aurelius, the great Roman Emperor, closest perhaps to the paradigm of the philosopher-king in Plato's *Republic*. Having mulled over my comments, Schall reminded, "You have to be careful with stoicism, because it is the gateway to pride." Here, he played the part of gadfly, as Socrates was once known millennia ago. How exactly did stoicism, inner strength manifested by the rejection of earthly glories, lead to pride?

Admittedly, this did take some time to think through. Eventually though, after a few lunch conversations, the issue grew clearer to me. It had a bit to do with the search for power mentioned earlier via Machiavelli. It is true, a Stoic is not Machiavelli's prince seeking only to hold fast to his earthly dominion. The stoic did not want the world at all, but rather to prove himself pitted against the world. The Stoic wanted not glimmering trophies, but the freedom to be unmoved by the world. Nevertheless, the Stoic then exclaims, "I have done it, all by myself." There is no need for any other human being. Nor is there a need for a loving God, who allows us to endure the travails of this world with the gift of His grace. Hence, in the end, the Prince and the Stoic—one seeking power over others, and the other the elevation of the self over the world—end up because of their pride in the same state: alone.

The other philosophical vein Fr. Schall often mined concerned not a sin such as pride, but rather a virtue, some would say one of the most sought after of all virtues. In the *Republic*, justice only comes to both an individual soul and a city if they are properly ordered. In the soul, reason must prevail, and the intellect and spirited emotions ought to rule over the appetites. In the city, the artisans, unable to rule themselves, depend on the guardians and rulers, with the latter's apex seen embodied by the philosopher-king, ruling wisely. Only then can a just person be among others living in a just city.

With this context in mind, Fr. Schall took great care in pointing out that, "Justice, though a virtue, is the most terrible of virtues." Here again was Schall as the American Chesterton. If virtues were the opposite of sins, which were of course, bad, how could virtues then be terrible? Although I always declined his offer of a Corona before lunch, this last line of reasoning almost had me reconsider the offer. This, simply on its face, did not make sense . . . until it did.

Fr. Schall often remarked on how much the Greeks, who had not yet received revelation, attained, seemingly with their reason alone. Yet, when he brought this up, he observed a quiet outcry on the Greeks' part for something which would complement reason. Justice, as a virtue from the Greco-Roman world, was seen as exceedingly rational. If a person lived with an ordered soul, then a just life would ensue. If a person lived with the chaotic wreckage of a soul wherein the appetites ruled, then personal ruination would follow. No loopholes, no appeals.

The terrible nature of this pitiless approach to others leads the mind to seek beyond the Greco-Roman virtues. It is with Christianity where mercy does not reject justice, but instead softens it. Mercy comes from God who does not have to give it, but nevertheless does. He gives it because it is not His wish to have His creations, human beings, end up alone like the sinful Prince or the virtuous Stoic.

I felt at times that the ills of the world could be cured just with the discussions held at a small table in the lunchroom of the Jesuit Center in Los Gatos. Of course, Schall had taught, lectured, and written for decades—much of it in the most powerful city in the world—and the world still has its ills. The writings he has left us in this book, too, appear only as one quiet "voice" in a world of shouting. As a scholar of the first order, but more importantly, a good man, Fr. James Schall knew of course the folly in thinking that grand human ideas could change the world. Instead, he ceaselessly worked toward the goal of inspiring people to see, in each other, the reflection of a loving Creator. So, instead of pursuing pride and selfish ends, they would be directed to their common end, to not be alone, and to be with the source of what is and what is good. May it be so for all those who read these pages.

José Maria J. Yulo

Editor's Preface

When I told Father Schall I was going to philosophy studies as a Jesuit scholastic, he told me: "Don't just study politics, or you'll be dumb."

That line epitomized Father Schall's approach to politics: he studied it with a profound love for all that is real. The themes of the chapters herein reflect that breadth, from Aristotle to Martin Luther to Leo Strauss. As he writes in "An Autobiographical Memoir" that prefaces this collection, "This delight that things are is not something that I impose on reality, but something reality incites in me. It always takes a human mind to recognize it."

The essays in this volume, including that short memoir, were selected and arranged by Father Schall himself prior to his passing, which is why the body text ends with a conclusion in his own hand. The book, as a whole as well as in its parts, is thus the product of his mind; editorial changes have been kept to a minimum. Whether it should therefore be considered his "last book" is left to the informed reader's judgment; Father Schall's inclusion of the memoir gives it a certain valedictory air.

Many of the names Father Schall invokes herein and throughout his works—Rommen, McCoy, Schumacher, Chesterton, Belloc—were thinkers with a similar propensity to engage the world. In that sense, to read Father Schall is to emulate him, as he always sought out writers who plumbed the breadth and depth of creation. Reading him grants us the same gift.

Father Schall's passionate pursuit of wisdom often led him back to the great question of Catholic theology: the relationship between faith and reason. Ultimately Father Schall sought to illuminate the universality of the faith and its harmony with reason. There was a critical element to this project, testing the rivalrous claims to universality of other enterprises, not unlike how Socrates explains his life's work in the *Apology*.

It was with such desires that Father Schall undertook a dialogue with Leo Strauss, a conversation in some ways exemplary of Father Schall's charitable but probing approach, but in other ways unique because of the importance of Strauss and his project. That importance comes through in the numerous references to Strauss in this volume, including an important review of *Leo Strauss and His Catholic Readers*.

Father Schall adopted a deferential tone toward Strauss because he wanted Catholics to take Strauss's concerns seriously, even if Father Schall did not agree fully with Strauss's conclusions. Indeed, a central message of Father Schall was the harmony of faith and reason. In this Father Schall was in profound accord with Pope Benedict XVI on the mutual purification of faith and reason. Pope Benedict's concerns about pathologies of faith and reason—as, for instance, he argued in his dialogue with Jürgen Habermas—were those of Father Schall as well.

As we continue to muddle through a world without Schall, we might ask again one of his favorite questions: Is there a Roman Catholic political philosophy? His answer was not straightforward. The great thinkers of classical political philosophy evidently developed through reason an extensive mastery of the question of how we ought to live. If Father Schall was not always impressed by the deliverances of modern political thinkers, it was because he viewed them as rejecting the classical tradition as much as they rejected Christianity.

And yet Christianity has had no little impact on the question of the good life. As Father Schall's great mentor Charles McCoy noted, revelation makes humans aware of their condition and their end, the former often obscuring their knowledge of the latter. Father Schall expressed his debt to McCoy through a focus on the "last things," a theme of his work from the beginning. Father Schall's legacy for us must include the challenge of how to speak of the last things in our own time, an epoch that like many others takes politics to be the sum total of reality.

This is no mean task. And so it is not irrelevant that, whatever the status of a Roman Catholic political philosophy, for Father Schall the Christian cannot engage in politics without hope. This is not hope that the eschaton will be fully immanentized—Father Schall did very much like that phrase of Voegelin—but neither is it the bloodless yearning for some final happiness with no bearing on the *hic et nunc*. It is a Paschal hope: that humans labor confident of the Lord's final victory. This hope is perhaps Father Schall's greatest gift in our time. For only hope allows us to face squarely the totality of reality, both the challenges of sin and the promise of our end in God.

There can only be one Father Schall. But the essays in this volume are offered in the hope that his wisdom will flourish long after his death. After all, it was never really his wisdom, but a participation in the divine, the divinity in which Father Schall assuredly now finds himself enveloped.

BILL MCCORMICK, SJ
Feast of the Blessed Virgin Mary,
Mother of the Society of Jesus 2021
Regis College, Toronto

Acknowledgments

The editor would like to thank the following journals for permission to reprint material that had originally appeared on their sites.

Catholic Social Science Review, Chapter 5, "Political Philosophy and Catholicism"

Catholic World Report, Chapter 9, "On 'Rights'" [Original title: "Modern 'Rights' and the Loss of Freedoms"]; Chapter 10, "On Politics and Salvation"

Christian World Imprints, Chapter 1, "The Nature of Political Philosophy"

Communio: International Catholic Review, Chapter 8, "A Happening that Really Took Place"

Crisis Magazine, Commentary 4, "On the Catholic Appreciation of Leo Strauss"

Faith & Reason, Chapter 14, "Luther and Political Philosophy: The Rise of Autonomous Man"

New Oxford Review, Chapter 6, "On Socratic Surprises" [Original title: "Ancient Perspective on the Modern Condition"]; Commentaries 2, "On Being and Politics (Walsh)"; Commentary 3, "The Shadow Over All Politics (von Heyking)"

Perspectives on Political Science, "An Autobiographical Memoir"; Chapter 7, "On the Completeness of Political Life and the Incompleteness of Political Philosophy"

Rowman & Littlefield, Chapter 4, "Political Theory: The Place of Christianity"; Chapter 13, "On the Place of Thomas More in Political Philosophy"

St. John Paul II Bioethics Center, Chapter 12, "Political Philosophy and Bioethics"

Telos, Chapter 2, "Why Precisely *Political* Philosophy?"

University Bookman, Commentary 1, "On Appreciating Aristotle (O'Rourke)"

VoegelinView Newsletter, Chapter 3, "On the Primary Experience of the Cosmos"

Studies

An Autobiographical Memoir

I.

To look forward to a life of thought and to gaze back on that same life from the perspective of old age cause me to ask myself: Did what I anticipated relate to what happened? It seldom does, I suppose. Yet, most lives, for good or ill, show a certain consistency over time. This consistency is probably what Aristotle meant in placing the end of all our practical actions in the kind of happiness we in fact make our end. The "means" that constitute the everyday of our lives revolve about that end for which we do all that we do. One thing is certain: it is the same mind of the same person that looks in either direction. We may change our minds, but we cannot change our being. Even a person's worst moments are part of this same life. Indeed, what we do about that which we should not have done often best defines what we are.

Prophecy, they say, is not so much the "prediction" of future events. It is more the retrospective understanding of the past when it was seen as the beginning of a future. Such a backward view can make our lives seem to be determined. But prophecy knows that we, with our wills, at each step might have made things otherwise. Besides the basic data of birth, place, kin, education, and deeds, the quickest overview of a life is to look at the bibliography, if any, that it has produced. A lady from Florida once told me that the only times that a proper Southern woman wanted to see her name in the press were when she was born, when she married, and when she died. Ultimate human dignity takes place in souls outside the public gaze of men. That is what the *Republic* of Plato was about. Unjudged lives are never complete. Aquinas noted that civil law cannot command our interior acts, though God can.

Avoiding attention does not so much hold with academic lives. Though prone to vanity, they too are spent in enclaves sufficiently withdrawn from ordinary life, hopefully to be free from fads and prejudices. Academics are to pursue things for their own sake. Their incomes are *honoraria*, not salaries or wages. If a professor, moreover, fails to tell us what he has learned, what he affirms, he is, as Frederick Wilhelmsen once put it in a passage I

* This chapter is revised from *Perspectives on Political Science* 45, no. 2 (2016): 106–12.

have often cited, simply "not a professor."[1] We need to add that the errors of the same professors are often as revealing as the truths, if any, that they do discover. It is the mission, indeed the duty, of the human race to know evil and error precisely as evil and error if it is ever to know the whole. The knowledge of evil, as such, is not evil. It was Aristotle, I recall, who said that good can know evil, but evil cannot know good.

The bibliography of my writings comes to some 150 pages of entry titles.[2] In retrospect, I wonder if I left anything unsaid. And since the purpose of writing is to be read, one wonders, even more, whether what he has written simply lies there somewhere, unread. A sentence is not a sentence; a book is not a book, until it is read. Yet all that any man writes is but a tiny blip on the vast screen of accumulated human knowledge. Awareness of the vastness of human knowledge is a cure for any temptation to pride. My listing, in any case, includes books, chapters in books, book reviews, academic and literary essays, periodical and online journalism, interviews, and letters to editors.[3] It does not include classroom notes, journals, personal letters, or cancelled emails. Several different sustained series of columns that lasted for some years were entitled "Schall on Chesterton," "Sense and Nonsense," "On Letters and Essays," "English Essays," "Schall on Belloc," "Last Things," and "Wit & Wisdom." Most of it in printed form is found in the Special Collection in the Lauinger Library at Georgetown University. Looking at this corpus of writings, I am astonished at being so verbose. Yet, I know that it is only by constantly rethinking and reformulating one's thoughts that a person will have any hope of that ultimate goal of all thinkers and writers, to be able to state the core of what one knows with some confidence that it is true and intelligible to whoever might come to read it.

The first published essays appeared in 1954 and 1955 and continue for some sixty years into the present (2019). I have published some forty-five books, many of which include previous essays, academic and popular. One begins a book by writing a sentence, then a paragraph. He often does not know that it is a book he is beginning. The book is where a beginning idea took him. I have especially enjoyed writing relatively short essays, as I

---

1 Frederick Wilhelmsen, "Great Books: Enemies of Freedom?," *Modern Age* 31 (Summer/Fall 1987): 323–31.

2 This bibliography can be found at www.moreC.com/schall.

3 See James V. Schall, "On Political Philosophy and the Understanding of Things: Reflections on Fifty Years of Writing," *Political Philosophy & Revelation: A Catholic Reading* (Washington, D.C.: The Catholic University of America Press, 2013), 227–39.

explain in the introductions to *Idylls & Rambles: Lighter Christian Essays* and *The Classical Moment: Essays on Knowledge and Its Pleasures.*

The title of one of my books, *On the Unseriousness of Human Affairs*, a phrase from Plato, will explain why, I hope, most of what I have written contains a certain lightsomeness in it. This delight that *things are* is not something that I impose on reality, but something that reality incites in me. It always takes a human mind to recognize it. Humor flows from seeing how things need not be the way they are or the way they are expressed. It is not a quirk, I think, that I often cite Samuel Johnson, P. G. Wodehouse, Will Cuppy, Charles Schulz, James Thurber, or G. K. Chesterton. Each of these men caught something of the delight of existence itself. The existing things we know need not exist, but they do.

An "autobiographical memoir" is a retrospective glance at what I have in fact said in various ways. It emphasizes what seems more important. I recall once reading that no man has more than one or two seminal ideas in his life. These ideas keep coming back to him in various ways. It is almost as if, once begun, they demand completion and judgment. A man is responsible for his own thoughts, where they lead, something he does not always see or admit. Obviously, Plato, Aristotle, and Aquinas had many ideas in all fields. Yet, each of them betrays a certain inner consistency that, over his lifetime, defines his work as his and no one else's. We associate "the good" with Plato, order with Aristotle, love with Augustine, and *esse* or being with Aquinas.

I keep returning in various ways to a few basic positions. If a thing is true, even the most devious route will lead one back to it. At whatever age, one begins with present insights. He will work his way back to the reason or occasion why such ideas initially occurred, to the reasons why they may or may not be true. He unfolds the reach and lineage of those ideas or truths that began his quest, with that "classical moment" that suddenly illuminated what it was that he was seeing. I have reflected on Etienne Gilson's remark that a man is free to select or choose his first principles. Once he chooses one, however, he is no longer free to think as he will but as he must.[4] A "first principle" is really a "first principle"; we cannot really avoid its truth. Our "chosen first principle," if wrong, will always run into a contradiction with the real "first principles," the things that cannot be denied without at the same time affirming them.

4 Etienne Gilson, *The Unity of Philosophical Experience* (San Francisco: Ignatius Press, 1999), 243.

II.

Even though I wrote a book entitled *The Life of the Mind*, I consider myself to be a relatively late starter in things literary and philosophical. In my Midwestern youth, I mostly lacked that formation in language, logic, rhetoric, memory, philosophy, and literary taste that should occupy one before he is twenty. We had no French *lycée* or German *gymnasium* on the Iowa prairies. Though by twenty I was able to read and write well enough, in fact I had not read much of anything. I had no real guidance about where to turn. This lack was not all bad. Something is to be said for floundering as well as for acquiring the other skills of a normal life. That we live in an imperfect world means that we live in a world that requires and invites our attention and our acting.

I cite fondly Yves Simon's remark that "nothing can save a young philosopher from giving himself over to an infelicitous professor."[5] The mind of a twenty-year-old can be and often is a jumble of knowledge and desire. It is not filled with what Dorothy Sayers called the "lost tools of learning."[6] What is needed is some authority or guidance to direct one to what is true, what is of greatest moment. It is not such a bad thing that each of us must begin life knowing nothing when before him lies the possibility of knowing everything—or better, that everything is there to be known. The myriads of things that I do not know and probably never will know are also blessings. If the world only knew what I or anyone else knows, it would have collapsed long ago. The most obvious limit to our knowledge is the length of our lives. This awareness is part of the reason why things like friendship and immortality frequently recur in my thinking.

This early experience of not-knowing was the origin of what I came to call in a book *Another Sort of Learning*. The Dominican Order's motto—*Contemplare et contemplata aliis tradere* (to pass on what one contemplates)—was a matter of experience. When we come across something true or something funny, or both at the same time, we want to tell it to someone else. This telling others carries with it a *caveat*. While writing something, we should not talk about it until it's finished. Otherwise, the drive to express it is spent in talk that passes away. And yet, it is this talk in which we want to engage ourselves.

---

5 Yves Simon, *A General Theory of Authority* (Notre Dame, Ind.: University of Notre Dame Press, 1980), 100.

6 Dorothy Sayers, *The Lost Tools of Learning* (London: Methuen, 1948). Multiple online versions are available.

All writing, no doubt, as Plato saw, is a struggle with *hubris*—that is, "a thing is true because I say it is true" versus "I say it is true because it is true." Words, I think, do not really "pass away." They always remain in being, formed by being, waiting for a mind to know them, and, through them, to proceed to that which they refer. The same Plato in his Seventh Letter affirmed that he never put what he really thought in writing. He was aware of how the written word could confuse or deceive us. On reading Plato many times, we still seek to know what he himself held. But if we did not have his written words, we would know much less of the grandeur of our being.

Yet, the enormous number of things to be known makes anything one writes seem futile or insignificant in light of the myriads of languages in which people speak and write their own words. Still, knowing these things, we go ahead anyhow. No one knows ahead of time whether anyone will ever read what he writes. This is not a reason to be silent. Words begin in silence and, after the light of their being read and comprehended, end in silence also, the silence of memory. Knowing points beyond one's-self to *what is*. Neither what I know nor my knowing power came from myself. All thought must take these two truths into consideration.

Without my having anything to do with it, I stand outside of nothingness as to what and who I am. Being and intellect were already there in my being waiting for me to exercise the powers given to me. I concluded from such musings that all of reality was in fact knowable. It beckoned me to know what I could of it. No one can be content with not knowing. Even if he thinks no truth can be found in things, or that reality is flux, he hastens to assure me that what he proposes is true. I watch what he does, not what he says.

III.

My doctoral dissertation (1960) was entitled "Immortality and the Foundations of Political Theory."[7] It was a distillation of what I had been thinking and learning from my twentieth to my thirty-second year. This title grew out of experiences of friendship. In years of teaching college students, I saw that friendship regularly perplexes and fascinates our kind. By the time that I began to think of these things, I was in the Society of Jesus with good guidance from some memorable professors. I had time to make up some of what I had missed in earlier years. I now knew of Aristotle and Aquinas, who

---

7 Later, with revisions, it was published as *Reason, Revelation, and the Foundations of Political Philosophy* (Baton Rouge: Louisiana State University Press, 1987).

also thought about these things. Friendship, it is said, exists in conversation, conversation about the highest things. Technically, by this time, I was also studying political philosophy. But fortunately, I had the opportunity to study other things, particularly philosophy itself. It turned out, as readers of Plato and Aristotle know, that friendship was a frequent topic of their concern.

The first autobiographical beginning that indicated to where I was intellectually going was the experience within friendship that sensed its concern with its permanence in the midst of a life that was obviously passing away. This issue was the key to much of what I later thought about. Indeed, it is at the center of what I think about political philosophy and its place in the overall understanding of things. The word "immortality" stood out in the title of my dissertation. Though as a young man I was not much his follower, still anyone who has read Plato will recall the word "immortality."

This subject was the one that Socrates dealt with on his last day in his conversation with the potential philosophers. They were perplexed by his calmness in the face of his upcoming death. How are we to deal with the relation of the "permanence" that we seek in friendship and the obvious mortality of our lives? If we look at the end of the *Apology*, Socrates tells us that, on his immanent death, he expects to continue what he had always done, to converse with the gods and the heroes he admired. His wife, Xanthippe, poignantly described the "last day that he would spend conversing with his friends."

Political philosophy, I thought, brought us to the deaths of Socrates and Christ. Both belonged together in this sense: the best men were killed, after a formal legal process, in the best existing cities of their time. But once they were killed, so what? Did it prove that it did not matter how we lived? If such is the fate of the best, why bother with the good? At first sight, it might seem that I have verged away from friendship. But at the time, what concerned me was whether the empirical desire for permanence in our loves and friendships was feasible. Or was it only an illusion? All cities of this world were composed of men and women constantly being born, living life's stages, and finally dying. This was the "mortality" of what Hannah Arendt called "the human condition," the condition of the city.[8] What ultimate difference did it make what we did if, in all actual regimes, the just were punished and the unjust rewarded? It made no sense to talk of a "right" way to live.

---

8 Hannah Arendt, *The Human Condition* (Garden City, N.Y.: Doubleday Anchor, 1959).

But this living and dying were the way things are. Politics described the cities of mortals who for the most part were not perfect in virtue. Justice and injustice would always be present among us. Such realism later was related to our freedom. I did know some Augustine, though not as well as I later came to know him. I was leery of that oft-repeated utopianism that sought to solve all our problems in this world by some political, economic, or psychological formula. My later book, *The Modern Age*, concerned this issue.

The reading of Marx's *Economic and Political Manuscripts of 1844* was instructive to me, as was Charles N. R. McCoy's *The Structure of Political Thought*. Marx was actually seeking a way to relate human diversity with some general unity that would overcome all the evils. Years later, I was glad to read in Strauss that perhaps we could look on Plato as telling us in the *Republic*, not that we could build the best city in this world, but that we cannot. To attempt to do so, as Aristotle intimated, resulted in a tyranny of the worst sort. But what was the problem and how did it relate to friendship? The problem concerned what the polity or civil state was.

IV.

In my Roman years, teaching at the Gregorian University (1965–77), thanks to earlier studies in Spokane (1952–55), I published "The Reality of Society according to St. Thomas" in the Italian journal *Divus Thomas*.[9] The reason I mention it here is because it pinpoints a central issue of political philosophy—namely, "What is the ontological status of a state?" The question was particularly interesting to me because two things besides the soul itself could be looked upon as "immortal." These were (1) the "species" and (2) the state itself. How so? How could this seemingly abstruse reflection have anything to do with friendship?

"Species" (also "genus") is a term that comes from logic, from the activity of the mind in knowing and classifying existing things. The "species man" means the idea that comprehends all the notes that make each living being of that species what it is. We implicitly include every actual individual who belongs to that species—in this case, man himself. It is the tool of our understanding of reality. It has a root in things. But its formal reality follows the nature of the mind. It abstracts from but does not negate the particular

9 See James V. Schall, "The Reality of Society according to St. Thomas," *The Politics of Heaven and Hell: Christian Themes from Classical, Medieval, and Modern Political Philosophy* (Lanham, Md.: University Press of America, 1984), 235–52.

matter by which things are concreate and visible in this world. It is concerned with "man," not John and Suzie in whom the form man is embodied as a cause. We are, in the order of logic, a perfectly valid aspect of reality. Nominalists want to deny any relation between reality and general ideas. For them, everything is directly related to God, or, if no god, to itself.

Marx's "species man" wanted to combine the whole human experience into each person. As McCoy pointed out, Marx confused logic and reality. He wanted in being the kind of reality he found in the mind. Wherever he looked, he wanted to see only man, no gods.[10] But the relation of logic to being is best handled by Aristotle. Knowledge does not change what a thing is. Knowledge is of *what is*, of existence. Knowledge only changes the knower. Knowledge ultimately explains why it is all right to be human. As Yves Simon said, each individual person can know the vast world that is not himself. He is not deprived or isolated by being a finite, particular human person. The being of the polity is a real relationship, and it can be known. When it is known, it exists in the mind with a basis in things. Polities are never independent substantial beings.

Immortality arises out of these reflections on knowledge. If a general truth is known, it is by means of a power that is not itself material. Hence, the soul is said to be immaterial, though, as such, it is the causal form of the body. Contrary to materialist assumptions, the body does not explain itself.[11] It is not an independent "substance," as Plato seems to have thought. The mortal being knows in a way that prescinds from matter without denying its reality. This is why it sees, and knows that it sees, how all the aspects of a thing belong together to form *what it is*. The soul, however, is never unrelated to its matter, even in death. This philosophical fact will return when we consider the relation of revelation to political philosophy.

The state is not a substance—that is, a complete autonomous being with its own self-moving, autonomous life. The medieval organic theory of the state sometimes held this odd position. Any theory that subsumes the citizens of the state into itself as parts of its being operates on a metaphysical error. The state falls in the metaphysical category of "relation." It is concerned with how things within a single being or among beings stand to each other. Its "being" depends on the beings that are related to each other.

---

10 Charles N. R. McCoy, *The Structure of Political Thought* (New York: McGraw-Hill 1963), 264–90.

11 See William Carroll, "Does a Biologist Need a Soul?," *Modern Age* 57 (Summer 2015): 17–31.

The polity is not another separate "thing" that is immortal in itself. Substantial immortality only belongs to human persons seen as citizens. Recent theories about "structures of sin" seem to attribute sin, a personal act, to a state which is not substantial being. These views confuse the Aristotelian notion of differing regimes determined by the freely chosen ends of its citizens—wealth, honor, pleasure, and contemplation—with the persons who choose these ends.

The polity, properly understood, did have an inner-worldly "immortality." It is the burden of political philosophy to distinguish these meanings of immortality and the realities, real or logical, to which they refer. In the great scene in the *Symposium*, what is begotten of love is not a polity or an idea, but a new human being. The state can properly be said to be "immortal," not as the soul, but in that it goes on and on down the ages. This or that citizen replaces another within the same arrangement of offices and ends. In this sense, the purpose of begetting is the "species," not the individual. It intends to keep human beings present even beyond the deaths of any given individuals. Citizens "bear" the relations in the polity. States cannot be "friends" with other states, except in a metaphorical fashion. Only individual persons can be friends.

V.

Socrates saw that the political conversation among citizens is limited and defined by their mortality. They must constantly prepare for the new and bid good-bye to the old. Human beings are the "mortals." They die and know that they will die. The sense of permanence in friendship, however, felt by Socrates on his last day, hints that death is not the end. Or, in Plato's sense, if it is the end, the world is not created in justice.

Political philosophy, from within its own experience, confronts two issues that no polity can meet by itself. The first is that justice, since it is not requited in this world, implies an immortality in which proper judgment is finally achieved, as Plato saw. Secondly, friendship, as Aristotle noted, implies a permanent living together. Something more is suggested than the "till death do us part" of the marriage vows. Indeed, it implies a completion of the marriage vows themselves.

Aristotle held that legislators are more concerned with friendship than with justice. Justice relations are harsh. Something beyond justice, something that softens it, is necessary for humans living together. This "beyond justice" experience explains why Aristotle spent two chapters of his *Ethics* on friendship but only one on justice. Thus, friendship has a legitimate, indeed necessary, place in the polity. But the polity cannot mandate it. It can only foster and encourage what is beyond its scope. The well-being of any polity requires something over which it has no direct control. This sphere has generally been called "the natural law" with intimations of revelation. A whole world of reality exists that the polity makes possible but does not control. This fact explains why the contemplative order is necessary if the practical order is to be itself and not a pseudo-metaphysics that tries to supply the substitute we have come to call "ideology."

The polity itself, however, possesses an inner-worldly "immortality." If it goes on for centuries, every citizen will be replaced through births and deaths. Citizens are "the mortals" amidst the immortalities of polities, souls, species, and the heavens. This political "immortality" is not Plato's "city in speech." Cities are founded to last. They are loci of memory, words, and events, of lives good and bad that occurred in them. Few cities and nations last more than three or four hundred years without a radical change in regime, according to Aristotle's classification of their diversity. The city's reality falls in the categories of action, passion, and relation. Living citizens follow laws and customs of their city.

The "species," to keep it in actual existence, also depends, though in a different way, on a succession of living persons. Their best span of years is usually the scriptural "four score years and ten." Plato's "city in speech" would be intelligible even if no actual human beings existed. Indeed, God could, without contradiction, understand a world that He did not put into existence. Without actual human beings, however, Aristotle's existing polities could not exist at all. We can speak, perhaps, of the Chinese "nation" lasting from 5000 BC, or the American nation lasting from 1789. Whether these are the same regimes even with the same names, as Aristotle saw, depends on whether the form (monarchy, aristocracy, polity/democracy, oligarchy, tyranny, or mixed) abides over time. It need not, but that it continues to exist is the "intention" of its founders. Radically different regimes can have the same names. We can hardly say that ancient China or Greece and modern China or Greece are the same polities, so much has their configuration changed.

These reflections refer back to the citizens of any regime, with their issues of justice and their friendships. Citizens die within imperfect regimes in which they lived. Modern political ideology mostly arose out of these issues of the nonachievement of justice and friendship. It sought to found an inner-worldly "perfect" regime of justice and friendship to last down the ages. Modern environmentalism supports this purpose, to provide grounds for an inner-worldly "immortality" on the planet. Such theories are parodies of the Christian notion of eternal life or the heavenly city. Eric Voegelin called it the "immanentization of the *eschaton*." That is, heaven, hell, death, and purgatory become inner-worldly goals of science, polity, and human configuration.

We can, in such a view, establish such a regime with our own powers if we just eradicate those causes that are preventing this attainable perfection. Most of the unexpected terror and absolutism of modern regimes arose from this source, this impatience to make us perfect in this world. But what is this effort? It is nothing more or less that a mislocation of the reaches of friendship and justice. It is buttressed by a deviant metaphysics that confuses being and thought. In this sense, it was not illogical for the Marxists to use the old monastic terms for each other—"Comrade," "Brother." These terms were implied in Plato. This effort to produce a "best regime" is a secular imitation of the condition of the end times.

VI.

Aristotle said that if man were the highest being, politics would be the highest science.[12] But since man is not the highest being, politics is not the highest science. What does this observation mean? How does it relate to immortality? Only human persons can be immortal in the substantial sense of remaining themselves even with death. States are not immortal in this sense, nor are logical species, however proper these terms are in their own orders. Here these autobiographical reflections reach their main point.

Basically, I suggest that reason and revelation are related to each other in a coherent, noncontradictory manner that does not corrupt either. Nor does it leave the intelligence found within the revelational narrative just sitting there unconsidered simply because of its source. The whole to which philosophy is intrinsically oriented cannot simply reject revelation if a coherent intelligence is found within it. Revelational answers are directed to the intelligence found in political things in their own metaphysical setting.

Modern political philosophy, with the aid of nothing but itself, has claimed to think of itself as completely able to answer the fundamental questions that concern the souls of men as they are manifested in political life.

12 Aristotle, *Ethics*, 1140b20–25.

When it claims that it can perform this feat, and this is my argument, it invariably lapses into some sort of actual tyranny, indeed a tyranny far surpassing any previous ones, including the communists and Nazis, though they are in the same line of thought.[13]

From the point of view of revelation, political life is a limited, though intelligible, understanding of how man rules himself while he is mortal in this world. Civil order thus requires our taking out of politics this recurring temptation to assign to itself the task of explaining and putting into effect everything about man. This limitation indicates the superiority of metaphysics to politics. But it doesn't deny what politics is about. Metaphysics frees politics to be politics. It restrains politics to deal only with that aspect of reality over which it is competent. But metaphysics itself attests to an order of being that is not subject to human willing. Charles N. R. McCoy remarked that politics becomes a pseudo-metaphysics when a transcendent order is denied.[14] This "pseudo-metaphysics" is the history of much modern thought, especially political thought.

What is the conclusion of these reflections? Justice in logic requires that unpunished injustices be requited and unassigned rewards be granted. This requirement is a function of political philosophy.[15] But its being carried out is only possible if each human being is forgiven, punished, or rewarded. This remedy has to apply to the person as a whole, not just a "soul." This requirement is only possible if such a thing as the resurrection of the body exists.

This consideration entails a permanent restoration of the individual person who was responsible as a whole for his own deeds. Aristotle saw that a complete human being was not just a "soul," which was the form of the body. The Christian revelation concerning the resurrection exactly addresses this requirement of reason. The reason of revelation is addressed to the perplexity of human finite reason. To see this relation, it is not necessary to "believe" in the truth of revelation. But one has to grant the truth of logic that sees the relation. It understands that politics raises issues it cannot answer by itself, but they are addressed and resolved in the intelligence found in revelation.

---

13 See Jennifer Roback Morse, *The Sexual State* (Charlotte, N.C.: TAN Books, 2018).

14 McCoy, *Structure of Political Thought.*

15 See James V. Schall, "On Retribution," *The Catholic Thing*, November 13, 2018, https://www.thecatholicthing.org/2018/11/06/on-retribution/.

Further, friendship seeks permanence with the exchange of the highest things. It also requires the everlasting life of friends. Aristotle had wondered about the loneliness of a god who had no friends. Thus, some defect supposedly existed in the Godhead. It lacked a perfection of our being. Revelation added to Aristotle's concern the doctrine of the Trinity. Within the Godhead there was a diversity of persons bound as one in being, love, and friendship. This Trinity stood at the origin of *what is*. The Incarnation of the Word, of the Second Person, was precisely to inform us that we are created to be friends, even friends of God, and this in everlasting life.

This understanding of the Godhead signifies that the intimations within friendship of a permanence and a relation to the very origin of friendship were valid. Political philosophy provides the context of these understandings. Where do these reflections leave us? We read in Plato that human affairs are not "serious." We should spend our lives "singing, dancing, and sacrificing."[16] At first sight, this position shocks us. We like to think in terms of "duty" and "right," whereas we should first think in terms of gift and abundance, not of what is "owed" to us, but what is given to us.

The resurrection of the body and the Trinitarian understanding of the inner life of the Godhead manifest a "reason" found within revelation that, when thought about, is exactly designed to complete enigmas found in all political life, in the lives lived by actual human beings. Such a conclusion does not mean that we can "argue" directly from truths of philosophy to truths of revelation. It does indicate, however, that within reality a coherent understanding of man, his thought, the content of revelation, and *all that is* exists in the light of man's political life itself.

The studies and comments of this volume reflect and complete many of the strands of thought to which political life gives rise. To be political we must also be more than political. The "incompleteness" of political philosophy is what man realizes when he understands precisely what the thinking of man in the polity means. It is not that politics lacks something due to it, but that man is, while being political, called to eternal life. Leon Kass's insightful title, *Leading a Worthy Life*, touches on the essential issue in political philosophy.[17] Not only is a worthy life good in itself; it is also a life that looks beyond itself in its very completion.

16 Plato, *Laws*, 803. This and all subsequent quotations from Plato are taken from Plato's *Complete Works* (Indianapolis: Hackett, 1997).

17 See James V. Schall, "The Plain Truth: Leon Kass on Just About Everything," *Catholic World Report*, May 31, 2018.

Socrates's farewell to the Athenian jury that tried him looked to the immortality of his soul. By accepting this farewell and looking to the resurrection, a more complete fullness of political philosophy is envisaged in revelation. The life to which each existing human being is originally and ultimately directed is a divine life, a life not "due" to him, but one given to him. The drama of human existence, and of political philosophy, depends on how he responds in his life, worthily or unworthily, to this invitation. In creating us free, God assured us that the story of our lives would not be the unfolding of a planned mechanism, but a drama of love and rejection that manifests itself in both the actual lives of citizens and in the laws of our human cities.

Chapter 1

The Nature of Political Philosophy

Then we're not legislating impossibilities or indulging in mere wishful thinking, since the law we established is in accord with nature. It is rather the way things are at present that seems to be against nature.

—Plato, *Republic*, 456c

I.

In this universe, members of the human race are the "mortals." That is, they are unique beings in the sense that they will die. But all living, corporeal beings, not just men, die. What is the difference? The difference is that men know that they will die. Understanding what a human being is, then, includes this awareness of its finitude in this world. The "when" one dies is not certain; the "that" is. Whether the fact of death might have been otherwise, whether a world lacking in death could exist, is an abiding topic of human speculation.

But even though science sometimes claims that we can lengthen human life to hundreds of years, a grasping for inner-worldly immortality, it is difficult to see how such a lengthy life would be anything but agonizing. Death in this light of ongoing existence in this world seems a blessing. This realization of some wisdom in death is why the second form of immortality—that of the soul or spirit—came into play. Immortality may be intimated by a conscious experience of knowing unchangeable being and principle. But it is also brought in view because of the general awareness that the injustice of individual human lives is not always punished and virtue not always rewarded in this life, no matter how long it lasts. Our lives, in other words, have something to do, not with how long we live, but with how we live while we are in this world for whatever length, wherever or whenever human beings live.

What human beings are plays itself out against the background of the particular death of each person who comes to be in the universe. Any society at any time, be it tribal or political, is filled with members who are being con-

* This chapter was previously published in *Prologue to Provocations: A Search for Truth in Christian Anthropology*, ed. Romero D'Souza (New Delhi: Christian World Imprints, 2016), 69–79.

ceived and born, growing up, reaching maturity, then old age, and death. The membership of any lasting society is transitory in this sense. Though civil polities themselves also pass away in time, usually they last well beyond the life span of given individuals who, at any given time, compose them. Members of any polity are here for a time; they then pass on. This mortal condition allows for both newness and tradition, for replacement and continuity.

Most people who have ever lived on this planet do not live out the famous "four score and ten" (90) years said to be allotted to some of the more vigorous. But few of those who live so long are able actively to participate in what might be called the "ordinary" affairs of mankind—that is, the economic efforts to keep alive and to prosper, the efforts to identify what is good and what is evil, and the efforts to attend to things of nobility and beauty. The classical comments of Socrates in book 1 of the *Republic* and of Cicero in his essay "On Old Age" were designed to address the issue of the importance of age and wisdom to a human community from which the individual citizens would sooner or later depart.[1]

Philosophy is said to be itself a "preparation" for death. Politics, however, is held to be what we do before death—that is, what we do during the period from our conception and birth through our education, public life, old age, and death. Politics concerns the life of the mortal being while he is "mortal," while he lives, flourishes, and declines. The connection between how we live and how we die is not arbitrary. The oft-repeated notion that "we die as we lived" is designed to stress this relationship. The notion of asking for "forgiveness" for aberrant personal acts implies an effort to reconnect how we did live to how we ought to have lived. One of the original purposes of having a political order in the first place was to establish a rule of law and justice whereby disorder could be punished and order restored. No political order in history has achieved more than limited success in this endeavor. This fact leaves the question of justice open to something beyond politics.

Man, though he belongs to the mortals, is not merely a "mortal." He is also seen to have something about him that is "divine" or "immortal." Politics has something to do with this "immortality." The human dignity of each person is related to the fact that something about him exists that is more than political or finite. The word "immortality" itself has two related

1 Plato, *Republic*, 328a–331d; Cicero, "On Old Age," *Selected Works*, trans. Michael Grant (Harmondsworth: Penguin, 1971), 211–50.

meanings. The polity was set up so that the passing words and deeds of men who lived in them would not be lost to the generations that followed them. This is why we have monuments, poems, and written words. To know what we are, we need to know what we have been and done. We need to know the record of great men and terrible tyrants, as well as the deeds and words of ordinary people.

Thus, we have an "inner-worldly" immortality that consists of our remembering those who have lived before us, who have shown by their lives and deeds what is great and what is heinous. Polities, consequently, are "founded" so that what we have done or what we ought to have done are not forgotten. Polities are constituted with "authority" to decide on what ways of action and word are to be followed and why. This "founding" is not arbitrary but has many elements that can vary. There are often many good ways of doing many differing things.

Likewise, many ways can be found to put into effect what is wrong or evil. The freedom that human beings possess is a freedom that follows on their intelligence, not a freedom that lacks any direction or order. Freedom means that we can do evil, but that we need not. Freedom does not make the difference between good and evil but recognizes it and seeks to act accordingly. Man is free to choose evil. But he is only free to choose it under the aspect of its being good. This fact is why the controversies of reason about what is true and good are unavoidable. A free polity is one that is open to such discussions as fundamental to its public order.

II.

When we inquire about the "nature" of something, we want to know and understand *what it is*. This endeavor to know what something, besides ourselves, is assumes that something exists in the universe that is worth knowing. We ourselves are legitimate members of this same universe. We can tell the difference between what is real and what is imagined. Once we know something is real, we can imagine something that is not real. Not to be able to tell the difference between what is real and what is imagined is a sign or madness or derangement.

We also observe that not everything is exactly the same, though all things do have some things about them that are rightly common. Nothing is so different that we have no way of identifying it. If each thing is simply unique and diverse, nothing can be said about it. All efforts to speak about it become artificial constructs with no relation to what is being identified.

It is not an accident that a polity is defined as a place where speech is to be grounded in a reality that can be verified as true. We can know what is "out there" and affirm its reality. The only way a polity can be held accountable for the acts of its leaders and citizens is if there is a standard in which all acts and words can be grounded.

Political entitles are not direct produces of nature like vegetation or animals. They are not "substances." But they are "natural" once we have human beings who can act together to achieve something—in this case, a common life. In this sense, politics are a reality but not a *substance*, not another "being" with a "life" independent of the citizens who compose it. Rather a polity describes rational beings insofar as they related to one another to form an association in which many goods can best be achieved, particularly the development of a virtuous life of the citizenry. To say that man is "political" by nature means that he will invariably put this organization into existence once he comes to a point where he needs to act in common to achieve goods that are worthwhile but impossible to achieve solely by himself.

In this sense, the polity is not set up as opposed to men's achieving what they can by themselves but as completing what they can achieve in a more complete form in union with others. Since man's life is finite and temporal insofar as he is mortal and political, the polity is a late arrival. Many things are necessary before it can fully develop, just as when it is finally organized, it is by its own nature open to something that is not properly itself. This is one reason why the academy, while a proper institution of any common good, is not itself simply another agency of rule. The academy is, or should be, a sphere in which not only politics but what is beyond politics can be freely and reasonably addressed. The good of any polity requires that it grant a space for what is not just political. Otherwise, it will not understand the limited sphere in which politics is to be itself.

By adding the word "political" to the word "philosophy," we do not intend to change the nature of either politics or of philosophy. We can say that "politics" is a legitimate object of philosophical inquiry. Likewise, we can say that the politician needs to know what intelligence and mind are about lest he misunderstand the nature and good of the citizens who are to be ruled and guided to the many ends to which they are open. The temptation to tyranny is, at its most dangerous, the subsumption of philosophy into a politics that allows no purpose but itself.

Politics are concerned with human action and interaction insofar as men are organized together by custom and law to attain a common good.

Private goods are perfectly valid and should be protected and encouraged. The common good is not a sum of private goods. The "nature" of each human being is such that he needs a polity to be what he ought to be. That good is not just any "good" or "desirable" thing. The common good is what is good for what it is to be a human being in all its variety and breadth. The common good means that there are goods that cannot be attained by oneself alone or even by small groupings, which are themselves necessary to any common good. Neither politics nor philosophy means anything if there is no mind to think them. The fact of beings with minds existing in the universe is not the result of human agency. It is a given. Thinking is not caused by politics. Politics is the result of thinking.

All things that flow from this givenness of human reality are themselves implicit in the original power to know. Among these powers that flow from reason is the use of the mind to relate human beings one to another in a coherent social unit in which beings with reason could participate because they could know. The origin of politics is not, as such, force. Force, though not intrinsically irrational in its use, always appears as the result of a failure to use reason with an effort to correct its improper use. To say that man is a "political being" means that he is a being capable of causing associations based on reason in order to achieve his further purposes. Most of the things most needed in life are only achieved with the ordered cooperation of others. This cooperation presumes intelligence and freedom, with a limit based on truth.

In other words, *what it is to be man* is not itself subject to the function of politics. It is assumed by it. If man were not already a rational being, politics could not make him so. Any politics that rests solely on force cannot transform itself into reason. But a reasonable being can understand why force is sometimes needed in every political order. In order to know the whole of "things political," we need to know not just the good or best regimes but also the worst and those in-between. The total comprehension of "things political" includes understanding the reasons for disordered regimes. Aristotle even explains, for our understanding, how to be a "good" tyrant, as if to say that the complete knowledge of what is good includes what is not good.[2]

Philosophy seeks the knowledge of the whole. Its proper object is *all that is*. Aristotle tells us that politics is the highest of the practical sciences

2 Aristotle, *Politics*, 1313a33–17b26.

but not the highest science.[3] The highest science is metaphysics or ontology, including the causes of being. Its object is being as such, *what* is. If we deny the force or existence of metaphysics, we automatically make politics into a pseudo-metaphysics that claims to be able to account for all things by its own practical methods. Politics is the highest "practical" science, not the highest science as such. Practical knowledge presupposes an end that is given to it, one not constructed or made by man. Politics deals with the means to attain a given end already contained in *what man is*. When politics claims to define ends and not means, it has absorbed metaphysics into itself.

When it is said that Machiavelli is the founder of "modern" political philosophy, it means that the "prudence" that guides particular human action to its highest good is replaced by the "art" whereby the politician artist directs the polity to an end defined by nothing but the ruler, whether he be prince or democrat. In this sense, modern politics is defined by the loss of a natural end that limits the politician to *what* is. This limitation is the charter of any possibility of a critique in the name of reason of any existing regime.[4] From Machiavelli's premise, carried forward by Hobbes, the good state is not that one in conformity with human nature. Rather it is one that corresponds to what the prince or democrat wants. In other words, the politician is not limited by anything but his own will. Such a view, as Aquinas had pointed out, goes back to the principle of Roman law that states, "Whatever the prince wills, is the law."[5] This recurrent position in the history of political philosophy is the origin of a voluntarism that has no reference to being as a check on its scope of power.

III.

Political philosophy begins with the trials of Socrates and Christ—that is, with the presence before the laws of an existing state of the philosopher or prophet for being what he claimed to be. Both Socrates and Christ obeyed the laws of the polity under which they were tried.[6] Their trials were not "illegal" in any technical sense. The Athenian jury and the Roman governor

---

3 Aristotle, *Ethics*, 1141a20–22.

4 See James V. Schall, *At the Limits of Political Philosophy* (Washington, D.C.: The Catholic University of America Press, 1996).

5 Thomas Aquinas, "Treatise on Law," *Summa Theologiae*, I-II, 90.1, obj. 3, ad 3.

6 See James V. Schall, *The Politics of Heaven and Hell: Christian Themes from Classical, Medieval, and Modern Political Philosophy* (Lanham, Md.: University Press of America, 1984), 21–38; Schall, *At the Limits of Political Philosophy*, 104–22.

did not violate any procedural laws in the course of either trial. But, as readers of accounts of these trials throughout subsequent history have recognized, there was obviously something wrong with both legal scenes. Was the problem in the laws themselves, which were generally considered the best laws of their time, or in the souls of those who executed authority?

Both Socrates and Christ died obeying the laws of the states in which they were executed. Paradoxically, the only way for them to leave the question open with regard to their innocence or guilt was to die willingly. Socrates lives, as he tells us in the *Crito*, according to the laws of Athens. He does not want to destroy its laws by refusing to obey them at his death. His death brings us back to the relation of mortality to immortality, as he tells us in his *Apology*.[7] Socrates dies in peace obeying the laws because he knows his death is itself a judgment of those who wrongly tried and executed him. Christ died before a Roman governor who was not sufficiently concerned with truth to find out what was happening before him.

Neither Socrates nor Christ wrote a book entitled *What Is Political Philosophy?*[8] Yet, we know about them because accounts of their trials were written by Plato and Xenophon, by Matthew, Mark, Luke, and John. Some there are, no doubt, who go away from these public trials and executions to conclude that both Socrates and Christ should have been sentenced. They were guilty of upsetting the settled political order of the polities in which they lived. The authorities were merely looking for public peace. "It is better that one man die than the whole nation perish" (John 11:50). Such a principle deftly bypasses the question of justice, which is what a city was set up to uphold. A polity has a "right" to defend itself against those who undermine the existing public order. The language of "rights" based on the will of the prince is consistent with itself but not with the truth. It is this latter principle that mostly measures political entities today. Obedience to the laws means accepting whatever the ruler "wills."

Others, knowing of the same trials, are thus less happy with their results. They are aware of a possible conflict between philosophy and polity. When,

---

7 Plato, *Crito*, 49a–54d; *Apology*, 38c–42a.

8 See Leo Strauss, "What Is Political Philosophy?," *What Is Political Philosophy? And Other Studies* (Glencoe, Ill.: Free Press, 1959), 5–55; Charles N. R. McCoy, *The Structure of Political Thought* (New York: McGraw-Hill, 1963); Robert Sokolowski, "The Human Person and Political Life," *Christian Faith and Human Understanding* (Washington, D.C.: The Catholic University of America Press, 2006), 179–98.

as a young man, Plato witnessed the fate of his mentor and friend Socrates, he could not but ask himself: Must it always happen this way? Will something like these trials eventually exist in and undermine every polity? Or, is there a place where philosophy and politics can exist in harmony? It is in this sense that the origin of political philosophy arose from the soul of the young Plato. He asked the questions that demanded reasonable answers, not just solutions of power.

Plato clearly concluded that only in argument, only in speech, could the conflict be resolved. And Christ taught, in effect, that only in the transcendent order could the practical conflicts ever be resolved. All existing political orders would be less than perfect. Indeed, the implication was that the most dangerous political order was in fact the one that did claim to be perfect in this world. More philosophers and prophets have been killed by regimes claiming perfection in this world than by the pragmatists such as Pilate, who was just trying to avoid problems. This conclusion meant, in practice, that all existing regimes would be more or less imperfect. This conclusion did not mean that some regimes were not better than others.

The description of regimes in terms of better or worse was one of the functions of Aristotle's *Politics*. He distinguished between good regimes that ruled according to law and bad regimes that ruled according to the end of the ruling man or body. What this classification meant, in effect, was that certain basic issues that every person had to cope with were, in principle, "beyond politics." But it also meant that existing regimes could be the context in which the fate of Socrates and Christ was repeated in other times and in other forms. Most regimes, even the worst, have in fact attempted to avoid being in the position of making martyrs of its philosophers and religious leaders. When they have been killed, it was usually on the same justification that Socrates and Christ were killed—namely, as threats to the state and its laws.

Modern democratic theory, in its own way, tried to avoid this confrontation by reducing to insignificance the import of metaphysics and revelation. But most modern democratic regimes came to base themselves on the principle that nothing was higher than the positive laws of the state. If something was "legal," it was therefore moral. Any disagreement would be considered a "private" matter. The classic problem of tyranny did not exempt democracies from its scope. Indeed, democratic tyrannies can prove to be even more dangerous than the classic ones

described by either Plato or Hobbes. Whether a king, a dictator, a parliament, or a democracy be the body that enforces the principle that the
positive laws of the state are the only laws, it will still be classified as a
tyranny in the broader understanding of that term. It means that the will
of the ruler is the law.

IV.

What much modern democratic theory and Islam have in common is a
form of philosophic voluntarism. In principle, both are rooted in the
pseudo-metaphysics that stems from denying that there is such a thing as a
human nature that is itself not subject to political manipulation. Put more
broadly, we have systems of voluntarism, whether rooted in the will of the
prince or the will of Allah, that deny the stable nature of any existing thing,
particularly of any human thing. Man is infinitely malleable. He can be the
opposite of what he is without inconsistency, or so it is claimed. There is no
standard or reason that measures actions other than of that authority that
can will the opposite of what it willed before.

In the initial passage cited from Plato, he remarks on the possibility that
the *things that are* at present are contrary to nature. What is he saying here?
He implies that nature can remain normative or ruling for human beings
in a polity even if the actual polities that they create and live in are in fact
contrary to the human nature that ought to be. This means that a criterion
whereby to judge disordered regimes was the major reason Plato wanted
everyone to have a "city in speech" that was capable of retaining an order of
good even if it did not exist in political reality. Without a city in speech or
mind, we are limited to the existing laws when it comes to evaluating their
justice. The figures of Socrates and Christ in political philosophy abidingly
stand as judgments on existing regimes.

Plato noted that the best regime was not just "wishful thinking." Indeed,
existing regimes are more in the nature of "wishful thinking" insofar as they
deviate from the good and insist on calling themselves the best practical
regimes about which nothing better can be imagined. This is Machiavelli's
regime that contains not what men ought to do but what they "do" do. In
other words, it is a regime that refuses any criticism of its laws based on a
higher law in which the sins and errors of actual regimes are requited, as
Plato argued they would be in the last book of the *Republic*. In this sense,
Plato's "city in speech" is not a utopia, a wishful thinking designed to be
embodied in this world, but a permanent criterion by which the dangers of

utopia in this world are recognized and existing regimes are not exempt from standards they do not formulate or observe.

Theoretic voluntarism was invented or argued from both political and theological sources. It meant that reason did not direct will but was subject to it, in its service. No "objective" truth or reality existed to correct what is willed. In the West, the line from Scotus, Occam, Marsilius of Padua, to Hobbes resulted in a concept of the good of the state as dependent on the will of the Leviathan. Eventually, this Leviathan could have monarchic, legislative, or democratic forms. The Roman law principle, "Whatever the prince wills, is the law," as we saw, had already envisioned this principle. It exempts the prince from any reference to a transcendent criterion that would limit his rule. The absolute supremacy of the English parliament was based on the same notion. In Islam, voluntarism arose because of contradictions in the Qur'an that needed to be justified.

If Allah could command both *jihad* and peace, both violence and non-violence, it was necessary to explain why this view was at all justifiable. If God or the Leviathan were pure will, and if reality itself had within it no order or natural law, then all that men could do would be to submit to the will of the god or ruler. Submission to the law, whatever it was, became the only "virtue" required. Men did not have to ask—indeed, they could not ask—whether the law of the state and the law of the god were in conflict with reason. Any grounds for asking such a question had been eliminated by the premises of voluntarism.

The well-being of men in polities depends, ultimately, on the thought on which their polities are built. But the thought behind polities is itself a result of thought about *what is*. It is not merely thought about politics alone. To understand politics, we always need to know more than politics. Aristotle had noticed in the last book of his *Politics* that what happens in a good regime is a passage from politics to leisure. The term "leisure" (*skole*) did not mean relaxation or laziness. It meant the intense activity and curiosity about all things that comes when material needs are met.

Mere physical well-being produces a life, as Glaucon said in the second book of the *Republic*, fit only for "pigs."[9] He did not mean that physical well-being was bad, but that it was just the foundation, the presupposition for considering what human life really meant. The key question became: "What do we do when all else is done?" We seek in peace, free from ordinary needs,

9 Plato, *Republic*, 372d.

to know the truth of things.[10] In this sense, the polity exists so that sufficient virtue might be present to transcend immediate needs and disorders of soul to arrive at a free and true understanding of *what is*.

When we have a good regime, what is it we "do"? In other words, are politics sufficient for man? In a famous passage in the *Politics*, Aristotle brought up the question of the "wickedness" that is found in every existing regime as rooted in human beings.[11] Such "wickedness" seems endemic to human nature as it actually exists. It is Machiavelli's justification for saying that politics do not deal with what men "ought" to do, but with what they do "do."[12] But if this *what men "do" do* becomes our criterion of rule, we necessarily end up justifying some evil in the name of what men "do" do instead of striving to correct it on the basis of a justice we know of from the city in speech or reason.

Aristotle suggested that, if the reason for this "wickedness" was that men were hungry, they could be given property to supply their needs by themselves. If it was because of pleasure, they could be taught virtue. But if this "wickedness" was just because men wanted power to do what they wanted, there was no solution but philosophy.[13] Why philosophy? Philosophy was the only discipline that could actually confront the adequacy of the reasons given for one's supposed self-rule over all of nature. Augustine was later to treat this issue under the notion of pride.

But there was one problem with this approach. It was a problem that every politician who was a good man but not a philosopher had to face. And a mistake here could be fatal for himself and his polity. This is the problem of the sophists, of the philosophers whose souls are corrupt or whose minds are themselves not ordered to any true good. This is, as it were, the Socratic political problem, the problem of Athens, the city of philosophy, the best existing city. It did not recognize the philosopher when he appeared before them. The citizens did not want to "examine their lives," as Socrates had often tried to incite them to do.[14]

If present societies are "against nature," as Plato suggested that they might well be, we will not likely find any society according to nature among the exist-

---

10 See Josef Pieper, *Leisure: The Basis of Culture* (San Francisco: Ignatius Press, 2009); James V. Schall, *On the Unseriousness of Human Affairs* (Wilmington, Del.: ISI Books, 2001).

11 Aristotle, *Politics*, 1263b20.

12 Niccolò Machiavelli, *The Prince* (London: Penguin 1999), chap. 15.

13 Aristotle, *Politics*, 1267a2–15.

14 Plato, *Apology*, 38a.

ing cities. This conclusion takes us back to the philosophers who are like the captain of the ship in book 6 of the *Republic*. The sailor/citizen thought him mad. They were not able to recognize him because their own souls were in disorder. Their state ships lurched randomly all over the range of evil and good.

Thus, in conclusion, we return to our original inquiry about "the nature of political philosophy." We must recognize that political philosophy is a discipline of thought. It recognizes not just that some regimes are better than others because we can know what is good, but also that some philosophical systems are truer than others. The politician knows how sophists, undisciplined or unwise academics, can undermine his polity. Philosophers know of Callicles, in the *Gorgias*, the handsome and intelligent politician who contemns any inquiry into any thought that might question his rule. He will not accept that mind can judge power. But the sophist will not admit that mind can judge mind either. The great battles of politics are first fought out in the minds of the dons and the thinkers seeking to explain *what is*.

In the end, political philosophy is a testimony that the final regime, the final happiness that we seek, is not political. The citizens and philosophers who recognize this truth are, nevertheless, all born into some actual polity, the kind of polity that did or could kill Socrates the philosopher or Christ the man-God. The premises that justify these killings are all based on a voluntarism that accepts the principle that whatever the prince or the democracy wills is the law. Yet, philosophy does not solve all its own problems, however open to reality it is. And this is the final theme that politics leaves with the philosopher who is concerned with *what is*.

Philosophy is open and true, when its practitioners rise out of a good polity, in leisure. Must they also be open to a revelation that addresses not only the "wickedness" of human nature but also the realization that some answers to philosophic questions come to it from outside philosophy, though not in contradiction to it? Both the political order and the philosophical order reach a point of incompleteness when they are in fact being good politicians and good philosophers. The nature of political philosophy, as well as that of philosophy, is to remain open to the whole, to what cannot be supplied by itself. This is why, in their depths, both politics and philosophy are gift oriented. Politics is both an end, a highest practical good, and a means to something beyond itself, to philosophy and truth. Political philosophy, at its best, recognizes its crucial contribution to the fulfillment of human nature. Understanding what politics is leaves man free to understand himself as oriented beyond death to something greater than, but not contradictory to, politics.

Chapter 2

Why Precisely *Political* Philosophy?

Philosophy is to remind us of the necessity in things: not just to the necessities to which we have to resign ourselves, but those we can find splendid.

—Robert Sokolowski, *Moral Action: A Phenomenological Study*

Now classical political philosophy has held that it is not any natural power that is first and properly the concern of the political art, but on the contrary, rational powers that are not determined to one particular action but are inclined indifferently to many. It is precisely their specification by free action—which cannot rely upon or imitate a principle of natural operation—that constitutes the proper art of politics.

—Charles N. R. McCoy, *The Structure of Political Thought*

"Political philosophy" means primarily not the philosophical consideration of politics, but the political, or popular, treatment of philosophy, or the political introduction to philosophy—the attempt to lead the qualified citizens, or rather their qualified sons, from the political life to the philosophic life.

—Leo Strauss, *What Is Political Philosophy? And Other Studies*

I.

In the dialogues on the trial and death of Socrates, the philosopher, in Athens, the best actual (not theoretic) city of its time, we recall two unforgettable themes. The first, from the *Crito*: "It is never right to do wrong."[1] This principle is the cornerstone of the city and civilization that received their vitality and order from this affirmation. It recognizes a radical distinction between what is good and what is evil, a distinction that is not simply man-made. It is, however, capable of being recognized by man. It is the most significant and basic distinction within cosmic existence, the one that gets closest to the reason why anything at all exists. Its ontological category is

---

* This chapter was previously published in *Telos* 183 (Summer 2018): 203–12.

[1] This and all subsequent quotations from Plato are taken from Plato's *Complete Works* (Indianapolis: Hackett, 1997).

found in the objective nature of moral things. They reveal an order not of their own making, but one to which all human actions ultimately refer for their meaning.

This order can be recognized by the human mind. Subsequent to this recognition, the distinction can be either affirmed or rejected. Such is the scope of the free nature given in human existence. It constitutes the drama and need for judgment that is manifested in each human life. This affirmation or rejection of a given order is seen in how we judge the multiple activities of a given human life. This issue is what the last myth in the *Republic* was about. Still the distinction of good and evil presumes that *what is*, including matter as such, is good.

Evil is always the privation or lack of a good that ought to be there. Moral evil is a privation in some otherwise good act or thing effected by acts of free will for a purpose. The moral and political world is filled with choices that ought not to have existed but do. Once they do exist, from them, as the Latin adage puts it, *sequitur et bonum et malum*. (Either good or evil can follow from either a good or evil thing). That is, evil choices do not prevent the world from going on. Without de facto evil choices, contrition, forgiveness, and just punishment would be meaningless.[2] Paradoxically, the scope and depth of existence is expanded when evil is allowed to happen within reality.

Evil is not another substantial being in the universe. The fact of evil existing in ontologically good things opens the possibility of intellectual and sacrificial forces that can redeem the good found in the being that lacks something that it ought to possess. Things can also become worse unless the evil is recognized and counteracted. Aristotle was right to look carefully at vice and at tyranny as examples of how bad things might eventually turn out. He was also right to see them as habits that were freely allowed to form in our being.

Aristotle's *Politics* described the souls of the citizens who constituted differing forms of polity—monarchy, aristocracy, polity, democracy, oligarchy, and tyranny, with mixed regimes capable of combining some of these into one regime. Regime distinctions were based on the citizens' conduct, on their habits and character, and ultimately on their relation to this principle that it is never right to do wrong and its origins. Thus, good and bad

---

2 See James V. Schall, *A Line Through the Human Heart: On Sinning & Being Forgiven* (Kettering, Ohio: Angelico Press, 2016).

regimes reflected the deliberately formed souls of the free citizens who made up any particular city. All good regimes sought a common good that was inclusive of the good of everyone, the human good that was found in nature. All bad regimes sought the good of the ruling principle over against a common good.

The end and, hence, the definition of a regime guided the number and configuration of the subordinate structures and offices within a given polity. A civil constitution was designed to bring about the options manifested by the actions flowing from the souls of its citizens. The *Ethics* of Aristotle was a detailed explication, seen through their moral actions, of why and how individuals belonging to the same human species differed in things falling under their power of choice. Basically this difference was manifested in the degree of virtue or vice that motivated the citizens in their varied actions within their polities and in their foreign relations.

Modern civilization since Machiavelli and Hobbes usually denies this principle that it is never right to do wrong. It claims the "freedom" to do wrong if needed. The classical city stands in constant conflict with the city in which this supposedly exhilarating liberty to do wrong is an option of the politician. The possibility of doing wrong is implicit in the nature of freedom. Its right ordering occurs through the acquiring of virtues. This "liberty" to do wrong, however, was postulated to assist the politician or the citizens to achieve their own chosen purposes, not those discovered to be good in the order of things. Glimpses of this recurring controversy were already found in the first book of the *Republic*. The current culture is best defined as the political effort to remove all natural relationships and institutions as impediments to a city wholly constructed by human choice subject to nothing but itself.

The second memorable and solemn passage, also from Plato, tells us that "Death is not the worst evil." Doing wrong, not just abstract wrong, is the worst evil. Thus, no evil can befall a good man. Death is not the worst evil. The ultimate power of the politician, the arbitrary power to inflict death on anyone, including the philosopher and the prophet, is rendered useless if fear of death is not effective, if one accepts death rather than does evil. When the good man says to the unprincipled politician, "Kill me then," the power of the politician is undermined. The power of the philosopher transcends his city and becomes known in the city of the world as the alternative to absolute power.

II.

Political philosophy is designed to understand this situation, this neglected relationship of philosophy to the city. As we learn in the *Gorgias*, the only defense the philosopher possesses before an armed politician who is not limited by the distinction of good and evil is the philosopher's power of speech, his power to speak the truth. All tyrants, even democratic ones, recognize their need to control speech. Once the politician no longer consents to examine his own soul, to listen to argument, the philosopher is dead. How we speak and how we listen are both moral activities by which we are judged.

But the philosopher's death is not the worst evil. By his stance, the philosopher has avoided that alternative of doing evil to save his life and his truth. His death results in upholding, before the public, before the world, the principle that it is never right to do wrong. This latter principle governs the city in "speech" to which the life of the philosopher haltingly points. Political philosophy seeks to turn, even slightly, the soul of the statesman toward the good of the philosophic life, to an awareness at least that more than politics is found even in politics.

Political philosophy has the happy burden of justifying itself both before philosophy and, more particularly, before political life itself. Its prime function is to convince the statesman, whose active life leaves him little real time for philosophy as such, that a realm beyond politics exists and does include what goes on in the political life of its citizens. Music, poetry, history, literature, and art, along with tragedies and comedies, can prepare and direct the statesman beyond his immediate interests. The virtues, and, yes, the frequent crimes of everyday life seen by the statesman also serve as a preparation for and intimation into the philosophical truths that the statesman has little time to contemplate.

In this philosophical realm, finally, all political acts, all moral acts, are judged in the light of what is good and what is evil. A polity without philosophy is a polity in which its own self-defined well-being takes the place of philosophy. Political philosophy wants to know: "What is the place, if any, of philosophy within the polity?" Why does the issue need attention? How do we go about establishing that philosophical issues are vital to the well-being of a polity?

Political philosophy initially must show why politics is normal for man, the political animal. Having granted this truth, though it is involved with things human, with things of this world, politics is still limited in such a way that it is not itself the explanation of the origin and meaning of every-thing human. Though it is the highest of the practical sciences, it does not explain everything that needs to be explained. It is this issue, when unad-dressed, that allows politics to conceive itself as a metaphysics, as itself com-petent to explain and construct in its own image all that is. Politics deals with man as mortal while he is in the condition of mortality. It is no accident that the subject brought up at the end of *The Apology of Socrates* was not mortality but immortality. This issue directly followed from experience of the city's killing the philosopher.

Secondly, political philosophy must reveal, in an intelligible manner, how politics by being what it is leaves open realms, the consideration of which is the proper subject matter of both philosophy and a theology directed back to both. Politics and philosophy, in other words, by being what they are, leave open perplexities that still need to be considered. Neither politics nor philosophy on their own terms explains *everything that is*. Political philosophy guarantees the legitimacy of both politics and phi-losophy by addressing itself to the reasons why politics is tempted to become itself metaphysics and, simultaneously, why philosophy seeks to become visible by incorporating mind into a city designed by philosophers.

Along with both philosophy and politics, political philosophy also must account for itself before various different theologies, themselves often tempted to imitate philosophy by building the holy city in this world. The statesman recognizes the dangers of philosophers who do not understand the practicalities of the actual human condition. In particular, why in prac-tice is it so difficult for most citizens to be virtuous? This concern always brings up the mystery and pertinence of the doctrine of original sin.

Anything that calls itself "philosophy," moreover, must also indicate where it fits in the whole that philosophy purports systematically to explore and whose truth it brings to light. What calls itself "political" must identify what it considers the metaphysical status of the *polis* to be. What exactly is that cor-porate entity that identifies itself as an organized body politic designed to foster the good of its citizens, who are certain kinds of beings by nature? The city is certainly not another substantial being with its own existence.

Man does not make man to be man, as Aristotle said, but taking him from nature as already man makes him to be good man.[3] But this "making" him to be good man is not conceived as a necessity that must happen. His

---

3 Aristotle, *Politics*, 1258a20–25.

goodness follows upon his freedom. But as McCoy noted, his freedom does not constitute the essence of his goodness. This later view is the "modern project," the effort of man to give himself his own goodness apart from the givenness of his already constituted nature as man.

Ontologically, the *polis* falls into the Aristotelian category of relation, *ad aliud*. It is not a substance.[4] As an ongoing ordered relation manifested in the actions of its citizens, the polity as such is immortal. But as a relation it depends on individual living substances that are themselves political animals, each one of them.

The individual citizens who ground the being of the *polis* are each immortal, as least in their souls (Plato). The question of the resurrection of the body relates both to the completeness of what a person is and to the possibility of a reunion. This consideration is what revelation is about and why it relates indirectly to political philosophy, which in its own order is unable to do anything but speculate on this possibility and see that it is not in principle incoherent. Logically, this will mean that Christian revelation does not contradict reason in its proposals about the location of a final end or happiness for each person in a gathering called classically the City of God.

Man is a political animal in two senses. In this life, to complete the potentialities found in him he needs a common good in which a wide variety of goods may be discovered and developed. In the beginning, man does not have any idea of the riches and complexity of what is available to him when he works and thinks about the world. Following the *Ethics*, his happiness even in this life consists in acquiring and practicing the virtues that enable him to rule himself. Laws are necessary to inform him in more detail what is just and unjust in his practice of virtue or lack of it. The virtues are concerned with the passions, those natural things found in us that need to be ruled in the light of reason.

The acquiring of habits, of virtue or vice, indicates the kind of material the polity has to work with in the formation of its constitution and way of life. Thus, we have the distinction of good and bad regimes and those in between. The discussion of continence and incontinence relates to the level most people will have in the status of their inner control. That is, few are virtuous or bestial; most fall in between. For the most part they are good or evil; sometimes they are the opposite of what we expect. The coercive aspect

4 See James V. Schall, "The Reality of Society according to St. Thomas," *The Politics of Heaven and Hell: Christian Themes from Classical, Medieval, and Modern Political Philosophy* (Lanham, Md.: University Press of America, 1984), 235–48.

of civil society arises when virtue is not acquired or practiced in individual or group cases. In that sense, coercive authority ought not to exist, but it is reasonable to do something about it in the order of pleasure or pain to see that others are not hurt by our vices.

Politics concerns man as a whole being. Hence, it is related to his sensory side as itself an instrument to his knowing and well-being. Man is the mortal. It is genuinely good that he is what he is. His ultimate life is not an effort to escape from the body as a preparation for its return in a transcendent order. The establishment and life of human cities, with the variety of goods that they can manifest, is what the polity is for. Things and institutions related to health, knowledge, beauty, and prosperity are what should come forth from his mortal existence.

The notion of democracy as the best and only legitimate regime is open to considerable doubt. Aristotle's mixed regime is not the modern democracy, even when it contains separation of powers. In Aristotle's best regime, the continuing sequence of begetting, infancy, adolescence, family, old age, and death continues. Thus, the regime stays the same, if the order of virtue or vice remains more or less the same. If it changes, the regime changes. This phenomenon is why in modern regimes we can have the same constitutional forms over time but with an inner personal order of citizens that passed from virtue to vice in the very definition of personal virtue.

The purpose of the actual political order is to manifest the level of virtue actually found in a given citizen body, as seen in the deeds, works, and speeches of its citizens. Each individual is thus, by being a political animal that needs to rule himself, able to reach a steady habit that defines his character or personality. Once this stage is reached, the question arises, What else is there to live for? Does the practical life, the life of arts and mechanics, of trade and technology, itself, at its best, point to something lacking not in the political life but in the lives of those who do politics?

III.

It is here that political philosophy as such most connects with mortal life and points to something that transcends it. The life of leisure, the contemplative life, is properly divine, as Aristotle said. This life wants to know just for its own sake. Political philosophy is not a substitute for philosophy or revelation.[5]

---

5 See James V. Schall, *Political Philosophy and Revelation: A Catholic Reading* (Washington, D.C.: The Catholic University of America Press, 2013).

What it does is explain to the politician why certain transcendent questions must be faced for the good of the polity itself, even though they are not as such political questions. But they are pertinent to every citizen and will eventually destroy any polity if they are not properly addressed.

Political philosophy explains to the prudent politician (that is, to the one who has acquired the highest practical virtues) why he must not kill Socrates or Christ. In turn, the politician explains to the philosopher that there are ideas and habits among the philosophers that are truly disruptive of any good life among the citizens. A certain healthy degree of good sense usually is found among normal citizens. Aberrant ideas, the statesman understands, need to be shown for what they are not just in their effects but in their own order. This is why good politics usually depends on good philosophy.

Thus making good philosophy present should be what a university is for. It is an institution both within and outside of the political order if it is true to what it is. When a university betrays its vocation, serious consequences follow for the body politic. The worst tyrants in this sense are usually philosopher-kings gone wrong, not dolts who just are greedy or vicious. All tyrants set up disordered civic orders in this world. All philosopher-kings lead men to virtue and through that allow them to be open to truths for their own sake.

The question of death—whether that of Socrates, of Christ, or of ordinary old age—is not finally answered by politics or philosophy. But that does not mean that this concern is irrational. It is not a vice, but a duty, a hope, to seek to find some final answer. This openness to questions that cannot be answered by human philosophy or politics is the indirect reason why revelation is legitimately related to these two areas of human life. Politics awaits the City of God. Philosophy awaits the encounter with the *Logos*.

As David Walsh showed in his *After Ideology*, these deeper questions arise most vividly in disordered politics when the good man is killed in them.[6] Is this injustice, this torture and inhumanity, simply in vain? To suspect that it is not is precisely one of the primary realizations we have when we see good men refuse to go along with specific evils. But in some form such experiences occur in every human life at its end, even the most peaceful one. The question of death is thus also a question of both politics and

---

6 David Walsh, *After Ideology: Recovering the Spiritual Foundations of Freedom* (San Francisco: HarperCollins, 1990).

philosophy. We are the mortals trying to understand what we are, what it means to be mortal.

The common good is that good of order that allows and encourages all other goods to come forth. It is a witness to the fact that abundance is more characteristic of our being than penury. But the historical experience of politics is replete with disordered regimes rooted in disordered souls. The mission each person is given at conception is that of reaching the final end for which he was created. This end is transcendent and is best described in the annals of revelation. It is the answer to the wonder about why we cannot be and are not completely happy in this life.

But Augustine was right. It is a very good idea not to expect too much in this world. Augustine was at the same time the greatest realist and the greatest revealer of our personal transcendent destiny. Political philosophy, hence, ought to be, if it is complete, a study of both the best and worst regimes, and all more or less good ones in between. The political life is the natural end of man while he is in this world. Philosophy is what goes on in this world when we realize that politics, though good, is not everything. Revelation is a knowledge that points to the limits of both politics and philosophy. In a sense, it confirms the validity of each in its own order.

Philosophy and revelation both limit politics. Politics is an extension and completion of ethics. It indicates how citizens in various ways deal with virtues and vices. Virtue makes it possible for us actually to be free enough from our own inner disorders to deal with what is there for its own sake. This is why the best actual regime is the one regime in which the mind of the citizens and philosophers is not turned to themselves, to their own self-glory, but to the wonder of *what is*. In this sense philosophy depends on ethics and politics. Both the statesman and the philosopher need first to rule themselves for them to see the good of what is not themselves.

But politics recognizes that some things are not in its capacity to resolve. This is why Carnes Lord said that the politician needs to know music and poetry.[7] The statesman is too busy to be a philosopher and too modest to think that he can build the kingdom of God in this world, which latter seems to be, in one form or another, the major enterprise of political philosophy since at least Machiavelli.

---

7 Carnes Lord, *Education and Culture in the Thought of Aristotle* (Ithaca, N.Y.: Cornell University Press, 1982).

In conclusion, what finally is the answer to the initial question: Why precisely do we have *political* philosophy? Political philosophy exists in speech firstly to protect the philosopher from the raw power of the politician. But more importantly, it exists to explain to the prudent and intelligent statesman why the life of philosophy is itself a good of the polity, the good of politics' knowing why it is not everything. But political philosophy does have a subsidiary function of protecting the polity from the aberrant philosopher. The statesman has to know enough of what is normal to see the damage that comes from the abnormal.

Both politics and philosophy, though open to what is good and indeed to *what is,* remain at a deep level perplexed. What is it all for, and why do we not have the ready-made tools to answer our own enigmas? At least one conceivable answer to this line of thought comes from revelation. Basically, it informs us that none of us is created simply for this world. That is why we cannot find our end, our *telos,* within it. Secondly, it tells us that the significance of our lives, what we do to ourselves and to one another, is the field in which what we finally will be is manifested. In the end, it says that we are made to be not souls alone but complete persons, body and soul, who have reached the end for which they were created.

What is remarkable about these three aspects of revelation is that they are formulated in such a way that they answer our own most perplexing questions about ourselves if we succeed in formulating and asking them. That is, if we succeed in being citizens and philosophers who have actually considered in our own experience and minds the curious insufficiency of our own reason to explain why we do not fully know ourselves. We do not fully know ourselves because we must first know what is not ourselves. This knowing what is not ourselves is precisely why we have minds.

The solution to the mystery of *what we are* is ultimately a gift to us. But it is a gift wholly in accord with what brings everything together and holds it together. It is a *Logos* that is addressed to our own minds when we are prepared and willing to receive it. Political philosophy is precisely what opens the city to what is beyond it. It is what keeps it open so that it can hear and accept the gift that explains to it why each citizen in any polity exists at all.

Chapter 3

On the Primary Experience
of the Cosmos

The experience of the cosmos existing in precarious balance on the edge
of emerging from nothing and returning to nothing must be acknowledged, therefore, as lying at the center of the primary experience of the
cosmos.

—Eric Voegelin, *Order and History*, in *The Collected Works*

I.

In a seminal passage, Eric Voegelin spoke of "the primary experience of the
cosmos." By this phrase, he did not mean that, to find it, we should hurry
to look through a space telescope, walk on a moon of Saturn, or grasp the
formulae of the constants of spatial order, not that there is anything wrong
with doing these things. He did indicate, however, that this experience of
the cosmos has a "center"—that is, a point, perhaps an intellectual point,
around which all else revolves. The existence of this cosmos, moreover, is
"precarious." We are aware that it is. It does not explain itself. This universe
need not be, but *is*.[1] It stands at the "edge" of nothingness. Without the sus-
tenance of that which brought it into being in the first place, it returns to
that same nothingness. That we can even understand the word "nothingness" implies that something, though it may be capable of being denied by
us, remains there before us, evident to us.

What precisely must we acknowledge about this cosmos? We must
affirm that it is contingent, that it need not be. This "need-not-be" condition
applies also to us, the knowers in the universe. We abide here one by one,
each briefly, within this same cosmos. We do "experience" this very cosmos.
We seek to know the status of its whole being together with that of all its

---

* This chapter was previously published online, *VoegelinView Newsletter*, August 28, 2018,
https://voegelinview.com/on-the-primary-experience-of-the-cosmos/.

1 See Robert Sokolowski, *The God of Faith and Reason* (Washington, D.C.: The Catholic University
of America Press, 1995).

parts. We want to know the order of things.[2] Why do some things fit
together, while others do not? We want to know why some things work,
while others do not. At the center of the things that we know, we find a con-
tinual passingness, itself surrounded by limits, what Aristotle called act,
potency, and change. This primary experience sets us to wonder about the
ground of this being of this cosmos in which we dwell, in which we know
that we too exist. We seek the source of the life and being that we behold
and confront that swells up within us. We know that we stand outside of
nothingness, on its "edge," as Voegelin put it.

Within this universe, man is designated as a "micro-cosmos"; a whole,
a small world is contained within himself. Even though he can imagine
other worlds, he is not in another world unrelated to the reality before him,
to *what is*. His micro-cosmos is confronted with the macro-cosmos before
him, the one in which he dwells, the "vast spaces" that frightened Pascal.[3]
He is not an illusion, nor is the cosmos. The uniqueness of his particular
standing within the universe means that within his reality are found the
other levels and forms of being. Understanding himself may be more difficult than understanding the rest of the cosmos. He is the being who has
weight, who vegetates, who senses in various ways, and who thinks, all in
one unified way. Each individual is a whole composed of diverse functioning parts that enable him to know and act. He realizes that he is like other
things and, at the same time, unlike them in his very likeness.

Man is distinguished most graphically because he knows that he knows.
He knows what is not himself; but his knowing does not change what is
known. It does change him, however. The primary object of his knowing is
what is not himself. His object of knowing is what is out there, whatever it
is. He only knows himself, and this reflectively, when he is knowing something that is not himself. *Know thyself! Know what is not thyself!* These are
the two upsetting, prodding, and delightful charges that we human beings
have been given from our beginning. We did not ourselves create them.
They could not have evolved from nothing—*ex nihilo nihil fit*. We found
them the same way we found ourselves, already there with these powers of
soul firmly implanted in us, already operating as we grow and age.

We can, perhaps, imagine the same cosmos that we know as existing
without any presence within it of a race of beings that have the power of

2 See James V. Schall, *The Order of Things* (San Francisco: Ignatius Press, 2007).
3 Blaise Pascal, *Pensées*, trans. W. F. Trotter (New York: Modern Library, 1941), 206.

knowing. But what possible purpose could such an empty cosmos have? Why would a divine being ever bother with it since He would already know it in knowing Himself? Rather, it seems that the cosmos exists also in order that it be known by a non-divine intelligence within it. This intelligence knows the world by living in it, working in it, and learning about it.

In this sense, the cosmos is not complete unless and until there exists within it a race of intelligent beings, whose purpose it is to learn what the world is from within it. Why is the human race the way that it is? Why is this thing not that thing? And if a finite, intelligent being did come to know the order of the world, would this satisfy it? Is this full knowledge of the cosmos, on completion, itself ordered to something else by being what it is? To know the cosmos from the inside would still leave us to wonder: Why is it there as it is? Why is it not configured otherwise?

II.

Yet, we can wonder more: Why do we have a world in which living finite beings slowly, over generations and eons, learn *what it is*? Their knowing includes the memory of their coming to know. Does this knowing have anything to do with the knowers, what they are? Why they are? It is not perhaps an accident that the race of men has sought to establish a city within the cosmos, a human city, a city of man at his best. In it, the most complicated individual beings within the same cosmos would order themselves into a series of relationships that would take care of their needs, their minds, and the work of their hands.

We are familiar with the notion in Genesis that man is given "dominion" over this creation that is spread out before him. He is to cultivate the earth and make it bear abundantly, as it was evidently made to do but only with man's input. He is to build homes in which he can beget and rear his children. He can let one generation pass to the next. He builds monuments lest he forget his past, writes books to retain what he has learned and what he knows. He organizes academies better to teach and learn in. The abundance of the cosmos is to be used, not simply preserved. The universe itself is ultimately finite. Its end times and man's end times, though related, are not necessarily the same. For man, the end times are laid in the judgment of each, one by one, as Plato saw at the end of the *Republic*.

Man is as much a part of this universe as any other being within it. Whatever caused the universe to be also caused him to be. Yet, even at his best, he has a sense of homelessness about him. He finds himself, as Chesterton once put it, homesick at home. But becoming what he ought to be and doing what he ought to do within the cosmos reveal to him that he is not only made for this world. Yet, what he does or does not do in the time he is individually given in this world seems to be the locus in which he reveals what he is to be permanently. It is possible for each existing man not to reach the end for which he exists. The only way this could happen would be for him to reject the reason for his being what he is. The real drama of the finite universe lies here.

One generation follows another. Nations rise and fall. First a few hundred thousand human beings appear on the planet, then millions, then tens and hundreds of millions, then billions. They leave records, words, artifacts, and bones. Some one hundred billion of our kind are estimated to have now lived on the planet Earth. Some seven billion are still alive. The rest are dead. They completed their initial purpose in their living. Today, we have never known more about our planet or the objects in space around it—comets, moons, planets, stars, and black holes. We know about distances in terms of light-years. Mankind does not exist as one single being. It exists in multiplicity. Each existing individual makes a mark, a dent in the cosmos, fleeting perhaps, but there. The whole seems to be something more than the sum of its parts. The universe stands on the edge of nothingness in order that what is not nothing may be present to it.

What is unique about the human "wholes," that is, persons, who are parts of the universe is that their final place in the whole is itself a function of their own choice. This truth brings us back to the question of why, within the universe, we have a race of beings that are delegated to know it from within it. The race of men is not placed in a perfect world. The cosmos, as it stands, needs completion by something within it. It is to this completing task that men are brought into existence in this world. Yet, this completing task is not merely an understanding of the makeup of the world by beings within it. The very carrying out of this completion reveals the souls of those who complete it at whatever level, small or great. The rational being must decide, each one, whether this life he has been given, this cosmos present before him, indicates to him what is to be understood and how he ought to live out his life when it is being understood.

III.

We can also approach the existence and purpose of the cosmos from outside of it, not merely at the "edge" of nothingness. We begin with the fullness of being. We begin with revelation and its manner of address to us. It has its own inner logic that is uncannily related to what we learn and do not learn about ourselves and our cosmos by our own efforts. We again affirm that the world need not exist. Nor does it somehow cause itself to spring out of nothingness. The world is not a necessary emanation from some necessary process. It is put into being for a purpose, a purpose that is not of its own making. Strictly speaking, by himself man could not see the exact purpose of his being made. It comes to him as a gift. Yet, vestiges of this origin are found within the world. The world reveals constant intimations of it. As Anaxagoras said, the world is full of mind, of intelligibility, that it received but did not make.

The seminal explanatory passage comes from Aquinas. It reads as follows: Aquinas, in the second question of his *De Caritate,* says that man is complete in his own order, but if he is invited to a higher destiny, as he is, something must be "added" to his nature. This addition is usually called grace. Natural man, as such, never existed in this universe. What existed from the beginning was man whose individual end was completed in transcendence, not merely in formation of the cities of this world. The existence of the world is, as it were, something of an afterthought. At the origin of being, God did not first create an empty cosmos and then, later, look around for something to put in it. The whole existence of the cosmos and what is contained within it is, as it were, related to a "drama" that took place within the Godhead. How to understand this drama?

God would be God even if the world did not exist.[4] God plus the world does not make God more God. God is not "part" of the world. God minus the world does not make God less God. Why is there a God plus the world when the world need not exist? Aristotle had wondered whether God was alone, whether He lacked that highest relation of friendship that we find in the finite, rational beings of the race of men. Just who could God be friends with? Two absolutely identical Gods are impossible to conceive.[5]

What Aristotle broached here, in an incipient way, was the nature of the Trinity. The Godhead was not inert but contained within itself an otherness

---

4 See Robert Sokolowski, *The God of Faith and Reason* (Washington, D.C.: The Catholic University of America Press, 1995).

5 See James V. Schall, "Two Gods," *Catholic World Report,* September 15, 2018.

of Persons who shared the same divine nature and life. God as God was not lonely. Hence, He did not need to create in order to complete something lacking in Himself. If anything besides God were to exist in the universe, it would have to exist by nonnecessity—that is, by abundance of being and gift. The being of real, finite things displays an openness to what is beyond itself in the realization that not everything is known about even the tiniest existing thing. Finite being stands outside of nothingness and outside of God.

In the beginning there was only God who lacked nothing. If something besides God were to exist, it would have, as it were, two aspects. It would appear against the background of nothingness. But it would also "be" with an origin in the cause of *what is*. If God would not create a universe in which a race of finite rational creatures existed, still He could, without contradiction, create a world in which they did exist. The essential question came down to this: Could God invite finite rational creatures to participate in the abundance of His own inner life? The key word here is "invite." The inner life of the Godhead is such that no one could be there who did not both know it and choose it. This is the key to the ultimate contingency in the universe, one of the reasons, as it were, why human nature exists in a vast multiplicity of finite persons over time.

The ultimate contingency, the risk of God in creation, is the fact that His invitation to the finite rational being to participate in His inner, Trinitarian life must be chosen and accepted by the finite creature during the course of his time within the cosmos.[6] What does this affirmation presuppose? In the beginning, there is God and nothingness. In the order of intention, God does not first think of creating a universe as a display of His power. He first thinks of associating within His inner life other beings that are capable of knowing and loving this life, these divine Persons, Father, Son, and Spirit. These knowing creatures are not gods. Unlike angels, human beings are naturally composed of body and soul as one being. They need not exist. From before creation, in God's plan, they are ordered to a supernatural life—that is, a life above that which is naturally due to their level of being. This order to something higher is possible because man is a being capable of knowing *all that is,* but this is possible only with added grace, which is there from the beginning. Any being who can know God by his own powers is, logically, already God.

---

6 See James V. Schall, *The Universe We Think In* (Washington, D.C.: The Catholic University of America Press, 2018), 121–32.

Thus, though a thinkable possibility, no purely "natural" human being ever existed in this cosmos. What existed were beings already from the beginning ordered to a life higher than their being would warrant. The cosmos that we contemplate is a consequence. In logic, it follows from this initial purpose of associating other free beings in the inner life of the God-head. What is first in intention can be last in execution. Man does not appear first but last in the order of time.

Once in existence, the cosmos is the arena in which this divine invitation is to be carried out and completed. This higher orientation of each person to an end beyond his given nature does not obviate the goodness of creation itself or the purpose of man to have dominion over the earth to carry out the task of completing within the world the building of a city worthy of human nature. Indeed, it is precisely within this city that the transcendent selection of each person is made about the ultimate state of his existence before God. He makes this choice in the light of the powers of his own reason and his response to the revelation that is given to him about what he is to know and how he is to live.

IV.

The particular universe we live in is one in which man initially rejected the invitation of God to live the inner life of the Godhead. In this sense, the universe we know is a remedial universe, after the Fall. That is, it is a universe in which God achieves His initial purpose even in the light of the rejection we know as original sin, the effects of which remain among us. That part of revelation known as redemption had to achieve its purpose while leaving intact the freedom of each man to accept or reject this invitation. Again, no one could be drawn into the life of the Godhead unwillingly. A coerced or determined friendship and love is not possible. It is on this basis that redemption, as we know it, was through the Cross. Man learns by suffering, as the Greeks said. But the worst evil was not suffering. It is better to suffer evil than to do it, as Socrates also taught.

The heart of redemption in the fullness of time is the divine intervention in history at the birth of Christ, the Word of the Father, made flesh. Looking at this event in history at a definite time and place, two things are clear. The first is that Christ is who He said He was. The second is that each finite human person must choose his own final end, as Plato also taught. Each person is to make this choice in the city in the time in which he lives.

He manifests his decision by the kind of life he leads in the city in which he dwells, by his response to reason and the commandments.

The this-worldly mission of man over time is to know the world, to have dominion over it, and to make it a city. In this way, a grounding or setting is established whereby myriads of human choices, good and bad, are carried out in time. The redemption is carried out in a context of forgiveness and repentance, of the abiding possibility that God brings out the good in which evil is manifested, a greater good. Each finite being is given every opportunity to accept the divine invitation, but it must be willed. What follows are death and judgment. Without these latter, the world cannot be complete or reach the end for which the universe exists—namely, as a locus in which finite beings are invited to accept the original divine intention and to plan for existence outside of nothingness. This whole scope of meaning is summed up in Ignatius of Loyola's famous principle: "Man is created to praise, reverence, and serve God our Lord, and by this means to save his soul."

One final thing needs to be added. All existing human beings die. No human being is complete that is not a whole, body and soul. In this sense, the resurrection of the body, the central teaching of Christianity about our final status, is needed to complete the initial divine purpose. This means that the logic of the resurrection confirms the experience of man in the cities of the world—namely, that he is not complete unless he is whole. The immortality of the soul is true but not enough. The primary experience of man in the cosmos includes Plato's concern that the world was unjust if the evils that occurred within it were not properly punished and the good properly rewarded.

But Plato's logic, while valid, was not quite complete. Though he could not see how, it needed the resurrection to complete the intelligibility of the initial divine intent in creation of the cosmos—namely, to associate finite, free, and rational beings into the life of the Godhead, a life that was a double gift: a gift of being what it was—man did not make man to be man—and a gift of redemption whereby in the end all things, including evil, are ordered to their initial purpose.

Chapter 4

Political Theory
The Place of Christianity

n his essay "Teaching History to the Rising Generation," Russell Kirk told of the textbook his daughter was assigned in the sixth grade of a Roman Catholic grammar school. "In the whole of the textbook, there is no mention of Christianity or Christ, no mention of Catholicism or of any other Christian or Jewish persuasion. . . . One is left to conclude that none of [the] large (historical) themes has been influenced by religion in any way."[1] The question can also be asked quite naturally at a higher educational level and not only in a parochial environment: Is the treatment of Christianity much better at the university level, and this not merely in history departments? In particular, is the academic discipline of political theory, with its various conferences, journals, departments, and curricula, so designed in practice that it can be presented as if Christianity did not and does not exist? Anyone familiar with the field, no doubt, will suspect that the latter is largely the case. Christianity is not in practice seen to be connected with the core integrity of the discipline itself. At most, it is a marginal theoretic issue, of some importance in certain past eras, quite often with harmful results. There is, it would seem, some need to state the opposite position, at least for the sake of argument—namely, that political philosophy cannot be fully itself without understanding the relationship of Christianity to its premises and contents. The relative neglect of Christianity must, then, itself be accounted for.

"Too much politics, like too much education, is a sign of social decline," V. A. Demant wrote in his essay "The Theology of Politics." "The temptation of the natural man is to seek one unifying principle short of God. This is sought in some immanent fact of the natural and historic process."[2] Politics

---

* This chapter was previously published in George Carey and James V. Schall, eds., *Essays on Christianity and Political Philosophy* (Lanham, Md.: University Press of America, 1984), 93–106.

1 Russell Kirk, "Teaching History to the Rising Generation," *Educational Update* (Winter 1980).

2 V. A. Demant, "The Theology of Politics," *Theology of Society* (London: Faber, 1947), 218.

remains the most natural and human substitute for God, since politics is, in its own right, a "unifying principle." This is why, intrinsic to itself, political theory requires a reason to be limited and *self*-limiting. The essential contribution of theology to political theory is, on this basis, philosophical. That is, by locating ultimate being outside of the legitimate tasks open to mankind to accomplish by its own efforts, theology at its best prevents political theory from becoming its own metaphysics, prevents it from being, again in Demant's words, "some immanent fact of the natural and historical process." For metaphysics, however it be called, is a discipline that presumes, on its own grounds, to account for all being—all natural and historical being, itself implicitly identified with *that which is*.[3] When this latter effort appears under the guise of political theory, it limits total reality to that which appears under the methodological processes available to the study of politics.

Without the transcendent, however, politics has no intrinsic limits, since in itself, it is, properly, the highest of the practical sciences, as both Aristotle and Aquinas held. Without a theoretic limit, politics naturally tends to become absolute, a discipline designed to place everything under its scope. On the other hand, an authentic political theory will be, even in its sense of its own reality, essentially "self"-limiting, to the extent it realizes that the whole of being and reality is *not* to be identified with that aspect of reality which is human, which deals with man as "the mortal," as Hannah Arendt used to say.[4] In this connection, then, we are able to suggest that to explore political theory is first to examine its natural and also extrinsic limits. The import of this position can clearly be sensed if we recall the traditional idea that theology was the "queen of the sciences."

We should not, then, easily pass over what Professor Leo Strauss wrote at the beginning of his *The City and Man*:

> It is not sufficient for everyone to obey and to listen to the Divine Message of the City of Righteousness, the Faithful City. In order to propagate that message among the heathen, nay, in order to understand it as clearly and as fully as is humanly possible, one must consider to what extent man could discover the outlines of that City if left to himself, to the proper exercise of his own powers. But in our age it is much less urgent to show that political philosophy is the indispensable handmaiden of theology

3 J. M. Bochenski, *Philosophy: An Introduction* (New York: Harper, 1972).
4 Hannah Arendt, *The Human Condition* (New York: Doubleday Anchor, 1959), 19.

than to show that political philosophy is the rightful queen of the social sciences, the sciences of man and of his affairs.[5]

Whether, some twenty years later, the urgency is still in the direction Professor Strauss suggested can be questioned. But anyone familiar with the central line of Western tradition will immediately recognize in his reflections themes from Aristotle and Augustine, Plato and Aquinas.

Yet it is safe to say that few Christian thinkers have recognized the enormous implications to theology contained in Leo Strauss's monumental works.[6] For his subtle argument was to ask about the limits of the "queen of the social sciences," political philosophy itself, in order to allow a space for revelation or at least its possibility. He understood, in other words, that even on its own grounds, political theory could not account for everything that guided and influenced nature and man. Hence, in urging political philosophers to "discover the outlines of that City if left" to themselves, Strauss recognized that self-limitation was the natural consequence in a discipline that was not itself a true metaphysics. This legitimated the enterprise of political theory itself, with its own relative autonomy—what the Christians called "rendering to Caesar"—while not requiring political philosophy to explain everything, *all that is*, a task proper to man, even though not a political task. This is why Aristotle said that even the little we could know of the divine things was worth all our efforts, even though politics was "proper" only to man.[7] In deemphasizing the "handmaiden" relationship, Strauss evidently made a place for the same function within the discipline of political philosophy itself, or at least tried to do so.

Political theory, for its part, has also something very basic to say to contemporary theology and religion. From the ordinary viewpoint of the political theorist, theology seems presently to state its case before the world precisely in political terms and guises, yet with few of the limits to which political reflection, at its best, is subjected. This makes theology seem more and more unreal, even naive. It often advocates lethal policies in the name of "justice" without ever even suspecting where political things actually go,

---

5 Leo Strauss, *The City and Man* (Chicago: University of Chicago Press, 1964), 1.

6 See James Steintrager, "Political Philosophy, Political Theology, and Morality," *The Thomist* 32, no. 3 (July 1968): 307–32; Charles N. R. McCoy, *The Structure of Political Thought* (New York: McGraw-Hill, 1963); David Lowenthal, "The Case for Teleology," *The Independent Journal of Philosophy* 2 (1978): 97.

7 Aristotle, *Metaphysics* 981b25–983b29; *Nicomachean Ethics* 1141a31.

without ever having heard of the chapters in Plato and Aristotle on the decline of states. Today, it is not the theologian who complains about the encroachment of politics. Rather, the political theorist, while surveying what is purported to be theological reflection, wonders if theology has anything at all to say other than the political, a political that seems but a determined image of contemporary ideology. The curricula of theology or religion departments and seminaries often vaguely parallel those of government departments, with little clear notion of any differences in content or procedure. From the viewpoint of academic political theory, then, the major encroachment today is not from the political to the theological, but (particularly in the area of economics and development and "rights," and in the founding and rule of the new and poorer nations) from the theological to the political. Theology almost seems to have admitted that politics is indeed an autonomous metaphysics, contrary to the tradition of Aristotle and Aquinas.[8] Today, there are priests who want to become politicians (even after the papal decree to the contrary).[9] In the Christian tradition, however, as in the case of Ambrose of Milan, it was the politicians who became bishops and priests. The hierarchy of value was reversed.

What political philosophy has to tell religion, then, is the grounded estimate, based on judgment, experience, and law, of what can be expected in terms of virtue and practice from the generality of mankind as each person exists in a given culture. Ironically, this is what religion used to tell politics, before religion began to claim for itself the advocacy of the ideal human good, as it has tended to do more and more in conformity with modern revolutionary utopias, especially Marxism.[10] To deny that men can always be "better" is, therefore, as "un-Christian" as to expect them actually to produce the kingdom of God on earth.[11] "We can hardly measure what the modern doctrine of individualism must owe to the Christian belief that men are spiritual beings, born for eternity, and having

8 James V. Schall, "The Recovery of Metaphysics," *Divinitas* 23, no. 2 (1979): 200–219.

9 John Paul II, Address, January 28, 1979, http://www.vatican.va/content/john-paul-ii/en/speeches/1979/january/documents/hf_jp-ii_spe_19790128_messico-puebla-episc-latam.html.

10 Cf. Roger Heckel, SJ, *The Theme of Liberation* (Vatican City: Pontifical Commission on Justice and Peace, 1980).

11 Cf. James V. Schall, "From 'Catholic Social Doctrine' to the Kingdom of God' on Earth," *Communio: International Catholic Review* 3 (Winter 1976): 284–300. Reprinted in *Readings in Moral Theology*, no. 5, ed. Charles E. Curran and Richard McCormick (New York: Paulist Press, 1986), 113–30.

a value incommensurate with anything else in the created universe," the great Protestant historian Professor Herbert Butterfield wrote in his essay "Christianity and Politics."[12] But, as he went on to suggest, the doctrine of universal sin, with particular attention to one's own sinfulness, was designed "to be a serious check on the many evils and mistakes in politics." Likewise, G. K. Chesterton, in his still even more formidable *Orthodoxy*, found the political connected with this doctrine: "Christianity is the only thing left that has any real right to question the power of the well-nurtured or the well-bred. . . . If we wish to pull down the prosperous oppressor we cannot do it with the new doctrine of human perfectibility; we can only do it with the old doctrine of Original Sin."[13] Only if all men and women are sinners can we realize that our governments, composed as they likewise are of these same men and women, must be designed to prevent these same people who actually rule us, even with our own advice and consent, from also abusing us.

Thus, by itself, politics could not know how valuable each person really was. All it could do is to project, with a Professor Rawls, that we all must be important because we all would, with various veils of ignorance, project the same fate for ourselves. Yet, by itself, politics could neither know nor account for the depths of evil and disorder that are operative and somehow expected among men. The holocausts we describe and acknowledge do not prevent their repetition among us. They only guarantee that the destiny of the sufferers cannot be finally accounted for by politics alone. The saint, Aquinas remarked, is above the law, because he observes the law and knows it, whereas the politician must account for the majority of us who are not saints.[14] The politician who does not understand how men can abuse one another, who does not believe that holocaust is possible, is simultaneously a bad politician and a bad theologian. He does not know how to rule because he does not know what to expect.[15] Thus, when once the truth of the value of each person and his concrete sinfulness is comprehended, it becomes the legitimate task of politics to account for their realities within

---

12 Herbert Butterfield, "Christianity and Politics," in *Writings on Christianity and History*, ed. C. T. McIntire (Oxford: Oxford University Press, 1979), 44.

13 G. K. Chesterton, *Orthodoxy* (New York: Doubleday Image, 1908), 116, 141.

14 Thomas Aquinas, *Summa Theologiae*, I-II, 96.2; 96.5.

15 Cf. Jeane Kirkpatrick, "Dictatorships and Double Standards," *Commentary* 31 (November 1979): 34–45.

the political realm, to account for the absolute dignity of human beings and for the possibility of mass political destruction and the more frequent lesser evils.[16] This is why politics ultimately does have something to teach theology even about itself. For it is the politician who must confront men also in their sinfulness, however it be called, while leaving a real space for their virtue, a space that does not "coerce" a particular definition of goodness on men. The politician must seek a "common good" even among the less than perfect, the kind of people Aquinas held to be the primary objects of civil law.[17] The task of political theory, as Plato had already intimated in the *Republic*, the first book of the discipline, is to find a place for the Good that transcends the ordinary political experience of the normalcy of men. Specifically Christian political theory begins with the Incarnation, with Augustine's realization that the Good, happiness, was indeed a necessary aspect of human reflection and endeavor, but that its fullness was not proper to this world, not achievable by human, particularly political, means.

In his still perceptive essay "Saint Augustine and His Age," the Catholic historian Christopher Dawson pointed out why the reality of transcendence, the dignity of the person, and the persistence of evil and sin—each a foundation of politics and of what is *beyond* politics—can become the basis of a new kind of social order that results from the effect of the Christian stimulus in the world. "In the West, however," Dawson wrote, "St. Augustine broke decisively with this tradition by depriving the state of its aura of divinity and seeking the principle of social order in the human will. In this way, the Augustinian theory, for all its otherworldliness, first made possible the ideal of a social order resting upon the free personality and a common effort towards moral ends."[18] This idea that the social order was to be based upon the dignity of individual persons, who had the capacity to "will"—the philosophical discovery the late Professor Hannah Arendt in her *The Life of the Mind* attributed directly to Christianity—this capacity to direct human actions to moral or immoral ends even within the political order, seemed to make political theory free from any scientific determinism, even from

---

16 Cf. James V. Schall, "Displacing Damnation: On the Neglect of Hell in Political Theory," *The Thomist* 44 (January 1980): 27–44.

17 Aquinas, *Summa Theologiae*, I-II, 96.2.

18 Christopher Dawson, "Saint Augustine and His Age," in *St. Augustine*, ed. M. C. D'Arcy (New York: Meridian Books, 1957), 77; cf. also John East, "The Political Relevance of St. Augustine," *Modern Age* 16 (Spring 1972): 170–71; Herbert Deane, *The Political and Social Ideas of St. Augustine* (New York: Columbia University Press, 1966).

sociology or psychology.[19] The "causes" of social disorder or progress, there-fore, had to be located in the vices or virtues, in the various definitions men gave to the actual existential happiness that they individually sought—choices eventually reflected, as Aristotle knew in the first book of his *Ethics*, in the forms of government described in *The Politics*.[20]

"Value-free" political theory, consequently, as Professor Strauss and Pro-fessor Voegelin were quick to note in famous studies, explained everything but politics and that which transcended it.[21] The late E. F. Schumacher, in his remarkable *A Guide for the Perplexed*, was thus mostly correct in his observation that "the modern experiment to live without religion has failed, and once we have understood this, we know what our 'post-modern' tasks really are."[22] The post-modern endeavor for political theory is, consequently, precisely the rediscovery of specifically Christian political theory, a theory which does not, when it is itself, allow politics to become effectively a secular religion or substitute metaphysics, as it has, in effect, tended to become in the recent past, particularly in academic political theory. This would, like-wise, be a theory that does not allow theology to destroy the things of Caesar.

There is, then, rather much truth in the ironical remark of Father Robert Sokolowski, professor of philosophy at Catholic University, when he said: "Perhaps we can say Christians forget that justice is a reflection of the image of the good and not the good itself. It is curious that Christians look for the divine in social order at a time when the social order itself has so much of the inhuman in it."[23] The rapid legalization of what were prop-erly called "vices" in classical natural law theory has made it more and more imperative that political theory retain its principled foothold in theology and metaphysics, in a source that would prevent it from completing Machi-avelli's modern project of identifying absolutely what men do with what they ought to do. The public order is more than ever being arranged so that we are not allowed to state the "untruth" of the laws and practices we have enacted against the classical norms.

19 Hannah Arendt, *The Life of the Mind*, vol. 2, *Willing* (New York: Harcourt, 1978); Vernon Bourke, *Will in Western Thought* (Chicago: Sheed and Ward, 1955).

20 Cf. James V. Schall, "The Best Form of Government," *The Review of Politics* 40 (January 1978): 97–123.

21 See Leo Strauss, *Natural Right and History* (Chicago: University of Chicago Press, 1953); Eric Voegelin, *The New Science of Politics* (Chicago: University of Chicago Press, 1952).

22 E. F. Schumacher, *A Guide for the Perplexed* (New York: Harper Colophon, 1977), 139.

23 Robert Sokolowski, letter to the author, 1979.

"To speak knowingly the truth, among prudent and dear men, about what is greatest and dear, is a thing that is safe and encouraging."[24] Such penetrating words of Socrates in the fifth book of Plato's *Republic* are, of course, very circumspect. For the number of "prudent and dear men," among whom Socrates felt himself to be discussing where political thought ultimately led, is indeed too few. When, however, this same truth is spoken among the multitudes, it can be quite dangerous, as Socrates himself soon was to find out. Realization of this very danger was the background of Professor Strauss's emphasis on "secret writing," about what he called "persecution and the art of writing."[25] The social sciences had to search their own limits because, if men suspected such limits led to or arose from revelation, they would, perhaps stubbornly, refuse the search for the truth. This is why it is no accident that both Paul VI, in the Vatican II document on religious liberty (1965), and John Paul II, in his address to the United Nations (October 2, 1979), took special and careful pains, from the side of religion, to insist upon the obligation of each person in himself not merely to pursue but to accept the truth on its own grounds, even the truth of revelation if it persuades. Truth may indeed make us free, but, as Solzhenitsyn and Strauss knew, it may also lead to persecution and tyranny by its rejection. The truth of political theory, from the viewpoint of the truth of original sin, may indeed lead to what does happen in actual political experience, to persecution of the just and the honest *because* they are just and honest. Man, in other words, always retains will as well as intellect.

The suspicion that the truth of political theory was bound up with the truth of metaphysics and revelation, then, has been the guiding principle of Western political theory—Christian, Jewish, and Muslim—until the modern era, until what the textbooks call, from Machiavelli, "modern" political theory.[26] The modern theoretical project, however, the one that now normally dominates the discipline, is based upon the intellectual "autonomy" of political theory. This means that the discipline contains within itself not only an historical *canon*, as Professor Pocock called it (a baker's dozen of basic authors from Plato to Augustine to Hobbes, Locke, Rousseau, and Mill,

---

24 This and all subsequent quotations from Plato are taken from Plato's *Complete Works* (Indianapolis: Hackett, 1997).

25 Leo Strauss, *Persecution and the Art of Writing* (Glencoe, Ill.: Free Press, 1952).

26 Ralph Lerner and Muhsin Mahdi, eds., *Medieval Political Philosophy* (Ithaca, N.Y.: Cornell University Press, 1972); Leo Strauss, *Thoughts on Machiavelli* (Chicago: Free Press, 1958); McCoy, *Structure of Political Thought*.

through which political theory is understood), but also a methodology and independent ground that is self-explanatory and self-justifying.[27] The extreme position was meant to be something quite different from Aristotle's notion of a "practical science," as he developed it in the sixth book of *Ethics*. It is different because, for Aristotle, the ends of the practical sciences were found in the metaphysical order.[28] Man did not "make" himself to be man, as Aristotle said, so that politics presupposed what made man to be man. Man's relation to himself, in other words, was not primarily one of self-making, but of self-discovery. And we can, properly, only "discover" what we ourselves do not make. Political theory appears in most academic and scholarly programs as the "history" of political theory, even though Professor Strauss warned that political philosophy ought not to be confused with the *history* of political thought.[29] Usually, political theory will be divided into the following categories: classical Greek and Roman; Jewish—early Christian—Roman Empire; Feudal and Christian Medieval; Modern; and Twentieth Century. However, the same enterprise can be divided in another fashion, according to the themes of "The Great Political Thinkers." The narrative histories of Professor Sabine or the more recent work of Professor Sibley would fill in the gaps of practice and theory for the less than "great."[30]

A third approach not infrequently used would be the "isms" analysis, as, for example, that used by the late Professor Ebenstein.[31] Here, attention would be paid rather to a single doctrine or ideology with its contents and problems. We would find in such an approach treatments of capitalism, democracy, communism, Nazism, fascism, socialism, nationalism, behaviorism, corporatism, authoritarianism, anarchism, internationalism, and, perhaps, "developmentism," in the various offshoots of Professor Rostow's now-famous pioneer thesis about the "five states" of economic growth.[32]

27 J. G. A. Pocock, *Politics, Language, and Time* (New York: Atheneum, 1973), 5–15.

28 McCoy, *Structure of Political Thought*, 29–60; E. B. F. Midgley, "Concerning the Modernist Subversion of Political Philosophy," *The New Scholasticism* 53, no. 2 (Spring 1979): 168–90.

29 Leo Strauss, *City and Man*, 8; Pocock, *Politics, Language, and Time*; Robert Dahl, *Modern Political Analysis* (Englewood Cliffs, N.J.: Prentice-Hall, 1976).

30 Cf. George Sabine, *A History of Political Theory*, 3rd ed. (New York: Holt, Rinehart & Winston, 1962); Mulford Sibley, *Political Ideas and Ideologies* (New York: Harper & Row, 1970); Michael Foster, *Masters of Political Thought* (Boston: Houghton-Mifflin, 1957); William Y. Elliot and Neil McDonald, *Western Political Heritage* (Englewood Cliffs, N.J.: Prentice-Hall, 1957); Lee McDonald, *Western Political Theory* (New York: Harcourt, 1968).

31 William Ebenstein, *Today's Isms* (Englewood Cliffs, N.J.: Prentice-Hall, 1973).

32 W. W. Rostow, *The Stages of Economic Growth* (London: Cambridge University Press, 1960).

Finally, not a few endeavors would like to exorcise altogether the "history" of political theory in order to replace it with some procedure subject to "verifiable," scientific tools. In this way, political theory would, presumably, declare its independence from the tyranny of the past, of revelation, of metaphysics, even of history.[33]

In recent years, in most academic programs and official political-science journals and associations, even in professedly "Christian" universities, a distinct intellectual "silence" has existed about the content and philosophical import of Christianity in political thought and affairs. One need only to inquire of good undergraduate classes—it is little better in graduate classes—about the identity of the Good Samaritan or the precise meaning of the Incarnation, original sin, or the "City of God," all the common fare of the West for centuries and centuries, to realize that the terms of shared discourse are no longer readily available in the general academic community.[34] Official political-science journals will too often—there are exceptions—return essays on formal Christian political theory and its implications in the discipline with the polite suggestion that they would be more "fitting" perhaps for theological journals. (And, alas, the quality of political discourse in the theological journals is often appalling.) We no longer suspect that William of Ockham, for example, in his analysis of the divine freedom, might have had something to do with the absoluteness of later, more modern political theory.[35] We do not see why the denial of the divinity of Christ is related to salvific ethos in much modern ideology.[36]

This severing of political theory from religion and theology, this studied "reductionism," however, has unfortunately served to separate them at a moment when religion, under the curious aegis of "liberation theology," is gaining an unprecedented political influence.[37] One has only to glance at the average weekly religious magazine, Protestant or Catholic, or diocesan

33 Cf. Heinz Eulau, *The Behavioral Persuasion in Politics* (New York: Random House, 1963).

34 Cf. James V. Schall, "On the Teaching of Ancient and Medieval Political Theory," *Modern Age* 19 (Spring 1975): 157–66. Reprinted in Schall, *Christianity and Politics* (Boston: St. Paul Editions, 1981), chap. 2.

35 Cf. Josef Pieper, *Scholasticism* (New York: McGraw-Hill, 1964).

36 Cf. Stanislaw Fracz, "Neomarxistisches Jesusbild," *Stimmen der Zeit* 198 (March 1980): 176–82.

37 Cf. Michael Dodson, "Prophetic Politics and Political Theory in Latin America," *Polity* 12 (Spring 1980): 388–408; Michael Novak, *The Theology of Democratic Capitalism* (New York: Simon and Schuster, 1982); James V. Schall, *Liberation Theology* (San Francisco: Ignatius Press, 1982).

newspaper, to realize that the major drift is political.[38] Political theorists, for their part, find themselves ill-equipped to handle the political overtones of the murder of an archbishop in a Central American cathedral, or the elevation of a revolutionary priest to the Office of Foreign Affairs, or why it is not "illiberal" for the Roman pope to exclude the clergy from politics in Brazil. Moreover, this self-isolation of political theory, the result of its own modernist methodology, is itself in part responsible for the radicalization of theology. This latter discipline almost never receives the sobering analysis that ought to come from political theory at its best about what we might expect of men in the world.[39] Thus, when it comes to politics, contemporary theologians too often are the successors of the Dr. Price who so incensed Edmund Burke in his *Reflections on the Revolution in France*: "It is somewhat remarkable that this Reverend Divine should be so earnest for setting up new churches, and so perfectly indifferent concerning the doctrine which may be taught in them."[40] Today's divines are equally earnest, though not equally unconcerned about the direction of the doctrines they espouse. Today, they are concerned with setting up not new churches, but new governments and nations. Rendering to Caesar has become, paradoxically, a clerical occupation, or at least a clerical ambition, as the cynics have always suspected it would.

Ironically, then, the classical roles are almost reversed, so that religion lacks the "realism" once expected of it, that source of sensibility Reinhold Niebuhr once found in Augustine.[41] The doctrine of the Fall did have political consequences in the very areas of property, coercive government, and labor, areas so related to modern theory and ideology.[42] Political theory, on

---

38 Cf. E. O. Norman, *Christianity and the World Order* (New York: Oxford University Press, 1979); Jacques Ellul, *The Betrayal of the West* (New York: Seabury Press, 1978); Ernest Lefever, *Amsterdam to Nairobi: The World Council of Churches and the Third World* (Washington, D.C.: Ethics and Public Policy Center, 1978); James Hitchcock, *Catholicism and Modernity* (New York: Seabury Press, 1979); James P. Hitchcock, "Will John Paul II Reorient a Church at Sea?" *National Review*, November 25, 1983.

39 Cf. Michael Novak, "The Politics of John Paul II," *Commentary* 31 (December 1979): 56–61; George Graham and George Carey, *The Post-Behavioral Era* (New York: David McKay, 1972); James Gould and Vincent Thursby, eds., *Contemporary Political Thought* (New York: Holt, Rinehart & Winston, 1969).

40 Edmund Burke, *Reflections on the Revolution in France* (Chicago: Gateway, 1955), 24.

41 Reinhold Niebuhr, *Perspectives on Political Philosophy* (1953; repr., New York: Holt, Rinehart & Winston, 1971), 1:243–57.

42 Cf. Schall, "Political Theory and Political Theology," *Laval Théologique et Philosophique* 31 (February 1975): 25–48.

the other hand, appears unable to articulate a coherent version of man or common good that would permit "the political" to be less than a substitute metaphysics, as it has become implicitly in so much contemporary theory. This would seem to suggest that, even for its own health, political theory must have addressed to it certain basic ideas and religious affirmations that would force and convince politics to limit itself to its own proper sphere.[43] Likewise, religion will not long remain balanced if the experience of politics is not included as a basic element in the analysis of how religion impacts the world and how human dignity is to be defended. The very nature of man's intellect does, in classical reflection, give him a real source for political knowledge.[44] "It may be accepting a miracle to believe in free will," G. K. Chesterton wrote in *The Well and the Shallows,*

> . . . but it is accepting madness, sooner or later, to disbelieve it. It may be a wild risk to take a vow, but it is quiet, crawling and inevitable ruin to refuse to make a vow. It may be incredible that one creed is the truth and others are relatively false; but it is not only incredible, but also intolerable, that there is no truth either in or out of creeds, and, all are equally false.[45]

The "miracles," "the wild risks," and the "incredibilities," which arise from a Western tradition that includes both faith and reason, seem to be those innovations that allow us to keep our politics sane and sensible.[46]

This, ultimately, is why Christianity cannot be avoided, along with the Old Testament, in the study of political theory—and why religion needs to acknowledge that Caesar is to be rendered unto, within limits, to be

43 Cf. Frederick Wilhelmsen, *Christianity and Political Philosophy* (Athens, Ga.: University of Georgia Press, 1978); Harry Jaffa, *Thomism and Aristotelianism* (1952; repr., Westport, Conn.: Greenwood Press, 1979).

44 Cf. Jacques Maritain, *The Social and Political Philosophy of Jacques Maritain* (1955; repr., Notre Dame, Ind.: University of Notre Dame Press, 1973); Josef Pieper, *The Silence of St. Thomas* (Chicago: Logos, 1957); Schumacher, *Guide for the Perplexed.*

45 G. K. Chesterton, *The Well and the Shallows* (New York: Sheed and Ward, 1937), 82.

46 Cf. Etienne Gilson, *Reason and Revelation in the Middle Ages* (1938; repr., New York: Scribner's, 1966); Pieper, *Scholasticism*; Pieper, *Silence of St. Thomas*; Maurice de Wulf, *Philosophy and Civilization in the Middle Ages* (1922; repr., New York: Dover, 1953); Charles Morris Cochrane, *Christianity and Classical Culture* (1940; repr., New York: Oxford University Press, 1977); Christopher Dawson, *Religion and the Rise of Western Culture* (Garden City, N.Y.: Doubleday Image, 1958); Gilbert Meilaender, *The Taste for the Other: The Social and Ethical Ideas of C. S. Lewis* (Grand Rapids, Mich.: Eerdmans, 1978); McCoy, *Structure of Political Thought*; John Senior, *The Death of Christian Culture* (New Rochelle, N.Y.: Arlington House, 1978); James V. Schall, *The Distinctiveness of Christianity* (San Francisco: Ignatius Press, 1983).

sure.[47] This is why, too, the most remarkable part of Christ's famous distinction was not that God was before Caesar, but that Caesar did have a place by right. In limiting politics, Christianity limited religion.[48] Christian political theory is the intellectual limitation of the political by removing from Caesar what is not his. In Aristotelian terms, this leaves the "highest of the practical sciences," the "queen of the social sciences," to be what it is. The "Divine Message of the City of Righteousness, the Faithful City," then, ought to be sought, even listened to by political theory, for that is part of its discovery of itself. This is the place of Christianity in political theory, and the place of political theory in Christianity.

47 Cf. James V. Schall, "The Old Testament and Political Theory," *The Homiletic and Pastoral Review* 80 (November 1979): 64–72.

48 Cf. James V. Schall, "The Death of Christ and Political Theory," *Worldview* 21 (March 1978): 18–22; "Political Philosophy and Christian Intelligence," *Catholicism-in-Crisis* 1 (November 1983): 26–30.

Chapter 5

Political Philosophy and Catholicism

"Political philosophy" means primarily not the philosophic treatment of politics, but the political, or popular, treatment of philosophy, or the political introduction to philosophy—the attempt to lead the qualified citizen, or rather their qualified sons, from the political life to the philosophic life.

> —Leo Strauss, "On Classical Political Philosophy,"
> in *What Is Political Philosophy? And Other Studies*

The end of the theoretic sciences is a good which lies outside the sphere of the human will; the truth of the theoretic (speculative) intellect. The contemplative life, most perfectly ordained to this intelligible good, is the life to which the political virtues and the arts themselves are ordered.

> —Charles N. R. McCoy, *The Structure of Political Thought*

I.

"Catholic social thought" is that body of official reflection—theological, philosophical, political, economic, social, familial—that has been presented as authoritative by bishops, the papacy, and national episcopal conferences. It is designed to give a reasoned explanation and justification of the Church's understanding of the public order and human life within it. Its sources are reason, tradition, Scripture, and experience. Political philosophy inquires about the place of the transcendent within the city. Though the two ought to be aware of each other, the object and the immediate sources of each are different and need to be distinguished. Philosophy strives to make distinctions clear so that we can know and speak accurately about *what is*. This knowing and speaking is what the mind is "for."

* This chapter was previously published in the *Catholic Social Science Review* 22 (2017): 147–56.

Catholic social thought is not exclusively a discipline of human origins. While upholding reason and recognizing its scope, it acknowledges and benefits from the information and inspiration found in revelation. It sees this source as a valid guide to understand the human enterprise. The present chapter concerns the way reason and revelation relate to each other in a noncontradictory manner. In this sense, it points to the "natural" end of what is implicit in political philosophy—namely, that its completion is not in philosophy itself. But philosophy enables us to see why a transcendent end is feasible. Charles N. R. McCoy made this point in the introductory quotation about the good that lies outside the will, not created by the will. To understand this relationship of political philosophy, philosophy, and revelation, one must begin with the contemplation "for its own sake" that is philosophy. Philosophy seeks a knowledge of the whole; yet the whole escapes it. This very escaping is the central problem of all of philosophy, the quest for the truth of things. It is likewise the reason why philosophy cannot exclude revelation and remain itself coherent. It cannot logically claim to be open to the whole while deliberately excluding something recurrent within the whole.

Man is by nature a "political animal," as Aristotle explained at the beginning of his *Politics*.[1] But each human being is a "whole."[2] He is primarily created for what transcends the city, for eternal life. Transcending the city does not mean bypassing it or denying it. The two ends of man—the political and the transcendent—are, in principle, compatible with each other. They have a common origin. They can diverge from their respective ends, however, because of free will, itself natural to what it is to be a human being. No rational being can achieve its end apart from its own knowing, choosing, and accepting it as given, as gift. The inner life of the human person as it is related to others, including the origin of being, is the locus of the primary "action" in the universe. This is the action wherein what is and what is not of God are decided. The universe exists in the first place in order that the drama and story of free persons be carried out in time. There is no collective inner-worldly entity that gathers together all human beings. The creation of such an entity is not the purpose of the existence of man in this world.

1 This and all subsequent quotations from Aristotle are taken from Aristotle's *Basic Works* (New York: Random House, 1941).

2 See David Walsh, *Politics of the Person as the Politics of Being* (Notre Dame, Ind.: University of Notre Dame Press, 2015).

An incident in the New Testament illustrates these points. The rich young man can be compared and contrasted with the young potential philosophers that populate Plato's dialogues. The rich young man, on considering what Christ requested of him, decided not to accept the invitation. No indication in the text suggests that he was not intelligent enough to know what was at stake—just the opposite. Subsequently we read—in memorable, even poignant, words—that, after his decision, he "went away sad" (Matthew 19:22). He did not take the nobler alternative to which he was invited. Most modern thought on the same subject would consider that actually embarking on the "higher road" offered to the rich young man was equivalent to rejecting man's autonomous and unlimited freedom. In this hypothesis, he should have gone away elated. He chose to be "his own man," as it were.

The rich young man, of course, was not, as in Plato, encouraged to become a philosopher or a politician. He was simply invited to sell what he possessed and follow Christ. The life that he was leading did not seem to be intrinsically disordered or evil. Still, we are made conscious that a conflict can exist between the good and the very good. This conflict resides in the order of rational freedom, of greater and lesser goods and abilities. We find no sign that, because of his choice not to follow Christ, the young man somehow lost his soul. He lost something, no doubt; and he could have lost his soul, but probably he didn't. Nevertheless, something greater that might have existed seems to have been lost by his choice to go away. Otherwise, he would not have been invited in the first place.

II.

What I want to indicate, by recalling this incident from Scripture, is the place of political philosophy as an intellectual discipline. Different issues are treated by different disciplines. Politics is not metaphysics. "Methods" only reveal what they are designed to reveal. No single "method" that we know of gives us access to everything *that is*. Reality is always more than the "methods" designed to know it. Much of reality remains outside of the methods used to understand some aspect of it. Disciplines can be distinguished and ranked according to their respective ends. We deal with things that are good, other things that are very good. We also classify, in the order of intelligibility, what is opposed to the good.

We might add that the world will not have ordinary people in it if it does not, at the same time, have extraordinary ones. This observation would include both the good and the evil. A realistic understanding of both the worst regime and the worst man is as important as an understanding of the best—and the proper location of each. Any discipline, when it does what it is designed to do, opens out onto what is beyond itself. Political philosophy is aware that philosophy exists, that it deals with *what is*, not just the order and end of the city. Political philosophy points to philosophy, but indirectly, by being aware of its own limits. It knows the implication of Aristotle's remark that "if man were the highest being, politics would be the highest science."[3] The politician who thinks politics is the highest science is the tyrant who finds the operative source of action in himself.

The way to deal with political things is not the way to deal with philosophic things. But it is possible to deal with both after their own manner. Nor is the purpose of political philosophy to make everyone either a philosopher or a statesman. A city containing only philosophers is not a city and could not last. A city also needs farmers, craftsmen, merchants, scientists, artists, and priests. Aristotle was not wrong to see that the common man could know many sane things without necessarily knowing complicated arguments about them. But a good politician is aware that, if we do not have in the city at least some philosophers who are engaged in concern for the truth of things for its own sake, the political order will be headless.

Speaking of Aristotle's notion of contemplation in relation to the city, Josef Pieper put the matter succinctly: "We suddenly see the new and forceful validity in the old principle: 'It is required for the good of the human community that there should be persons who devote themselves to the life of contemplation.' It is contemplation which preserves in the midst of human society the truth which is at one and the same time useless and the yardstick of every possible use; so it is also contemplation which keeps the true end in sight, gives meaning to every practical fact of life."[4] Aristotle is also aware with Plato that prideful philosophers, whose end is themselves, can destroy a city. No city exists without an explicit or implicit philosophy to justify its order of rule, some to its glory, and others to its destruction. The educated or, better, prudential politician, the statesman, must know enough not to kill the philosopher and also enough not to let the corrupt sophist rule.

Political philosophy, then, looks at the city; yet, it is aware that not everything belongs to the city. It understands the often-justified mistrust

3 Aristotle, *Ethics*, 1141a20–22.

4 Josef Pieper, *Josef Pieper: An Anthology* (San Francisco: Ignatius Press, 1989), 123.

that good statesmen and ordinary citizens have for those who call themselves wise, something classically recalled in books 8 and 9 of the *Republic*. The most serious long-range danger to cities arises first in the souls of philosophers. The statesman or ruler is not himself a philosopher, though he does have good prudential judgment. He recognizes the insufficiency of politics to be the highest science, even though it is the highest of the practical sciences, the sphere of the human actions of mortal men in this world. The statesman understands the importance of and difficulty of citizens to acquire the virtues, including especially the friendship that relates to virtue.[5] He also understands that virtue itself makes possible the consideration of things for their own sakes.

The philosopher sees that the best regime exists only in speech. The better actual regimes are worthy of ruling. But even the best of them is not to be confused with the best regime in speech. In the later Christian view, this distinction was the basis of Augustine's gloss on the *Republic* in his *City of God*. The best regime was not a regime in this world. To try to make it so, the temptation of modern political thought, led both to the destruction of worthy cities and to ideological efforts to reconstruct not just the polity but man himself.[6] No human philosophic reconstruction of man is better than what man is by nature. The history of political philosophy, with its "brilliant errors," as Strauss called them, is basically an empirical proof of this position.

III.

The task of political philosophy is to convince the politician that, while he has authority along with power over life and death, he is not the highest authority.[7] Even as statesman or ruler he is subject to the order of both political and natural things. How the city and its politicians understand the place of philosophy itself is what concerns political philosophy. It first arises out of the deaths of Socrates and Christ at the hands of the best existing cities of their time—the Greek polity, the Roman law. Both men were condemned to death in legal trials for the act of upholding the truth before the law.

---

5 See John von Heyking, *The Form of Politics: Aristotle and Plato on Friendship* (Montreal: McGill-Queen's University Press, 2016).

6 See Leo Strauss, *The City and Man* (Chicago: University of Chicago Press, 1964); James V. Schall, *The Modern Age* (South Bend, Ind.: St. Augustine's Press, 2011).

7 See Yves Simon, *A General Theory of Authority* (Notre Dame, Ind.: University of Notre Dame Press, 1980).

Christ, in a memorable phrase, acknowledges that Pilate, the Roman governor, does have authority. But the authority he has is "given to him" by Christ's Father (John 19:11). That is, political authority is itself subject to a higher law and falls within it in its proper exercise.

As he affirmed in the *Apology* and *Crito*, the principle that Socrates stood for, at the cost of his life, was "that it was never right to do wrong."[8] This principle is the foundation of all civilization. To empower the prince to use evil to rule is to destroy any grounded appeal to justice. But, as Socrates put it, nothing evil could happen to the good man. Death is not the greatest evil. Doing what is wrong is the greatest evil. Such an evil must always be a chosen thing by one free person. Contrary to Hobbes later on, the greatest evil is not violent death. The greatest evil consists in denying truth by doing what is objectively wrong.

But, as Plato clearly saw, unless these principles are upheld—that is, seen as intelligible—the world is incoherent. One can do wrong with ultimate impunity if there is no final sanction to violations of justice. Both the death of Socrates and that of Christ are central to political philosophy because they affirm that, after death, a judgment of moral and political things, both good and evil things, will occur. Ultimately things do cohere. Our understanding of this world is not adequate unless the deeds of those who have, in freedom, lived in it are judged. The significance of actual human lives must be resolved in terms of what they were in their choices.[9]

In this context, what might Catholicism have to do with precisely political philosophy? Should not political philosophy be independent of any revelational considerations? In fact, very little about politics is found in the New Testament. There are, to be sure, some things that give pause—the recognition that Caesar has things due to him. At Jesus Christ's trial, at one point Pilate, the Roman governor in charge of the formalities of the actual trial, responds famously, "What is truth?" as if to imply that he is not bound by something that he does not admit. The issue is pretty much the same as that of Socrates. The first book of the *Republic* is devoted to the question of whether might is right. When it came to the question of Socrates's condemnation at his trial, the majority of citizens present voted for his death. In the case of Christ, the crowd affirmed that they "had no king but Caesar" (John 19:15).

8 This and all subsequent quotations from Plato are taken from Plato's *Complete Works* (Indianapolis: Hackett, 1997).

9 See James V. Schall, "The Death of Christ and the Death of Socrates," *At the Limits of Political Philosophy* (Washington, D.C.: The Catholic University of America Press, 1996), 123–44.

Subsequent readers of these trials sense that justice was not observed in them. Can we leave it at that? The issue can be universalized: "The good man will be killed in all existing cities, even the best ones." This view was already present in the second book of the *Republic*. In all existing polities, the just man would be killed and the evil man prosper. This result is essentially why the issue of the best regime, which is the central question of political science, had to be seen as a city in speech. It was not an actual city with the normal variety of human characters and occupations. It takes this diversity of endeavor to make up a city. But a city in speech, in the mind, is not an illusion. Its existence in the mind is a real intelligibility, the conclusion of a logic. Its existence is argued, not founded in a given place and time. It serves as a standard both to see actual regimes more clearly and to judge them. But it also points beyond the political regimes of mortal men.

The human mind, as Plato saw, cannot accept the fact that those who do injustices will simply get by with them. In this sense, the doctrine of the immortality of the soul is a philosophic doctrine. It is posited because of the insufficiency of human cities as manifested in the trials of Socrates and Christ. Unless the immortality of the soul is true, no city of speech can be thought. Or better, immortality is itself contained in the logic of the best regime and its proper location. Evils have to be punished and good deeds rewarded properly. Otherwise, the world is incoherent. We cannot live with that thought.

IV.

The essence of the Christian teaching is that Christ, true God and true man, suffered, died, was buried, rose again, and ascended into heaven, from whence He shall come to judge the living and the dead. This cycle indicated the completion of a plan that found its origins in the Old Testament and ultimately in the Godhead itself. The central events depicted are facts, not myths. It will be immediately noticed, however, that Christianity does not rest its case on the immortality of the soul but on the resurrection of the body. It is not that the Greek reflection on immortality is wrong or not also accepted in Christian terms.[10] What is striking about it and its reality is how this teaching is a key issue in political philosophy. How so?

---

10 See James V. Schall, "On the Uniqueness of Socrates: Political Philosophy and the Resurrection of the Human Body," *Gregorianum* 76, no. 2 (1995): 343–62, reprinted in Schall, *The Mind That Is Catholic: Philosophical & Political Essays* (Washington, D.C.: The Catholic University of America Press, 2008), 61–79.

The proposition that the resurrection pertains to political philosophy will naturally be greeted skeptically. It should be. But let me at least sketch why the link between political philosophy, existing polities, and the resurrection of the body may make some unexpected sense. Let me begin with the end of the *Republic*. In the Platonic corpus, what was this ending about? It was literally the answer to a perplexity that Plato saw in existing cities. On hearing the issues at stake, most citizens would grant that good men do not survive in cities and that bad ones are rewarded. If this understanding be so, little case can be made for being just or good or for encouraging others to be so. If there is existentially no requiting of justice, no ultimate difference between right and wrong, we must grant incoherence to the world. The doctrine of immortality was designed to show that evil deeds are finally punished and good ones rewarded. But for this judgment to take place, the soul had to continue after death. This point was the significance of Socrates's comment to the jury after they voted to execute him. He simply said that "no evil can come to a good man."[11] The evil came to the unjust. In the meantime, Socrates would probably be conferring with friends and gods.

If we assume the logic of this argument, and it is very well formulated, why not rest there? Is there, in other words, anything yet to be considered that would link Christianity directly to political philosophy in a way not already established by Plato? What we need to establish is that something more needs to be attended to. What is this? First, there is the Aristotelian argument that what it is to be man is not simply to be a soul, however much that soul also needs accounting for. What is it, in other words, that is lacking? The first thing has to do with the critique of Plato. Man is body and soul, not just soul. His acts are the acts of his person, the whole of his being what he is.[12]

Logically, this recognition means that justice cannot be requited by considering the soul alone. The soul by itself was not what acted. It was the whole person who acted either for virtue or against it. If this approach be valid, then the justice and injustice experienced in the city—hence politics as the arena of human action—cannot be fully requited or rewarded unless the person who performed the act is fully present in judgment. In this sense,

---

11 Plato, *Crito*, 47e ff.

12 See David Walsh, *Politics of the Person as the Politics of Being* (Notre Dame, Ind.: University of Notre Dame Press, 2015); Robert Sokolowski, *The Phenomenology of the Human Person* (New York: Cambridge University Press, 2008).

the resurrection of the body is a proper response to an enigma that was already present in classical political philosophy. We need not argue that Christ's resurrection was directly intended as a contribution to political philosophy. What we do need to aver is that something unanswered or unattended to in political philosophy was completed by the fact of the resurrection of the body.

On this point, we might also refer to the story in the *Phaedo* of the man being punished in the rivers of the underworld for his crime of murder. He is to remain there in punishment until the man whom he murdered forgives him. From a Christian view, while agreeing on the point of forgiveness, this account has one major defect.[13] A sin or crime is not solely against the person who suffers from the unjust act. God also "suffers" from this act. In this sense, our sins reach beyond our present lives. They require divine forgiveness, which is made present in the suffering and death of Christ.

Ultimate justice is restored in this way, through suffering, as the Greeks also understood. What follows from this connection is that both Christ and we ourselves must forgive when forgiveness is asked. Forgiveness cannot be blanket. It requires some input on the part of the one who puts disorder into the universe. This is what sin is: the failure to put good in the world so that our acts have a lack of what ought to be there. Evil, recall, is the lack of a good that ought to be there. Justice, in principle, is restored the moment the one who does evil recognizes and admits that what he did was wrong. He recognizes, in other words, that the world is not incoherent, that it has an order.

V.

The resurrection of the body, in conclusion, restored the whole person who committed the evil act or did the good one. Without this final wholeness, the world is still incoherent. Modern trans-humanism, which is essentially a parody of the doctrine of resurrection, seems to recognize this in its efforts to keep the individual person alive down the ages. The revelational teaching or fact of the resurrection of the body is a requirement that arises out of politics itself, out of the inability of any existing city to punish all crimes or reward all virtue. Both the Platonic and Christian positions are needed for a complete whole. We might add that the doctrine of the immortality of the soul, from a Christian point of view, guarantees that the resurrected person

13 See James V. Schall, *A Line Through the Human Heart: On Sinning & Being Forgiven* (Kettering, Ohio: Angelico Press, 2016).

will be the same one that died and was the one that animated the person to good or evil acts. Whatever might be said for or against the relation of political philosophy to revelation, it seems clear that they belong to one and the same logical order and discourse. The exclusion of revelational considerations thus is a deliberate refusal of philosophy to open itself to the whole.

The final link is also found in Aristotle's notion that what exists as fully human is a single substance, body and soul, not just a soul using a body. The fact that legislators, in Aristotle's view, are more concerned with friendship than justice takes the final step. We can arrive at the intelligibility of resurrection beginning from sin or disorder of soul. But we can also arrive at it from reflection on friendship. In all true friendship, we find a sense of lastingness. It is not just the principle that "greater love than this no man hath but to lay down his life for his friend"—though it certainly includes this understanding. Aristotle had speculated about the apparent lack of friendship in the First Mover. It seemed odd that what was the perfection of human virtuous communication would be lacking in the divine.

Aristotle was right. It was a theoretic lack. The response of revelation was, essentially, in retrospect, a carrying out of Aristotle's notion of God as "thought thinking itself."[14] The revelational fact was that God was not monolithic, not intrinsically lonely, but an order of personal being and love that was complete in itself in such a manner that God did not really "need" the universe or men in it. This recognition meant logically that the world existed as an ordered gift, not as a necessity due to some lack in the divinity. The importance of political philosophy is the way it serves as a link between the issues that arise in the cities of the world and the transcendent whole that is each person in his final meaning as a finite, free being who does not, in the end, return to nothingness.

What, then, should remain clear is that political philosophy as an effort to understand all of reality through what happens in actual cities brings forth its own concerns. It arrives at enigmas that it cannot itself fully comprehend. Yet it can formulate what the problem consists in. Revelation is its own account of reality. Within it are certain events and understandings that illuminate what they are. They have their own intelligibility. We cannot argue from reason to revelation. We do find, however, elements in revelation that are also open to reason. The purpose of revelation is not directly political, but its truths do make clear many things.

14 Aristotle, *Metaphysics*, bk. 12, chaps. 7 and 9.

What is striking is that certain truths found in revelation provide sensible answers to the main perplexities of justice and friendship that political philosophy does not by its own methods solve but does inquire about. I would conclude from these considerations that reason and revelation, political philosophy and the city, are intelligibly related. Each, by being what it is, illuminates the other. Both by being themselves are required fully to explain man's philosophic, social, human, and transcendent life in its ultimate status—called, in the tradition, "eternal life." The plan of the universe from the beginning included each human person and was to bring about this end. It is in the mind holding all these things together in which we can see the surprising coherence of all things.

Chapter 6

On Socratic Surprises

The *Cleitophon* is the shortest of the Platonic dialogues, one from which we might not expect too much, though it is always dangerous in reading Plato to anticipate too little. Socrates barely appears in this dialogue, though he is the subject of criticism. As I like to say, no such thing as a university is possible unless we find there a constant reading of Plato by both faculty and students. Plato is not primarily for specialists. The same thing could be said of Aristotle, Augustine, and Aquinas, but they all knew their Plato. The history of philosophy might be said to be a reading of those who have themselves, sometimes wisely, sometimes not, read Plato. The fact is that if my criterion is valid, we have very few real universities in the land.

Lexington Books published *Plato's Cleitophon: On Socrates and the Modern Mind*.[1] The book contains a translation of the text, plus three essays by good scholars (David Roochnik, Clifford Orwin, and Jan Blits) on the dialogue. What, we might ask, could Plato's shortest dialogue possibly do with the "modern mind," such as it is? The answer is, I think, surprising.

In the introduction, Mark Kremer writes: "The drama between Cleitophon and Socrates is not unlike the drama of Western civilization itself in its relation to Socrates, and one can see from the relation between Cleitophon and Socrates that Plato anticipated the possibility of modernity and its decline into the postmodern hatred of reason or the affirmation of the will to power. The study of the *Cleitophon* is a point of entry into the ancient prospective on our modern and postmodern condition."[2] That passage is quite remarkable and surprises us about what is going on in this brief dialogue. We like to think that modernity is, well, modernity, that no one, least of all Plato, ever thought of its basic principles before. But as we read him again and again, we slowly discover that very little can be found that Plato did not anticipate.

* This chapter was previously published as "Ancient Perspectives on the Postmodern Condition," *New Oxford Review* 79 (July–August 2012): 30–34.

1 Plato, *Plato's Cleitophon: On Socrates and the Modern Mind*, ed. Mark Kremer (Lanham, Md.: Lexington Books, 2004).

2 Kremer, introduction, *Plato's Cleitophon*, 3.

Recently, I did write the introduction to the St. Augustine Press translation of Josef Pieper's *Platonic Myths*, a remarkable study.[3] It is quite clear that Plato's so-called "myths," especially his eschatological myths in the *Phaedo, Republic,* and *Gorgias*, were designed to get at truths for which Plato searched but could not quite grasp. Benedict XVI, who often cites Plato, in *Spe Salvi* approached these eschatological questions pretty much as they are found in Plato and reappear in different forms in modern science and ideology. The central concern in the soul of Plato was whether the world was created in injustice. If it was, the world would be incoherent. The whole issue of the immortality of the soul and its implications, especially regarding the resurrection of the body, arises out of this issue of whether the world was created in injustice that finds its initial formulation or realization in the actual political life of men in which not all crimes are punished nor all good deeds rewarded.

Cleitophon appears in book 1 of the *Republic*. He is one of the young men present at the house of Cephalus in Piraeus on the first night of discussion. He replies in Thrasymachus's favor later on in the first book. Thrasymachus holds that justice is the interest of the stronger, a classic position that will reappear in, not be invented by, Machiavelli and his followers.

Socrates wants to know if a tyrant can be deceived about his interest, in which case he would not be the strongest. Polemarchus, who has corralled Socrates into coming to visit his father's house, admits that Socrates has a point. Here, Cleitophon "interrupts." He accuses Polemarchus of being a "witness" for Socrates. Later, Cleitophon defends Thrasymachus about only seeming to know interests of the stronger. From these brief passages we catch a hint of the soul of Cleitophon. He is not impressed by Socrates.

In Clifford Orwin's essay on the *Cleitophon* in the same book, he notes, "This dialogue is the only one that features an unanswered blame of Socrates."[4] Many scholars have tried to show, on this account, that this cannot be an authentic dialogue of Plato, but this seems not to be true. This dialogue immediately leads into the *Republic*. It too is about justice. Cleitophon, Socrates, Lysias, and Thrasymachus all figure also in the *Republic*. It is said that we find three "trials" of Socrates: before the jury in the *Apology*, before Crito himself, and before the potential philosophers in the *Phaedo*. But we also seem to have something of a trial of Socrates for his positions before Cleitophon.

---

3 Josef Pieper, *The Platonic Myths* (South Bend, Ind.: St. Augustine's Press, 2011).
4 Clifford Orwin, "On the Cleitophon," in Kremer, *Plato's Cleitophon*, 59.

Socrates begins the dialogue by charging that Cleitophon has been giving speeches against him, or against his speeches. This accusation sounds a bit strange in the light of Socrates's oft-repeated insistence that he did not give speeches. It seems that Cleitophon never had a real dialogue with Socrates, so that he was a listener from outside, like the young men in the *Apology* who listened to Socrates quizzing their fathers about what they knew. To a listener, it would sound like speeches were exchanged, not arguments. In any case, Cleitophon tells us, on the contrary, that while he admittedly did not praise Socrates for everything, Cleitophon maintains that Socrates did not hear the whole truth of what he said (*Cleitophon*, 406).

Cleitophon frankly acknowledges that he was often "struck by amazement" by what Socrates said (407a). Socrates rises "above all other men with his speeches." He is like a god above the "tragic stage." He could inspire, demand attention. Socrates specifically denies in the *Apology* that he can speak well, unless of course simply "telling the truth" is good oratory. Socrates spends his whole life criticizing the Sophists, those precursors of college professors, with their long speeches. He tells the dangerous Callicles in the *Gorgias* not to give long speeches. Truth is found in conversation, in direct speech.

Socrates tells men in the city that they are doing nothing of what they ought to do. Everyone is about wealth, but how to use it justly does not concern them. Who will teach justice? Who will put it in effect? Here is the rub. Socrates has trained no one for justice, not even himself (407b). This seems the core of Cleitophon's complaint. He wants justice now and is impatient to get it, whatever human nature allows. Cleitophon, along with Machiavelli, displays a passion, not for ideal justice, but for "real" justice. He is impatient with all this soul talk.

But is an education in grammar, gymnastics, and art sufficient to achieve virtue? The young men have turned out to be ill-adapted to using wealth by this program. Men are at strife with one another, not at peace. "You [Socrates] say that men are unjust because they want to be, not because they are ignorant or uneducated. But then you have the effrontery, on the other hand, to say that injustice is shameful and hateful to the gods. Well, then, how could anyone willingly choose such an evil?" (407e). Is it by pleasure? What Cleitophon evidently complains about is that Socrates has not come up with a way to avoid these evils. Note the utopian streak in Cleitophon's argument. Socrates, you give a great talk about justice but you never produce it. We are impatient. We demand results.

Such is the substance of the accusation. Socrates replies that if you do not know how to use a thing, don't use it. ("If it ain't broke, don't fix it.") Cleitophon applies this principle to Socrates's speech. The man knows how to talk, but not to produce virtue (408a). Cleitophon is summing up his arguments as a lawyer. "I dare say I never objected or, I believe, ever will object to these arguments, nor to many other eloquent ones like them, to the effect that virtue is teachable and that more care should be devoted to one's self than to anything else" (408b).

Socrates can wake us up. "They [his speeches] can really rouse us as if we'd been sleeping" (408c). This is the great power of rhetoric. Cleitophon examines Socrates's friends to see if they practiced what he preached. (This same problem exists in Christianity.) If the practice of virtue is said to improve us, why are there not more examples of it? The Socratic answer is the same as that of Christianity. We all do not choose to live as we ought. We cannot be "forced" to be free or virtuous.

Cleitophon gives another short exhortation. "O you most distinguished gentlemen, what are we actually to make of Socrates's exhorting of us to pursue virtue?" (408d). Is it just talk? Is nothing going to happen? Will we just convert others to the "pursuit" of virtue but never find it? The key question is this: How are we to learn what justice is? (408e). This passage is obviously a connection to the *Republic* that follows. It is like discovering all the skills to improve the body but neglecting to use them. "What is the skill that concerns the virtue of the soul?" (409a).

Modern political philosophy wanted to be practical, to improve man's estate. It wanted to get out of the ideal state, as it were, and make everyone good. It chose to do this by lowering our sights. We no longer think of the higher things but of the bodily things that we have in common. If we have these, we will be happy and content. Disputes about the truth are dangerous, so let's not talk about them.

Socrates ("the man who appeared the most formidable among your companions") tells Cleitophon that this skill is "justice itself." What teaches this justice, its substance? (409b). It is to be a product of a skill, a technique. "Let's assume that one result of justice is also to produce just men." If justice is just beneficial or appropriate, it does not distinguish justice from other skills. "What is the product of justice?" (409d).

Here one of Socrates's friends said that the product of justice is friendship. (Recall the relation of justice and friendship in both Aristotle and the other dialogues, especially the *Phaedrus*.) Socrates insists that friendship is always good. He has to clarify friendships that do not lead to good. The people listening to this argument feel now that it is getting nowhere (410a). What is justice aiming at?

"So, Socrates, finally I [Cleitophon] asked you yourself these questions and you told me that the aim of justice is to hurt one's enemies and help one's friends" (410b). This definition comes up often in Plato, but as not the exact definition. It is Polemarchus's definition in book 1 and the military guardians' in book 2 of the *Republic*. In these places, Socrates does not hold this position. Then later, Cleitophon recounts, Socrates changed his mind and held, as he did in the *Republic*, that "the just man never harms anyone, since everything he does is for the benefit of all" (410b).

> Cleitophon next tells us that he got tired of asking Socrates what was the result of justice: I came to the conclusion that while you're [Socrates] better than anyone in turning anyone towards the pursuit of virtue, one of two things must be the case: either this is all you can do, nothing more—as might happen with any other skill, for example, when someone who's not a pilot rehearses a speech in praise of the pilot's skill as something of great worth to men; the same could also be done for any other skill. And someone might accuse you of being in the same position with justice, that your ability to praise it so well does not make you any more knowledgeable about it. Now that's not my own view, but these are only two possibilities: either you don't know it, or you don't want to share it with me. (410c)

We might note here that in Augustine the same question arises. The classics could teach what virtue is, but they could not figure out a way to practice it. The Christian would argue for the help of grace. But even with grace things go wrong. Behind this consideration is the original sin question, and behind it is the free will of each actual person.

In the last paragraph, we have a surprising conclusion. Cleitophon tells us that because Socrates could not guarantee a way for everyone actually to become just, Cleitophon would turn to the position of Thrasymachus that what is left to rearrange things is power. He has listened to enough speechmaking. Cleitophon agrees that we should not neglect the "soul itself while concerning ourselves solely with what we work hard to acquire for its sake" (410d).

Finally, Cleitophon repeats his defense that he only criticized Socrates for some things, but praised him for others. This is the conclusion: "For I will say this, Socrates, that while you're worth the world to someone who hasn't yet been converted to the pursuit of virtue, to someone who's already been converted you rather get in the way of his attaining happiness by reaching the goal of virtue."

At this ending, again, we might ask: Why is this shortest of dialogues considered to be prophetic of the trend of the modern mind? Being "Socratic" means that we never know everything. It also means that the best city is in speech. All existing cities, and men in them, are endowed with a will that means we cannot guarantee that things won't go wrong. To chafe at this limit is to challenge our finiteness.

When Cleitophon insists that he is "moved" by Socratic speeches, and he evidently is, we catch a note of disappointment in him. The only thing he has to fall back on is to change the definition of justice to the one Thrasymachus (and most of modernity) held, that it is power. If it is power, we can get things done without having to worry about choosing to be just in the Socratic sense. This result was basically what Leo Strauss called "the modern project." It was to achieve justice by our own definition and means, limited by no natural distinctions of good and evil, possibility or impossibility.

This conclusion still tells us why Socrates stands in the way of the modern notion of perfection. He insists that "it is never right to do wrong." Cleitophon is convinced that Socrates's speeches exhort him to want to put justice in place. He is impatient. He wants world order. He wants results. He does not listen carefully to the Socratic "speeches." He does not ask, as the *Republic* intimates, why the best city exists only in speech. Nor does he ask, as they did at the end of the *Republic*, about the presence of the best city among all existing cities. The result is still, to recall Glaucon in book 2 of the *Republic*, the real deaths of Christ and Socrates in existing cities of their time. They are not seen or acknowledged because we define what it is we want to see and what it is we want to call a human being and a city. We do not acknowledge that "what is a human being" and "what is a city" are not simply products of our own willing.

Chapter 7

On the Completion of Political Life and the Incompleteness of Political Philosophy

But we must not follow those who advise us, being men, to think of human things, and, being mortal, of mortal things, but must, so far as we can, make ourselves immortal, and strain every nerve to live in accordance with the best thing in us; for even if it be small in bulk, much more in power and worth does it surpass everything.
—Aristotle, *Nicomachean Ethics*, X, 7, 1177b31–78a2

Aristotle thus does not conceal the strange character and the precarious status of the science he is founding. Whereas there is no science but of what is general and no action that is not concrete and determined, the science he is founding is to be a science of action in general, that is, a science capable of determining what concrete action the acting human being should produce, and not therefore a general action or an action in conformity with some general rule, but a determinate action appropriate to the characteristics of the agent and the circumstances of the action.
—Pierre Manent, *Seeing Things Politically*

I.

The effort to define and classify how human beings have organized themselves over the centuries is what is normally called political science. The initial effort does not strive to explain that for which men ought to associate themselves together. Rather, it professes to show that they do in fact organize themselves in various, usually recurring, ways. It soon becomes obvious in this effort that some configurations are better than others. Observers

* This chapter was previously published in *Perspectives on Political Science* 47, no. 4 (September 26, 2018): 257–63, available at https://www.tandfonline.com/doi/full/10.1080/10457097.2018.1494427.

implicitly recognize that these organizational differences are not morally neutral, like classifying the varieties of flying bats or roses. Some ways of human polity seem better than others. This position, *pace* Machiavelli, seems to reflect a prior endeavor to identify what it means to be a good or a bad man. It is at this point that political philosophy arose, in Plato's awareness that the city is man's soul writ large.

Tyrannies were quickly identified and considered to be the worst regimes. Yet, Aristotle was able to speak of good and bad tyrants. The good tyrants, while retaining their self-centered end, in some fashion ruled after the manner of good monarchs. Soon we had different kinds of good and bad regimes. They could be classified according to the number participating in the decision-making authority or by the regime's purpose. All good regimes were for a common good under a definite law; all bad regimes were for the private good or interest of the ruling principle itself. In this latter case, the citizens were ruled for the particular good of the ruling principle, not for a common good that included the good of everyone including the rulers. There could be varieties of oligarchies or democracies. Various types of regimes could be mixed to foster goods or counteract evils that needed specific attention if the polity were to exist and flourish.

In the title of these reflections, I have spoken of the "completeness of political life" as contrasted with the "incompleteness of political philosophy." I do not consider this latter incompleteness to be a defect in the discipline but something that properly belongs to its nature. Indeed, a political philosophy that sees itself as a complete explanation of all that man can be is the proper definition of an ideology. Completeness and incompleteness are related to each other in a way that illuminates what I conceive to be the relation of political philosophy to philosophy itself and of both to revelation. I do not conceive revelation to be a myth or a subjective feeling. It is a way of life with transcendent origins that can be also articulated in terms of reason. Its parameters are open to anyone, not merely to those who have the said faith in which they are made known. The first step, then, concerns the meaning of "the completeness of political life." This completeness is not the same as the "completeness of political philosophy." Political science is complete when it gives an adequate description of the variety of civic possibilities.

The latter completeness, of political science, means that our survey and classification of differing regimes and their pasts is basically accurate. It explains what men did do, and recurringly do, in political life as it was lived in actual regimes. It describes differing regimes over time and place. Thus, an oligarchy was an accurate and intelligible term for certain types of regime in which wealth, its accumulation and protection, was the clear motive of the adopted political authority and usually also the souls of the citizens found in it, including the poor. It accurately reflected the habits of its citizens. The information that allowed such classification was based on observation and analysis of how men did act in relation to one another in political regimes.

Regime changes were also noted. Such changes were the result of shifts in the concept and practice of virtue among citizens of a given regime. Oligarchies could become democracies. Tyrants usually arose from democracies. The ultimate agents of change in regimes were found in the souls, in the virtues and vices, in the habits that are revealed in their living. Political science in this sense manifested a certain cyclic change. No actual regime was so stable that it never changed, though Aristotle was able to point out ways to preserve for a time even tyrannical regime.

The "completion of political life," by contrast, arises from another perspective. This completeness is primarily about the human beings, the unique persons, who are the acting subjects of political life. The "state," to use a modern, and perhaps confusing, term for it, is not a substantial being that bears its own reality and destiny over and above that of the individual citizens. Any organized civil community falls in the category of "relation." It is not itself a "what." It is an "order" of parts to each other and to a whole as displayed in the actions and interactions of the citizens. Each of its "parts," its citizens, has an end that, while properly passing through it, transcends the political order. But political order is not nothing. Its "order" makes a real difference in how people live and act, whether well or ill. But the more recent notions of social justice and structural "sin" or guilt are, as I see it, quite misplaced and have been the cause of untold confusion in political affairs and human life.

Justice in whatever form is always a personal virtue and cannot, without causing serious confusion, be posited of a regime independently of a personal virtue manifest in the souls of actual persons. The notion of corporate guilt, especially corporate guilt over the ages so that the sins of the fathers are real sins in the sons, was already rejected on the grounds of its injustice in the Old Testament. To see it recur in the form of reparations in more modern political thought is an instructive lesson in the decline of good regimes to those of less and less excellence. Individual persons are replaced by class, gender, race, or other nonfree, nonconcrete determinations. By that remark, I wish to alert us to the notion that modern political philosophy, as I argued in *The Modern Age*, is itself a profound metaphysical mis-location of man's personal transcendent end.[1] Man's final end is replaced by an organized social structure that identifies man's end with the perfect state to be achieved down the ages in this life.

II.

What does one mean by "a complete human life" that is carried out within the boundaries of every man's political situation? First of all, any existing human life from conception to when it dies or is killed is complete. In this sense, every human life is complete at its termination no matter how long it lives, even for a few moments. Such is all the life that it will have in this world. However long or short, it is what it is, for better or worse. Few human beings live out their four score years and ten that we associate with a long life.

Yet, the term "a complete human life" connotes actually living through the stages of life—conception, birth, adolescence, maturity, and old age. Relatively few human beings last the allotted years. That too is a fact of existence that does not necessarily contradict the fullness of the life lived. Those who die nobly in a brief life, as Aristotle thought, do sum up their complete existence. Moreover, if we include sickness, injustices, sins, and other factors present in most given lives, few lives are without sickness, grief, and toil. A given span of life is all that each particular person has to live and complete the life actually given to him. Man is the only being in the cosmos that is "mortal," the only one who knows that he is mortal, that he himself will die. He lives as an alien in the shadow of death amid the "immortals."

The gods are immortal. The stars turn in the heavens in unending cycles that seem to go on forever. In terms of the other species of living things, man is different, without being completely unlike them. The purpose of any species is to keep itself in being down the ages of time. This continuation is accomplished by whatever reproductive mechanism and life span are found within each species from trees to butterflies to trout to deer. In this sense, the individual exists for the species. Individuals die and pass on; the species remains. But the species is not something wholly apart as another being from the individuals who compose it.

Amid this changelessness and the cycles of immortal things from the cosmos itself to the creatures within each species, we have man. He seeks to know and explain to himself what reality is, *what he is*. His personal being is

1 See James V. Schall, *The Modern Age* (South Bend, Ind.: St. Augustine's Press, 2011).

as a member of an ongoing species in time that has constantly replaced itself for millennia of years with new passing individual persons. He exists concretely as an individual person. He also exists for his own sake as well as for the ongoing species. As such, he continues and reverses the priority of individual to species. He brings up the question of his own permanence. The continuing existence of new, distinct individuals in this world is dependent on a cycle of begetting, birth, and death of individual human beings.

In this sense, the human race has continued on this planet for eons, as have other species of living things. Theories that deny a personal afterlife to individual persons or that absorb particular human beings with names into an "all" of the species or cosmos itself can have no meaning to individual human lives other than as flicks of memory about what a passing individual might have thought or done. The only "immortality" left is an inner-worldly one, a mere memory or record of human events, good and bad. There is no concern with the person as such once he has passed away. The cyclic history in Thucydides and in Ecclesiastes or the exemplar history of Herodotus or Tacitus record these things for us as witness of what will return. What remains is a "utopia" or perfect society that is being brought forth down the ages to which all previous human lives are sacrificed.

The "complete human life" with which politics directly deal is the one that takes for granted the recurring process of begetting, birth, infancy, adolescence, education, family, work, old age, and death. A "complete life" meant the passing through these natural stages of life and death. No man was called happy until he was dead. This sober reminder also meant that what counted was not just the passing through these stages of life. What each person did while he was living it needed to be accounted for. This record, this tale of the acting person's "actions," was what distinguished one human being from another in the story of his deeds and thoughts.

Often, something disturbing or glorious was found about the record of each life, including the lives of the ordinary, of the common men and women encountered in any polity in any time or place. The completion of political life meant both the passing through the stages of human growth from conception to death and its record in terms of good and evil that was manifested by each person in the given polity in which each life was lived. Good lives could be found in terrible polities; bad lives could be found in good polities. The polity itself had no claim to substantial being, but its order could aid or hinder a life of virtue. Existence, transcendent being, was the issue of each person.

III.

Politics and political philosophy came together at this point. The issue was best formulated by Plato's brothers in the second book of the *Republic*. It was the common opinion that a just man who appeared in any existing polity would be treated unjustly, that the unjust prospered and the just suffered as a result. Since this situation seemed to recur throughout time and in all existing polities, the only logical conclusion that one could make was that the world was created in injustice. Such considerations were not incompatible with the revelational notions of a good creation and a fall from grace within that created cosmos.

Ademantus, Plato's brother, testified that the poets praised injustice and intimated that the good did not prosper. Logically, this conclusion, as it stands, meant, since the consequences were the same, that no ultimate distinction could be made between what was just and unjust. No further consequence followed from either one. This position became a recurring one in the history of political philosophy. If the unjust could live their lives in prosperity and die in it, what more could be said but that their lives were as complete as those who lived justly? Justice was a word that had no meaning if the consequences of both the just and the unjust life was the same. The world, in other words, was founded in injustice. Human life, whether lived justly or unjustly, was essentially the same. This understanding was Plato's dilemma.

Political philosophy arose out of such reflections on political science and life in actual regimes. Socrates, at his last day, spoke of the immortality of the soul. Thereby, he directly confronted the notion that the world was created in injustice. He maintained that it was never right to do wrong. No evil could come to the just man. Death was thus not an evil. Doing wrong to escape it was. Socrates did not escape death. He did escape doing evil. He maintained that justice could be upheld only if the actual consequences of completed lives were judged, rewarded or punished. Understanding of the nature and reality of the soul grew out of the dilemma of the completeness of each human life in its living in this world.

But the next question arose: What, then, is the soul? This topic is the link between political philosophy and metaphysics. It sets the stage for the relation of metaphysics to revelation. Thus, to speak of the "incompleteness of political philosophy" implies that, being what it is, it validates the implications of its own arguments. Such arguments lead somewhere it cannot itself go. But this inability in no way implies that the arguments as such are not true. Modern political philosophy, in its treatment of an inner-worldly city down the ages, tries to complete what cannot be completed by philosophy. In its logic, related to Plato's city in speech, it thus has to invent what Charles N. R. McCoy called a "substitute intelligence," one not based on *what is*.[2] No mind can accept incompleteness. The question is: What completes it?

Consequently, I would argue that the inability of political philosophy to do no more than make the case for immortality defines its place, a perfectly valid place, in the order of intellectual things. I will argue that when political science seeks to become itself a metaphysics, it will postulate the completion of political philosophy as a political mission in this world down the ages. In so doing, it fulfills the requirements of logic by denying the ontological status of the human soul and, more importantly, the body of the person it animates. When I say that the principles of logic are retained, I mean that once we deny the immortality of each particular citizen in the face of his mortality, his death, we subsume the individuals back into the "species" man. This species is in turn embodied in the ongoing human race in this world. In a proper political philosophy and metaphysics, the species only has a logical existence. What is demanded intellectually, however, concerns the permanence not of the species but of the individual persons with a name and a story.

What needs to be added at this stage of the argument is that the normal reality of ordinary human living results in many crimes unpunished and many good things unrewarded. Such a situation is clearly unjust. Once a transcendent order is rejected, what takes its place, as I have indicated, is the search for a perfect order in this world, one that has no transcendent criterion of good and evil, one that does not see the individual as anything but an instance of a species. The individual is for the species, not vice versa. It is this reversal of the understanding of being and thought that gives priority to logic and not to existence that must be dealt with. But how?

To the question of whether there ought to be both a transcendent completion of a human polity as implied in the City of God of Augustine and an inner-worldly example of "the best regime" that was proposed by Aristotle can briefly answered. One notes that it was once religion that was concerned most with the transcendent City of God. In sundry ecological concepts, we now hear of religion that postulates the care of the earth as its most important project. The implication of this view is that once we solve the ecological or political problem, we will solve the moral problem. Yet,

---

2 Charles N. R. McCoy, *The Structure of Political Thought* (New York: McGraw-Hill, 1963), 6.

people lose their souls in the best regimes and save them in the worst. That is, the human drama before the divine judgment takes place in all existing regimes in which actual persons have lived and died.

IV.

It is here, I think, that the real solution to the incompleteness of political philosophy can be found. Recall that this incompleteness was seen in what was the best regime of its time. It had to do with how one lived in any actual regime. The best that political philosophy could propose was the immortality of the soul as precisely a solution to an accusation of injustice against the gods. If the soul was immortal, however, and there were arguments that suggested that it was, the sins could be requited and the good actions rewarded in the Isles of the Blest, which were not conceived as mortal.

Yet, this solution left a nagging problem. The soul was not the complete man, as Aristotle pointed out. The complete man was this particular whole, body and soul, with all the storied deeds and thoughts of the being that the individual person bore in this world. The classical treatises on friendship intimated that this mutual love we call friendship was more than a passing thing. But how could this be if it included only the soul? It is into this situation that revelation addresses itself. I would argue that revelation did not in fact occur until such a time that its meaning could be grasped from the side of human living and philosophy. This point arrived in the fullness of time at the deaths of Socrates and, more particularly, of Christ. The last thing that the disciples expected was the resurrection of the body, foolishness to the Greeks and a scandal to the Jews. And yet, it is only with the resurrection of the body that the issues brought up by the incompleteness of political philosophy and the completeness of political life can be clearly seen. It is the complete person who sins or acts virtuously. It is this life that needs to be judged.

Political philosophy, in its natural logic, is completed by the resurrection of the body. While it could not plan for this completion on its own grounds, such philosophy could on reflection see that what it did arrive at was incomplete. It could likewise see that the alternatives proposed in time as rejections of revelational doctrines invariably lead to something worse in the political order itself.

What this conclusion suggests is a more sober look at political life, a realism, as it were, that does not propose negations of the commandments and human virtues in the name of man's self-perfecting himself. On this basis, the revelational response cannot be rejected out of hand as irrational. It is a reasoned response to an intrinsic incompleteness always found in political philosophy itself. If it is not accepted, it cannot be rejected on the grounds that the solution revelation provided was itself irrational.

The regimes of this world are passing ones. Each citizen who lives in one of them is mortal. The individuals who live in them reach resurrection and judgment in the revelational tradition precisely as a consequence of the dignity in which they were each created in this world. This dignity gave each person the freedom and the responsibility for deciding, in the polities of this world in which each lives his life, how he stands to the transcendent order to which his very personal being points.

V.

In this context, what is the precise meaning of the incompleteness of political philosophy? Again, I do not conceive this incompleteness to be a defect but a virtue. It stands at the limits of human reason by not affirming what it cannot affirm about reality. To affirm that we do not know what we do not know is a sign of intelligence. This view does not imply, however, that there is nothing left to be known. We simply do not know everything that is there to be known. It would in fact be a defect if political philosophy did claim to be able to complete itself, to explain reasonably all things about actual human life. Yet, modern political philosophy does organize itself around various forms of this claim to be able fully to explain and, if applied, to achieve what man is about in this world. The vision of the City of God haunts even the most rabid secularist in his very denial of any transcendent end. The transcendent end simply becomes terrestrial without changing its spots.

In this sense, political philosophy is a "theory" or an "idea" not drawn from *what is*. It is an artistically architectonic end-form originating in the human mind. In rejecting metaphysics and revelation, such a philosophy demands action embracing all men, not thought about what actually exists. Ultimately, as McCoy has held, modern political philosophy is the result of a reversal of the theoretic and the practical orders in which, within the practical order, art is already placed over prudence. In this reversal, however, a theoretic model of a perfect kingdom remains to be fulfilled in practice as a human project. Classical political philosophy was content to let the mind admit that there were things it did not know and knew that it did not know. It is this very awareness of the precise nature of what it did not know that allowed for the reasonableness of revelation at least to address itself to the human mind without any contradiction in being.

In modern philosophy's understanding of itself, the world lacks an intrinsic and objective "natural order" to which man's mind is open to *what is*. The source of truth for the human mind is not itself. It is open to the given reality before it. Political philosophy becomes itself a human construct, not a search for truth that is not itself. Man seeks to create himself in such a way that the experienced evils that he himself causes will be eliminated in this world through the application of correct ideas of economics, politics, and sociology. To accomplish this goal, we must eliminate virtue and the personal discipline that enables us to recognize and practice it. This is the "modern project" in its most intelligible form. As a result, political philosophy is thought to be able to complete itself, its own goal, with no appeal to any higher philosophical or divine order.

As a prerequisite to this completion, the "complete political life" of the normal citizen in any existing polity must be relativized so that it has no transcendent significance. Nothing "absolute" can be found within it. The stories of individual human lives and literature do not record any ultimate drama before the divinity. No citizen can be addressed by the Socratic affirmation "It is never right to do wrong."[3] This is not a reason for rejecting the new order of things fashioned by the human mind. In other words, both the classical philosophical affirmation of the immortality of the soul and the revelational affirmation of the resurrection of the body must be specifically denied. Both affirmations imply absolutes within each human, personal life that constitute its essential being. What replaces individual lives is the image of the ongoing human race down the ages of this world, an inner-worldly collective goal achievable by human effort alone. It is a goal proposed in defiance of the gods. The gods are now judged to be responsible for human ills because they allowed evil in the world. The classic image of Prometheus is not entirely inappropriate here. The fact that the gods also allowed personal free will and its relation to evil is overlooked.

I have remarked that revelation allows politics to be politics. How does it do this? Essentially, it does it by properly defining what man is expected to do as a mortal in this world. It allows for a proper theoretical order as the end of the political life. Political life by being itself points to the specu-

---

3 Plato, *Crito*, 49a–b. This and all subsequent quotations from Plato are taken from Plato's *Complete Works* (Indianapolis: Hackett, 1997).

lative life, the life proper to the gods. This is the life that Aristotle told us to direct our lives to, however little of it we could know. Also with the revelational tradition as a background, politics acknowledges a freedom that can choose against the good, for there is also a repentance that can strive to repair voluntary disorder. The life of leisure, as Aristotle understood it, meant that besides politics, itself a legitimate thing, the knowing of *what is* was also an essential feature of what it was to be a human being. Political philosophy was expected to know the truth of man.

But by separating politics and metaphysics, political philosophy was fortunately prevented from becoming a substitute metaphysics that is not concerned with achieving the real limited good to which man is ordained in his political life. Rather, this substitute metaphysics of modern political philosophy strives to transform man's being. In doing so, it misplaces the locus of his happiness. In this sense, revelation, by presenting a true description of man's end, allows the reading of Aristotle's *Politics* to be an accurate account of real regimes, including the best practical regime, and the virtuous or nonvirtuous actions of citizens within them. Actual politics are thus not overburdened with a theoretical construct that claims to be able to reform the citizen in such a way that his human condition, a condition that includes his evil actions and their existential consequences, is allowed to carry itself out to the citizen's natural death. Death is the end of citizenship, but not the end of actions carried out within each polity by individual citizens. Nor is death the worst evil. Doing wrong is the greatest evil, as Plato taught.

The "moderation" or realism of politics means that we have in the theoretical realm a proper, intelligible explanation of the order of things, including divine and human things. Politics ought to be free of the metaphysical and revelational notions that would tempt it to claim for itself to be first philosophy. Aristotle's *Politics* and his *Metaphysics* are not the same books because the realities to which they refer are not the same. But they are related. In the most obvious sense, as Aristotle also pointed out, disordered souls in the practical ethical order will lead to lives that seek to justify their aberrant deeds in the theoretic order. It is striking that ways of life that Aristotle would consider abnormal are the very ones that most often seek to impose their self-justifications on others through laws. Error cannot stand to be known as error. All error presents itself as truth and, in fact, will always contain some truth, but in a distorted way.

The incompleteness of political philosophy, its confrontation with the deaths of Socrates and Christ about the fate of the good man in all existing societies, leaves it with a certainty that its own questions, though properly asked, are not solved by itself. The issue is not the fate of "mankind," the collective universal, but what is the meaning of the death of Socrates, Mary, and Samuel in their unique personhood in any existing city. We do not confront the realities of human life until we admit that all citizens die individually. This fact is in part why a few modern scientists and entrepreneurs make it a project to get rid of death, or to bring back bodies to life after the manner of Lazarus in the New Testament, an existence in this world for a few more years or centuries. If the center of both political life and beatitude is not in the species but in each individual including his death in a given polity, then political philosophy is properly a discipline that lies open to a response to its own enigma.

Political philosophy at its best can see the reasonableness of rejecting the modern project. It can also understand, even if it does not believe, that there is a line of intelligence within revelation. This intelligence is itself directed to reason, the same reason that exists in each individual person when he actually understands what is at stake. One does not have to be a believer to understand that the resurrection of the body is itself directed to a human reason that has developed to the point of understanding the significance of each human life, including the souls of those who, in the best regimes of their time, consented to kill Socrates and Christ for maintaining the fundamental principle of our civilization—that it is never right to do wrong.

Once political philosophy has arrived at this understanding, it can see that its incompleteness is not a sign of incoherence in the universe but a sign that the human mind itself awaited an explanation of why it reached issues that it could not itself completely understand. This is why, as Aristotle himself once remarked, that happiness seems to be the one thing the gods would give us if they could. The whole struggle over modernity, and indeed over all human political philosophy and metaphysics, is over the "reasonableness" of the revelation that was handed down to us.

Man arrived at a point at which he could formulate what it was to be mortal and human. Almost at this very time, he was confronted with a revelation that addressed itself to what he could not figure out by himself. Many revelations and false gods appeared, many philosophies arose, but only one addressed the issue as asked. Political philosophy, at its best, in its very natural incompleteness, lies at the heart of the affirmation that all things of reason, of *logos*, do belong together. To see this truth is the great adventure of political philosophy and of the mind that we neglect at our peril.

Chapter 8

A Happening That Really Took Place

"The Adventure of Thinking"—Ratzinger on Reason and Revelation

It should really not be necessary to point out that all these assertions (in the Creed) only have a meaning on the assumption that *the happening whose meaning they seek to elucidate really took place*. They are the interpretations of an event; if that event is removed they become empty talk which would have to be described not only as frivolous but as downright dishonest.

—Joseph Ratzinger, *Introduction to Christianity*

I'd also already read some philosophy of religion in Freising; but I went about it differently from scratch. This gave much delight both to me and to the students, so I had a sizeable, lively popularity. . . . I was experiencing now *the adventure of thinking*, of knowledge, of advancing toward and entering deeply into things.

—Benedict XVI, *Last Testament in His Own Words*

I.

In his *Last Testament*, we find a passage that is most revealing of the man who was Joseph Ratzinger, now an aging pope emeritus. Looking back on his life, he was asked: "What would you have liked to occupy yourself with in life?" This question is obviously a delicate one to ask a pope who seems to have accepted the papal office willingly if somewhat resignedly. But Benedict is honest and frank. "What I could do was, as I said, something other than what I wanted—I wanted my whole life long to be a real professor—but afterwards I see it was good how it went."[1]

---

* This chapter was previously published in *Communio: International Catholic Review* 44 (Summer 2017): 224–41.

1 Benedict XVI, *Last Testament in His Own Words*, with Peter Seewald (London: Bloomsbury, 2016), 235.

On looking back at the eight-year papacy of Benedict XVI, it is difficult to say that, by being pope, he ceased to be a professor. All popes leave marks and legacies on things that they do better or less well. Some popes are linguists, some orators, some administrators, and some thinkers. The legacy left by Benedict is surely that intelligence and revelation belong together in a coherent manner. This view does not rest on sentimental but on objectively valid grounds. The validity of these grounds is what Joseph Ratzinger sought to establish or reaffirm precisely as something reasonably related to the integrity of all things human.

Not everyone needs to be, can be, or even wants to be a philosopher. Philosophy, the quest for a knowledge of the whole, as most other human things, takes the genius, work, and discipline of many minds. Myriads of sundry things need to be addressed full-time if the varied complexity of reality and human society is to be explained and understood. Things other than intellectual, things to be made and things to be accomplished, exist in the rich and varied cosmos that we human beings, to our surprise, inhabit. Yet, it remains true that, within any society, for its own integrity, we need those who are able to devote some or all of their time to the pursuit of knowledge and wisdom, to the accurate description of *the things that are*. Some things we want to know just to know them, their truth.

The Church's monastic tradition in part attested to this realization, as did the academic tradition in the ancient city. Intelligence, indeed, is not the exclusive property of philosophers or theologians. It would be doubly dangerous if it were. Almost everyone has some touch of it. Often the technically unlearned are wise enough to figure out basic things or to identify contradictions or vanities in the learned when they see them. This fact at least hints at the reason why revelation was addressed to all men, not just to the academics. Benedict's study *Jesus of Nazareth*, for example, is a scholarly book, finished after he assumed the papacy.[2] Yet, most people can understand it with great profit if they put their mind to it. Christianity is a religion of intelligence at every level, as John Paul II's *Fides et Ratio* reminds us.[3]

---

2 Benedict XVI, *Jesus of Nazareth*, vol. I: *From the Baptism of Jesus to the Transfiguration*, trans. Adrian J. Walker (New York: Doubleday, 2007); vol. II: *Holy Week: From the Entrance to Jerusalem to the Resurrection* (San Francisco: Ignatius Press, 2011); vol. III: *Jesus of Nazareth: The Infancy Narrative*, trans. Philip J. Whitmore (New York: Image, 2012).

3 John Paul II, *Fides et Ratio: On the Relationship between Faith and Reason* (Boston: Pauline Books & Media, 1998).

As such, Christianity presupposes and insists that reason be used to the best of our abilities, even in the considerations of revealed things. This is, after all, why we have "creeds." Ratzinger put it this way in an incisive comment in *Milestones*: "Revelation is always a concept denoting an act. The word refers to the act in which God shows himself, not to the objectified result of this act. And because this is so, the receiving subject is always also a part of the concept of 'revelation'. Where there is no one to perceive 'revelation', no re-*vel*-ation has occurred, because no *veil* has been removed. By definition, revelation requires a someone to apprehend it."[4] It requires an intelligence capable of distinguishing what it is that addresses it. Man is more than reason, but he becomes less human to the degree that he neglects its tenets in how he lives and what he thinks.

II.

Many ways can be found to approach and understand Joseph Ratzinger's basic insights. Everyone knows of his ability to play the piano and his love of music, especially Mozart.[5] Perhaps it is well to begin here. In an essay on "Art and Prayer," Benedict wrote that the way to God and truth is often a *via pulchritudinis*, a way that leads trough beauty. We find ourselves, he tells us, deeply moved by "a few verses of a poem or a piece of music." What is this experience that can "touch the heart . . . uplift the mind?" Benedict is aware of his own experience. "A work of art is a product of the creative capacity of the human being who is questioning visible reality, seeks to discern its deep meaning, and to communicate it through the language of forms, color, and sound. Art is able to manifest and make visible the human need to surpass the visible; it expresses the thirst and the quest for the infinite."[6] This "quest for the infinite" describes, perhaps better than anything, the character of Benedict's mind.

This approach through beauty is instructive. It is an example of something often found in Joseph Ratzinger's thought—namely, that reality, by being what it is, always points beyond itself. In his discussion of mathematics, for instance, he points out that mathematics deals with quantified

4 Joseph Ratzinger, *Milestones, Memoirs: 1927–1997*, trans. Erasmo Leiva-Merikakis (San Francisco: Ignatius Press 1997), 108.

5 James V. Schall, "The Universal Language of Beauty," *Homiletic & Pastoral Review* 108, no. 6 (2008): 20–23.

6 Benedict XVI, "Art and Prayer" (General Audience, August 31, 2011), in *Prayer* (San Francisco: Ignatius Press, 2013), 62–63.

matter. This is what it should do. But not everything is material. So there are methods of knowing things that are not essentially based on mathematics. When we have discovered the mathematical principles of a physical thing, we have not discovered everything about it, nor do we know the truth of nonmathematical things by our knowledge of mathematics.[7] Indeed, the knowledge of any existing thing, including one with quantity, is not wholly explained by the mathematical formulae found in it. The questions of "Why is it this way, not that way?" or "Why does it exist at all?" remain.

But when we talk of art, we talk of practical intellect, as Aristotle called it, of the *recta ratio factibilium*, of the right reason of things to be made. It is no accident that God is conceived as the Divine Artist on the analogy of man's craft and artistic capabilities. This very analogy implies that the source of order of any artifact is in the creative power of the mind that made it, that gives it its form. From the viewpoint of the rational being, the mind searches for any order that is found in the *things that are*. It searches for something that is already there, not for something it puts there. Truth then becomes the conformity of our minds with what is there. Wherever we find an order that does not explain itself, we look for something that does explain it. In this sense, the Divine Artist becomes the cause or source of the actual order that we find already out there among things. It explains why this thing is not that thing. It is concerned with why things that cannot and do not explain their own being look outside of themselves to an appropriate origin or cause.

III.

In his *"In the Beginning,"* Ratzinger wrote: "Holy Scripture in its entirety was not written from beginning to end like a novel or a textbook. . . . The Bible is the story of God's struggle with human beings to make himself understandable to them over the course of time; but it is also the story of their struggle to seize hold of God over the course of time."[8] Two things of interest can be noted of this passage. One is that the story of creation is not conceived to be a one-way street. It is not simply a question of man's efforts to know the whole in which he is involved. It is also God's effort to make Him-

7 Benedict XVI, Address in Verona, October 19, 2006. See James V. Schall, "Mathematics," *Crisis* 28 (January 2007): 63.

8 Joseph Ratzinger, *"In the Beginning . . . ": A Catholic Understanding of the Story of Creation and the Fall*, trans. Boniface Ramsey, OP (Huntington, Ind.: Our Sunday Visitor Publishing, 1990), 18.

self known to man both through the *things that are* and, if necessary, through a more direct revelation.

This twofold relationship would evidently imply that, unless man makes some effort to figure out what he can know about his condition, he will not recognize that God is endeavoring to make Himself known to him. This view would imply that the effort of philosophy to know as much as it can about man himself and the world is presupposed to God's endeavor to make Himself known to man. This point does not mean that the purpose of revelation is not also of concern to the nonphilosopher. But it does suggest that if man does not make an effort to know God and the order of things, he will not "know himself," nor will he easily recognize revelation when and if it does occur.

Ratzinger thus is aware, as were Plato and Aristotle, that some correspondence is found between how we live and what we know, or better, what we are willing to know. The view that the cosmos and man are essentially divine artifacts is opposed to the notion that they are simply haphazard things with no causal origins or interrelatedness. We can see this better in the way modern legal systems have come to eliminate the distinction of good and evil, a distinction that arises from reality. The law thus seeks to avoid the notion of "guilt," which arises because we are aware of doing something wrong.

Ratzinger's analysis of how this process works is perceptive, particularly in its awareness of the indifference of statistics to good and evil.

> It is preferable to turn to sociological language which turns the concept of good and evil into statistics and in its place distinguishes between normative and non-normative behavior. Implicit here is the possibility that the statistical proportions will themselves change: what is presently non-normative could one day become the rule . . . the whole idea of the moral has accordingly been abandoned. This is a logical development if it is true that there is no standard for human beings to use as a model. . . . People today know of no standard; to be sure, they do not want to know of any because they see standards as threats to their freedom.[9]

This is an accurate description of the logical consequences of denying any order in nature or in man. What is to be particularly noted is the last comment about people not wanting to know because such knowing would interfere with their freedom.

9 Ratzinger, *"In the Beginning,"* 79.

We might ask at this point: What do we mean by a measure or a standard? Technically, it means something against which we can judge the meaning of what we do or make. What "measures" our minds is the reality that it discovers and knows. Ratzinger's point about sociological statistics is that these are measures of what Machiavelli called "what men 'do' do." We conclude from what they "do" do to what is all right for them to do. It is true that we know a thing from what it does. In the case of man, however, what he does and what is right for him to do need not correspond even if they should.

Becoming virtuous or human means to rule ourselves so that we can live to the standard of what we ought to do in this or that particular case. It is not something that happens automatically. It is a sign that becoming what is human, what we ought to be, is something we ourselves must attend to. We are to live up to the measure of what we are, a measure that is not arbitrarily defined by our freedom as such but by the Divine Artist. We are already what we are. We are, as it were, measured. We are this thing, not that thing. Our freedom consists in following or rejecting the measure, not in replacing it with a measure of our own making, though it is possible for us to do that also. If we do follow our own standards, we thereby cease to be what we ought to be, what is best for us to be.

IV.

The end or purpose of both reason and revelation is that we know the truth of things. Ratzinger was struck by the pluralism of modern thought but even more so by its greater tendency to unity, even uniformity. He noticed that we can speak of French, German, Italian, and Spanish theology, perhaps even of African, Latin American, and Asian theology. These differing traditions by having a local basis arise, if they are sound, to something beyond themselves, something that unifies them with one another. In *The Nature and Mission of Theology*, Ratzinger wrote: "In reality we have not reached the pinnacle by having affirmed *ourselves*, set forth *ourselves* and raised monuments to *ourselves*—we have attained it when we have drawn closer to the truth. The truth is never monotonous, nor is it ever exhausted in a single form, because our mind holds it only in fragments, yet at the same time it is the power which unifies us. And only pluralism in relation to unity is great."[10]

---

10 Joseph Cardinal Ratzinger, *The Nature and Mission of Theology: Approaches to Understanding Its Role in the Light of Present Controversies,* trans. Adrian Walker (San Francisco: Ignatius Press, 1995), 97–98.

The theme that fragments of truth exist everywhere, but that truth itself binds all diverse approaches of philosophy and theology into a coherent whole, is the constant teaching of Joseph Ratzinger.

What is even more characteristic of Joseph Ratzinger is his capacity to follow theological ideas when they pass the limits of orthodoxy. Such ideas usually do not die but take on a new, usually deviant, life of their own. In this sense, *Eschatology: Death and Eternal Life*, together with the encyclicals on the theological virtues, especially *Spe Salvi,* are of fundamental importance. The effort to know and to keep the truth as passed down turns out to be of much more importance and of more difficulty than we might otherwise expect. The modern world, in a paradoxical and subtle way, is largely an effort to achieve or adapt to this world what we have known as the "four last things"—heaven, hell, death, and purgatory. Their modernization rejects the means of achieving them by means of prayer, sacrament, and reason. Rather, they are to be achieved by man's own political, scientific, and economic endeavors as these are seen to be independent of any natural order or revelation.

Perhaps the key figure here is the medieval Franciscan monk Joachim of Flora (1135–1202 AD). He proposed that the ages of the Father and the Son will be surpassed by an age of the Spirit. We now live in his third age. This Spirit will be independent of the previous ages and the limits imposed by reason and revelation, which evidently hold mankind back rather than cause it to flourish. Transformed man will be free to replace what went before with a new and unlimited kind of freedom. "The hope aroused by Joachim's teaching was first taken up by a segment of the Franciscan Order, but subsequently underwent increasing secularization until eventually it was turned into political utopia," Ratzinger wrote. "The goad of the utopian vision remained embedded in western consciousness, stimulating a quest for its own realization and preparing the way for that interest in concrete utopia which has become such a determinative element in political thought since the nineteenth century. This secularization of Christian eschatological thought has clearly sucked the life out of faith awareness."[11] Revelation posed these four last things to reason—a reason, as Ratzinger will indicate in his Regensburg Lecture, that was already somewhat prepared for it by certain strands in the Old Testament and by Greek philosophy.

11 Joseph Ratzinger, *Eschatology: Death and Eternal Life*, trans. Michael Waldstein (Washington, D.C.: The Catholic University of America Press, 1988), 13. See James V. Schall, *The Modern Age* (South Bend, Ind.: St. Augustine's Press, 2011).

What we have here in this reflection on Joachim and modern utopias is what happens to reason when it retains these eschatological goals but endeavors to pursue them independently of their transcendent means and implications. We might say that the attempt to escape from the transcendent but real aims of Christianity in the four last things is not successful. Or perhaps, better, it is successful but ends up by creating a closed, totalitarian society impervious to any transcendent purpose in the context of normal human lives. Eschatology reappears in a distorted but comprehensible form. Ratzinger's almost incidental conclusion is most perceptive. The secular utopia, designed finally to bring about a permanent and perfect inner-worldly society, sucks the life out of the "faith awareness" of these same realities. It is a "goad" that, in lieu of its proper location, seeks one visible to it in this world. We will return to the particulars of this secular and scientific eschatology below when we consider *Spe Salvi*.

V.

In this context, however, it is important to recognize the difference between the theological impetus of Joachim, which now reappears in Catholic circles under the guise of the Spirit's guidance away from the tradition that is handed down as well as from the philosophical impetus of Plato and Aristotle. This deviation is why the account of Western philosophical history in the Regensburg Lecture is of such significance. In this succinct and now famous lecture, Benedict, returning briefly to his old professorial post in Germany, in a formal academic lecture, addressed the reason and revelation issue in a unique manner. He presented the issue as if it is revelation itself that is most concerned to validate and address itself to reason. It is as if revelation all along was formed to propose to reason what seemed unintelligible to it. The very structure of revelation, in other words, betrayed the same ultimate origin as reason. It seemed to anticipate that things could and would go wrong with the free being so that remedial initiative was possible and needed from the beginning.

Leo Strauss, in his reflections on the difference between Jerusalem and Athens, had argued that revelation and reason operated in different worlds.[12]

---

12 Leo Strauss, "Jerusalem and Athens: Some Introductory Reflections," *Commentary* 43 (June 1, 1967): 45–57. See Susan Orr, *Jerusalem and Athens: Reason and Revelation in the Thought of Leo Strauss* (Lanham, Md.: Rowman & Littlefield, 1995); James V. Schall, "Jerusalem, Athens, Rome," *Reason, Revelation, and the Foundations of Political Philosophy* (Baton Rouge: Louisiana State University Press, 1987), 182–224.

One was intrinsically incompatible with the other. One argued from reason, the other from the faith. Each had a different view of reality. As a result, they could not "refute" each other. This inability to resolve which way was superior, or how they were related in a noncontradictory manner, left the believer to his way and the philosopher to his. They had to settle for a mutual tolerance of each other, both skeptical of the other's validity. No hope of a unified relationship was possible.

The Catholic position, especially in Augustine and Aquinas, however, did not see these two approaches to be incompatible. But it was incompatible with the Muslim notion of its revelation that had no real room for a stable reason once the voluntarism of Al-Ghazali became dominant. This latter voluntarist view became important in the light of its similarity to what happened in Western thought after Duns Scotus and Occam. Benedict saw Western ideology and Islam to draw from the same well, either a world with no intrinsic order or a world that could change into its opposite at any moment.

In the Regensburg Lecture, Benedict points out a curious thing about the mission of the Apostles, especially Paul's. The mission of Peter was to the Jews; that of Paul was to the Gentiles. But to what Gentiles and in what priority was the assignment given? After all, the Apostles were told to go to the ends of the earth, to all nations. What difference did it make where they went first? It turns out, in Benedict's view, that it made all the difference in the world. Paul was told to go not to India or to China or even to Persia, but to Macedonia. Macedonia was in Greece. The city of the philosophers was Athens, even though Paul was not particularly impressed with their wisdom. Yet, "the encounter between the Biblical message and Greek thought did not happen by chance," Benedict affirmed in the Regensburg Lecture (19).[13]

In Benedict's view, however, the first priority of the Christian endeavor was to deal with philosophy. And, as it turns out, not any philosophy, but that genuine philosophy that understood the basic processes and truths open to human reason on its own terms. It was important, in other words, that Athens, unlike Jerusalem, did not claim to have a particular revelation. The myths that it did have were questioned by its philosophers, especially Plato. Thus, philosophy was able to provide a basis on which it was possible to deal with anyone, no matter what his religion, civil society, or location.

---

13 See James V. Schall, *The Regensburg Lecture* (South Bend, Ind.: St. Augustine's Press, 2007). The text of Benedict XVI's lecture is in the appendix of Schall's *Regensburg Lecture*, 130–48. All lecture quotations are taken from this text, given in parenthetical citations with section number.

Philosophy dealt with those things men could reason to, could figure out by themselves. Revelation was not designed to replace reason but to heal and clarify it in its own order. Revelation was remedial to reason as well as transcending it. It did not contradict it. It would be the task of later Christian thinkers to spell out more fully this relationship. The symbolic first encounter with the philosophers, however, in Ratzinger's view, was not accidental. The first task of revelation was to relate itself in a coherent manner to reason when it was being strictly reasonable.

Moreover, when Benedict examined the Jewish revelation, the Old Testament, he found that it was not wholly closed to reason. In fact, he found the classical virtues and the commandments addressed themselves to mostly the same ways of living courageously, moderately, justly, and prudently. Even more crucial was the passage in Exodus wherein God identifies Himself as "I am" or "I am who am." This famous passage turned out to provide a key metaphysical insight into being that served to make philosophy more philosophical. It also broached not only the relation of reason to Jewish revelation but the relation of revelation itself to reason. The Word, the *Logos*, in which all things were created, turned out to be precisely what measured of *all that is*. Revelation is presented thus not as will but as reason, as mind addressed to mind. What was significant for philosophy was Augustine's account that he found "Word" in the Platonists, but not the "Word made flesh."

The subsequent burden of the Regensburg Lecture was to consider the Muslim understanding of Allah. He first appeared as approving unjustified violence. But mostly there was a denial of secondary causality and therefore reason itself. The power of Allah was in his will. This will is bound by nothing but itself. It can will contradictories. Otherwise it would not be all-powerful. No solidity is found in things. The Muslim notion of piety and even of civil society becomes that of submitting all to the will of Allah. This will is not bound by any limits of the reason based on *Logos*. But, in this lecture, Benedict is more concerned with the West than with Islam. Within a few years, after large-scale Muslim presence in Europe, the concern of the West would more and more be with Islam itself. In the meantime, Ratzinger was attentive to what had happened to Europe, especially to the European mind.

VI.

Benedict explains what happened to the Western mind in terms of "dehellenization"—that is, in terms of removing Greek (read universal) reason that was now seen to be the cause of corruption to faith (32–35). The Reformers wanted faith to be presented in its purity as if it were sufficient by itself. Revelation is claimed to have no relation to reason. By ridding revelation of any relation to metaphysics and the theoretic order, following Kant, faith became something "exclusively in practical reason, denying it access to reality as a whole" (35).

"Practical reason," as we noted above, is the realm of art and ethics, of things to be done and made. These practical virtues are responsible for directing means to the end. They do not themselves make the ends but acquire them from nature or prior artistic forms. With no access to reality as a whole, we have no way of measuring the deeds and works of practical intellect. The effect, in other words, is to remove any limit to what we do or make. Both faith and practice become impervious to a theoretic reason that seeks to know *what is*. The unity of the whole that includes theoretic and practical reason as well as revelation is broken.

The second stage of dehellenization followed these premises whereby reason and revelation were separated from each other. Benedict recalls Pascal's "god of the philosophers" and "god of Abraham, Isaac, and Jacob," gods that do not relate to each other. Adolf Harnack wanted to return to the simple message of the Gospels. Hence, he wanted a Jesus not seen in the light of metaphysics or thought about what exactly He was. We did not "worship" Jesus, as He was not divine. He was merely an example of morality. Jesus is just a man, the model of humanity (37). Jesus was now able to join modern humanity. He was not divine. Jesus was an historical figure and was thus open to scientific investigation. All theoretic explanations were mythic. Jesus became a model of a worthy man, not the Word or the Word made flesh.

The model of science was based on mathematics, on quantified matter. If something could not be explained by this method, it was said to be unscientific. This claim meant that questions of great concern to most men in most historic cultures, like "Why do I exist?" "Who is God?" and "What ought I to do or hope for?", were considered unscientific. Whole realms of reality were thus ignored as unscientific by the methods allowed to be used. Parallel to this was a Platonism in which ideas had no relation to reality. Man was free to manipulate these ideas as he wished. This ungrounded idealism becomes in part the basis of the utopianism that we see coming back into modernity's effort to establish its own version of eschatology as a human project.

The third step in the process of dehellenization sought to remove any relation of revelation to Greek intellectual foundations. Theology cannot be considered a science since it has no relation to the sort of reason on which modern science is based, which is mathematical. This relationship of Greece to Christianity was considered to be merely incidental. Paul had no particular reason to go to Macedonia. Faith is considered to be wholly independent of reason, including its relation to philosophy. However, as Ratzinger put it, "The fundamental decisions about the relationship between faith and the use of human reason are part of the faith itself; they are developments consonant with the nature of faith itself" (53). Reason was not an extraneous, foreign element to revelation but intrinsic to it on its own terms. This position does not mean that something is wrong with accepting many of the discoveries of modern science and technology. Insofar as science is itself open to truth, it is already a work of reason. Reason seen in quantified reality is still reason, just not all of reason.

Benedict thus envisions a science that is itself open to all truth, not just those based on mathematics and quantified matter. The essential things of mind and spirit are not based on matter. They require other methods to deal with them, methods that do not reduce them to what they are not. Benedict points out that most of the world believes in other realities besides material ones. These cultures too must be approached in ways that are not simply those of modern science (58). "Modern scientific reason quite simply has to accept the rational structure of matter and the correspondence between our spirt and the prevailing rational structure of nature as a given, on which its methodology has to be based" (59). This passage is but another way of recalling Aquinas's definition that truth is "the conformity of mind and reality." The reality and its order are already there. We have minds to learn what they are. The intelligibility is already there. We can know it, but we do not put it there.

What Benedict has done in the Regensburg Lecture is to reorient our minds, to recall that both theology and philosophy, in their own ways, are open to *all that is*. The experience of what men do with and without faith is itself subject to rational analysis. It constitutes empirical evidence of what happens when it is and is not present in the souls of men. It is at this point that Benedict cites not Paul but Socrates in the *Phaedo* (90c–d). He wondered why, if reality was so intelligible, so many errors and prejudices followed. The temptation is to reject philosophy forever.

But, true to his own methods in this lecture, Benedict sees that this overt rejection would be a great loss because, in tracing the paths of error, we do learn much about what is true (61). What is most dangerous to our culture is not to understand the foundations of reason, including the reason to which revelation manifests and is directed. It is perhaps ironic that it is a pope who is also a philosopher who points this connection out to us, who spells it out for us to see. What the tradition also is aware of, even on empirical and rational grounds, is that we can reject what is true if we will a personal or cultural end that is not reasonable in terms of the end for which reality exists.

VII.

What remains to consider is the central thesis of *Spe Salvi*, Benedict's encyclical on hope.[14] We have mentioned that modern political thought and activity has become an effort to secularize what in tradition were called the four last things. The traditional four last things, to recall, are heaven, hell, death, and purgatory. At first sight, it will appear that such events belong to the realm of faith with no scientific or political overtones. However, when spelled out, they serve to make clear in a unique way the significance of reason and revelation in their relation to each other. Benedict's thesis is not unfamiliar in political philosophy. Going all the way back from Joachim of Fiore to J. B. Bury's book on *The Idea of Progress*, it is clear that, by denying the peculiar Christian interpretation of these events, it does not follow that the issue that they strove to deal with disappears.[15]

What Benedict has done briefly is to sketch out how these notions reappear in modern scientific and political thought when they do not have the restraints and goals of their classical understanding.[16] The Regensburg Lecture was Benedict's account of the separation of reason from revelation. It resulted in a concept of reason that was limited to only a part of reality and a revelation that was mythical or Averroistic, one that had no relation to the common reality of ordinary men unless it was imposed on it by ideological choice and usually political force.

---

14 Benedict XVI, *Spe Salvi (Saved in Hope)* (Boston: Pauline Books & Media, 2007). See also Benedict's *God Is Love (Deus Caritas Est)* (San Francisco: Ignatius Press, 2006); *Charity in Truth (Caritas in Veritate)* (San Francisco: Ignatius Press, 2009); and *The Transforming Power of Faith* (San Francisco: Ignatius Press, 2013).

15 See discussion of Joachim of Fiore in Eric Voegelin, *The New Science of Politics* (Chicago: University of Chicago Press, 1952); and J. B. Bury, *The Idea of Progress: An Inquiry into Its Origins and Growth* (London: Macmillan, 1920).

16 This whole topic is developed more thoroughly in Benedict's *Eschatology*.

The modern concept of the purpose of the human race is not eternal life for each human person who chooses it. Rather, it is a perfect society within time down the ages. All previous societies exist to make this future kingdom in this world possible. It is the function of the *polis* to identify and eliminate the causes of human disorder that are not internal to each person as in Greek and Christian thought. This goal justifies the necessary actions that remove the individuals or classes who are thought to stand in the way of this purpose. Generally, this future-oriented goal falls within ecological estimates about the number of human beings the resources of the planet can support. The purpose of mankind comes to be the keeping of a few billion "perfect" individuals down the ages for as long as possible. In this sense, the notion of heaven is secularized into a movement to keep some human beings alive on the planet and in the universe for as long as possible.

Since death is seen to be the end of human life with no transcendent purpose, the scientific project becomes an effort to lengthen the life of each individual to hundreds of years. Benedict points out that merely stretching out human life is really an endless hell on earth. Death has two purposes, one of which is to end a life that has achieved its purpose of deciding what it is. With no death we have little need for new births, which fall under the jurisdiction not of the individual persons in families but the state to decide their numbers and qualities. We see increasing proposals that even want to make all births under the control of the state. Sex becomes a frivolous enterprise with no visible effects in the world. Children become engineered in laboratories according to specification of the political need of keeping the race going on earth.

Benedict points out that the result of such theories has the effect of making the lives of many people a hell on earth. Once we deny a transcendent end for each human person, he ceases to be an end in himself. The Christian doctrine of the resurrection of the body becomes crucial. Plato had been concerned with the question of whether the world was created in vain. It was if the crimes within it were not punished or good rewarded. The immortality of the soul was proposed in this political context of the polity's inability to produce true justice. What Benedict sees with the help of the two Marxist philosophers, Adorno and Horkheimer, is that the disorders of the real world involved the complete person, not just the soul.[17]

Spelled out, the logic of this reflection leads precisely to a final judgment and the resurrection of the body. That is to say, the Christian solution does

---

17 Benedict XVI, *Spe Salvi*, para. 42.

address itself to the demands of reason. It is interesting, as some trans-human theorists now insist, that it is not the human race that must continue in this world down the ages, but each individual person.[18] When thought out, this position is simply a parody of the Christian doctrine of the resurrection of the body transferred to this world.

In conclusion, Ratzinger's "event that really took place," the Incarnation and redemption, what is, constitutes the great "adventure in thinking" that joins reason to revelation, not as myth to philosophy or irrationality to truth, but as philosophy to the intelligibility found in revelation that is already directed to a human reasoning waiting to be developed and understood. This human reasoning itself depends on its discovery of the things that already are, what they are. This approach is neither fideism nor is it rationalism. It is a realistic look at *what is*, a look that is not afraid to gaze upon the whole. This whole includes all the intelligibility available, not just that which our narrow methods allow to us. "The highest claim of revelation," Benedict tells us, "the 'I am he' and the Cross of Jesus are inseparably one. What we find here is not metaphysical speculation, but the self-revelation of God's reality in the midst of history for us."[19] This "self-revelation" was also meant, *modo humano*, to be understood as true. This exploration of reason and revelation brings to life Benedict's "adventure in thinking."

---

18 See Peter Augustine Lawler, *American Heresies and Higher Education* (South Bend, Ind.: St. Augustine's Press, 2016), 121–24.

19 Benedict XVI, *Jesus of Nazareth*, vol. I, 349.

Chapter 9

On "Rights"

I.

Our political rhetoric is no longer formed in terms of virtue and vice but in terms of "rights."[1] A virtue requires that we take a careful look at ourselves. We intuitively see that we need to have some insight into our actual tendencies, where they lead. We need to control and guide our desires. Other people will often frankly tell us of the dire effects of our skewered actions that we are not willing to see. We thus need to develop a habit of controlling feelings and passions so that we deal in a just, courageous, moderate, or prudent way in our relations with one another. We can be helped (or hindered) by laws and customs that indicate to us what is good or evil in our actions. We are praised or blamed for how we act. A vice is simply forming a habit of doing what is disordered to the degree that we no longer see it as evil. Habits, both good and bad, indicate what we conceive as our good, the principle of our important activities.

A "right" can be defined, presumably, as what is due to something because of *what it is*. This view assumes that different things exist in an order. Existing things ought to be what they are. The differences found among things are contributory to a common good that enables the differing realities to come to their best functioning. Nothing exists in complete isolation. Our thoughts have generally expected results, but only when we choose to put them in the world. We thus have "human rights." We have "rights" to life, to defend ourselves, to liberty, property, religious freedom, and freedom of expression. Our law books have hundreds, even thousands, of "rights." A human being can be defined as a "bearer" of rights.

---

* This chapter was previously published in *Catholic World Report*, September 1, 2016, https://www.catholicworldreport.com/2016/09/01/modern-rights-and-the-loss-of-freedoms/.

1 See Pierre Manent, *La loi naturelle et les droits de l'homme* (Paris: Presses Universitaires de France, 2018); Robert Sokolowski, "Discovery and Obligation in Natural Law," *Natural Law in Contemporary Society*, ed. Holger Zaborowski (Washington, D.C.: The Catholic University of America Press, 2010), 24–42; James V. Schall, "The Natural Law—Natural Rights Dilemma," *Jacques Maritain: The Philosopher in the City* (Lanham, Md.: Rowman & Littlefield, 1998), 79–98.

In Los Angeles in July, the National Conference on Animal Rights was held. I am not sure whether insects are included in these rights. But I am sure that the mosquito as a species has a "right" to exist even while I swat one landing on my arm. After all, mosquitos are feed for reptiles and fish. It is good that they are around, though not, perhaps, in our screened-in porches. Plants and trees are also said to have "rights." We cannot just root them out or saw them down even if we own the land on which they grow. Yet, trees also age. It is possible to plant forests and see them grow.

The term "mineral rights" usually means that the owner of an extent of surface ground owns the material below the surface such as coal, oil, or gold. Many states, however, separate by positive law who owns the surface and who owns what is below the surface. It usually turns out, no surprise, that it is the government that ends up with control of the oil or valuable underground minerals and assets. The control of water is probably the next big step in state control of population. We can perhaps also speak of the "right" of iron to be iron or the "right" of a volcano to be a volcano. But this terminology means little less than saying that iron or the volcano is what it is. I do not think anyone has yet come up with the idea that it is against the "right" of iron to be mined or made into say a steel component, though many theories of limited resources tend in this direction.

We also hear of "rights" to abortion, to a living wage, to a job, to health care, to immigrate, to organize, to free education, and to choose our own gender. We speak of a "right" to die and even the "right" to a dead child when abortion fails. From all these now familiar usages, it is clear that the concept and language of "rights" is something of an intellectual minefield. "Rights" are, no doubt, a growth industry in liberal democracies, with new ones constantly being declared or legislated.

At one time, even while granting that "free will" was part of our essential structure, we talked about "gaining" our freedom. This phrase meant that freedom in the public order was something that we had to work for, even fight for. It was not simply given to us. The term "emancipation," however, meant that someone who was not legally free was liberated from bondage. It was something conferred on someone else by someone with the power to do so. The terms "rights" and "freedoms" were often interchangeable—a "right" to worship, a "freedom" to worship, a right to speak, a freedom to speak.

In this sense, it was possible to have a "right" without the "freedom" to exercise it. We can even imagine a "freedom" that is not based on a right, as in the parable in the Gospel of the owner of the vineyard. He gave equal wages to his workers no matter how long or little they worked in a day. He was being just to some but generous to others who did not have a "right" to his generosity (Matthew 20:1–16). Indeed, generosity implies some area of reality beyond the right and just. It is this area that the current practice of rights is quickly closing off as it implies something outside of state control, which now claims a monopoly also over benevolence.

II.

The idea behind the concept of freedom as emancipation was that we were "born" free, but found ourselves in chains, to recall Rousseau's famous words. Someone had taken something away from us that was ours by nature. Politics came to mean giving us our "rights" and protecting them when we acquired them. Attention was shifted from gaining "rights" to "receiving" them. The first usage meant working to acquire what we did not yet possess. The latter meant receiving from the government what it gave to us based on its estimate of what was available to everyone.

But if we deny, as we do today, that there is such a binding but freeing thing as a "nature" that is normative to us in reason, we cannot appeal to a standard of something objectively "due" to us in virtue of what we are. Generally speaking, natural law is denied not because there is no evidence that it exists but because it prevents us from doing whatever we want. With this background, the word "rights" takes on its practical and operative meaning in our society that it has today. It is what Hobbes pointed out most clearly. "Rights" have no objective meaning or content. No objective and discoverable reality can be acknowledged outside of our desires. At first sight, this view appears to be a new and exhilarating freedom. We do not have to answer to anything but ourselves. We are free to do what was once called evil. A "right" is whatever we think that we need for our preservation and flourishing.

The only trouble with this apparently exalted view is that everyone else has the same rights that we do. And since there is no common agreement on who should have what, we need to found an institution that will adjudicate for us what we can have lest we be constantly at war with one another. Suddenly, "rights" shift from what we supposedly want and need for ourselves based on our own estimates of need to what the state will allow us to have. "Rights" become a list of state regulatory decrees that we have established to prevent us from fighting and killing one another over conflicting rights. The individuals within the state become the raw material, as it were, for fashioning and refashioning the citizens into whatever configuration or way of life that seems viable to the government.

III.

The "right" to religion in this type of thinking now means, at least negatively, that the state defines what religion cannot hold and do within the existing polity. Neither the so-called freedom of religion nor freedom of speech takes any precedence over the positive law. If they exist at all, they are concessions of man-made positive, changeable law. Religion is civic, not transcendent. Any religion that holds tenets that are contrary to the enforced public law cannot receive any public standing, recognition, or assistance. A religion, such as Christianity, must be looked upon as hostile to the state if it claims transcendence for its morals and beliefs. If there is a state sanctioned "right" to something, it is divisive and intolerant to oppose it on the grounds of any transcendent or natural truth. A "natural law" or an abiding human nature is nonexistent in public law. No higher authority exists to which anyone might appeal in case of conflict. A written constitution is no longer a criterion or standard. It is replaced by a living constitution that is defined by public opinion, legislative and judicial law, and ad hoc presidential decrees and edicts.

The Qur'an has legal standing and is enforced in Muslim states, but the Bible has no such standing in any Western society. Even if it inspired much of what we know as constitutionalism, it is not recognized as a source of information about human worth. If it contains principles or laws contrary to civil law, it is thereby unfit for citizens who are always free to hold what they want, provided the state sanctions what they want with positive law and penalties. The state does not officially "persecute" Christians or others. They are welcome to live in peace provided they do not attempt to criticize or oppose the laws on the basis of some presumed "higher law."

It is not enough simply not to oppose these laws of the state. It is considered "hate language" to maintain that there is something immoral or unreasonable about them. This language causes unsettlement among the citizens and creates unnecessary tensions. In this sense, it is a great evil to oppose or criticize abortion or single-sex relationships. Such speech will be considered unpatriotic, inhuman, and destructive of civil peace. These are now the terms that rule the civil polity. Man lives in this world and for this world. These are the terms; this is the civil contract of his present being.

The Catholic Church, in most of its official documents and in much of its apologetics, has tried to retain the "rights" talk but give it another grounding. It sought to find a way to keep a terminology but eliminate from it any pejorative meanings. What seems to have happened is that many of its citizens have accepted the more modern meaning of "rights" so that opposition to abortion, gay marriage, or other such moral issues is seen as opposing the common good which has come to be identified with what the state requires. The majority of Catholics in most countries now accept or do not oppose most of the "modern" rights that were once vigorously opposed. Most Catholic citizens, if we go by their voting records, no longer form a single cohesive body of citizens agreed on certain truths rooted in natural and divine law. We can now affirm that, for the most part, modern natural "rights" rule the public order.

Chapter 10

On Politics and Salvation

Beloved, our Lord Jesus Christ, the eternal creator of all things, today became our Savior by being born of a mother. Of his own will he was born for us today, in time, so that he could lead us to his Father's eternity. God became man so that man might become God.

—Saint Augustine, Sermon 13 *de Tempore*, in Breviary, from Saturday before Epiphany, *PL* 39:1097–1098

Islam is not a religion in the way Americans understand the term. It governs every action and seeps into every thought process. It is a religion, yes, but also a political system, a legal system, a social system—in short, a total way of life.

—Derya Little, *From Islam to Christ*

I.

Of the basic texts that identify Western civilization, we usually name the first to be that affirmation of Socrates in the *Crito* where he affirms that *it is never right to do wrong*.[1] Every endeavor to undermine the civilization has to attack this principle. But a second, more modern, text can be named. The second text initially seems to clash with the Socratic principle. When sorted out, however, it implies the same thing.

In Dostoyevsky's *Brother Karamazov*, the Grand Inquisitor reviewed what he considered to be Christ's principal failure in understanding the nature of men. Given a choice between the freedom that Christ brought and bread, men *would invariably choose bread*, the Inquisitor maintained. They would freely accept whatever goes along with such a choice—namely, the abject submission to those who promise to fulfill their "rights" and needs in exchange for their liberty.

---

* This chapter was previously published online as "On the Purpose of Politics and the Salvation of Souls," *Catholic World Report*, January 11, 2018, https://www.catholicworldreport.com/2018/01/11/on-the-purpose-of-politics-and-the-salvation-of-souls/.

1 Plato, *Crito*, 49a–b. This and all subsequent quotations from Plato are taken from Plato's *Complete Works* (Indianapolis: Hackett, 1997).

The Christian distinction between the things of Caesar and the things of God argues that politics and religion, though both deal legitimately with an aspect of human reality, are different enterprises. Sometimes they became confused and entangled, but the real intellectual and practical task was to give to each it's due.

Indeed, the Christian religion was the first and still the only revelation that ever acknowledged as a theological datum some basic autonomy to the civil power. The latter power did not arise from revelation or religion. It originated in the very conditions of rational beings living together. Man was "by nature" a political animal, as Aristotle famously put it. To understand politics, we needed to see that it was a work of practical reason that dealt with the being and well-being of mortal human beings *while* they were alive and present in this world.

Plato and Aristotle could see that something in the very constitution of what it is to be man was open to a higher or transcendent order of things that could not be otherwise. Man had, as it were, two natural "goods." One was the work of life that could be expected among men who were finite, not perfect. This civil life in history was manifested in many different national and civilizational contexts. What they all had in common was that each person would be identified by the record of his life in the city or civilization in which he lived his finite life. All men would die. Thus, each existing civil society was composed of a constantly changing population of those being born and those dying.

The theoretic or contemplative order, the order to which in its own way politics pointed as a limit of itself, seemed always present. It promised a higher order of being and truth to which the human being seemed open. The significance of Plato's *Republic* was precisely that it posed a relation between these two orders. Plato recognized that, in the dynamic of actual regimes, many crimes went unpunished and many noble deeds went unrewarded. The notion of the immortality of the soul, wherein this disorder could be reconciled in a final judgment, arose out of this political dilemma. If no way to resolve the justice problem that occurred in every actual regime could be found, then we had to conclude that the world was made in injustice, an injustice that had its origin in the very constitution of reality.

II.

We have always had theories, either from philosophy or from revelation, that denied any supernatural or transcendent order. Religion and metaphysics were held to be illusions, projections of desires onto reality. Man only had this life before him. The ancient Epicureans, whom Marx studied, thought it was so bad that the only rational course was to withdraw from politics altogether to live a quiet life unperturbed by the turmoil of politics. Religion was invented to keep the masses content with illusions.

When Christianity came along, it addressed itself primarily to the final destiny to which man, in his creation, had been ordered. The purpose of Christian revelation was not to improve the world but to explain the final destiny of each existing person. The purpose of human life is finally to decide whether a person will or will not accept the invitation to eternal life for which he was created. This choice was to be made in whatever polity or civilization a person lived his life in, the best, the worst, or one in-between.

Thus, throughout its history, Christianity has reminded man that the purpose of his life is to save his soul. The Gospels begin with "repent" (Mark 1:15; Matthew 2:17). And in Christian terms, this salvation included the resurrection of the body, which was included in the eternal life to which each person was invited and ordered. The City of God is not composed of ghosts or abstractions. Christianity did not neglect the mortal life. Its admonitions to love the neighbor in a practical sense had the effect of remedying many misconceptions about one's relation to others. The commandments and natural morality were also remedying additions to any civil order.

Beginning with strands in the Enlightenment, the transcendent and salvific goals of Christianity gradually became this-worldly oriented. The supernatural ends were transformed into economic and politically achievable goals to make the world better. Men lost faith in their relation to the transcendent order and the salvation of their souls. The dead end of this endeavor to transform the supernatural end into a perfect order in this world, a parody on Plato, became visible in the twentieth century. The reinvigoration of Islam in the twenty-first century is but a revision of a religion that sought to control the whole world in every aspect for a religious purpose, submission to Allah. What we do not see is a corresponding return of Christianity to its roots wherein salvation after death is seen to be the primary purpose in revelation.

Rather, what we see is something quite different and perhaps quite logical. The efforts surrounding Vatican II endeavored to give both Caesar and God their respective dues. But the drift of contemporary culture is not in this direction. What we see is something quite new.

We do not see, as in Islam, a religion that quite openly subordinates everything to itself and its theology. Nor do we see a distinction or separation of church and state into legitimate fields of competency. Nor do we see the Benedict or Epicurean option of withdrawing from the public order as itself hopelessly corrupt. What we seem to be seeing, rather, is a use of Christian theology as itself the primary instrument to achieve political goals, an effort that becomes the essential purpose of Christianity. We do not speak of salvation or eternal life but speak of the transformation and preservation of the world itself. Morality is refashioned in this light.

This new mood is not the eighteenth-century attempt to set up a kingdom of God in this world as itself the meaning of man's purpose. Benedict pointed out in *Spe Salvi* that we now look to science to achieve something like a deathless life in this world. Trans-humanism, in a parody of the resurrection, even wants to preserve within time the individual, not just the species. No, Christianity is something different now. It is not dependent on preserving for the human good some unchangeable revelation from an initial divine/human event in the time of Caesar Augustus. We need to do for our time what Christ did for His time—namely, look at the things that need to be done for man here and now. The center of concern is not salvation and eternal life. Theology is rather a guide in achieving political goals for men in time.

To conclude, Augustine put it nicely. God became man so that man could become God. He meant, of course, that man could live the Trinitarian life for which he was initially created. The old refrain from Ignatius of Loyola that man was made to praise, reverence, and serve God and thereby save his soul remains the dividing line between what is and what is not Christian. The purpose of revelation is not politics. But the purpose of politics is to provide an arena in time wherein each existing person decides what he shall be forever. In this sense, revelation can "heal" politics, but only if we remember that revelation is about eternal life and not directly about politics itself.

Chapter 11

On Secondary Causes

I.

The long controversy occasioned by Hume about whether we can affirm that a "cause" of any sort exists still floats in the intellectual air of our time. We only see, it is claimed, that one thing "follows" another. This result happens on the "occasion" of that other thing happening. The alternative to an explanation that uses causes is a determinism. Just what "determined" what to be this way and not that way is not addressed. But the fact that this thing happened because that thing caused it to change seems and remains obvious enough. It is always a better explanation than the denial that any causes at all exist.

The term "secondary cause" obviously implies a first or primary cause. The primary cause of something explains what and why a given thing is. The "secondary cause" presumes the existence of something else besides primary being itself. Once something exists outside of nothingness as a certain kind of thing—as a "this thing," not "that thing"—secondary causality refers to what it does that is unique to itself. Its activities flow from its being. The old saying goes: "You do not get blood out of a turnip." What a thing does flows from *what it is*. The world, as we encounter it, is thus a vast interlocking network of secondary causes. In various ways, finite things can cause something to happen in other finite things. Change can be accounted for.

To put it graphically, the "secondary cause" of a dog's barking is the dog. The dog does not bring itself into existence or give itself the capacity to bark. But, once being what it is, a dog, it barks or does not bark under its own power. Clearly, if the dog did not exist, or if it did not exist as a dog, it could not bark. We do not have "barking" just floating about out there with no dog in sight. When we hear a dog howl or bark in the night, we know that we are not "listening" to the quack of a duck, the moo of a cow, or the drone of an airplane.

Such reflections seem obvious enough. Why bother with them? It seems odd to bring them up. Yet, it is a dangerous thing to leave things unthought-out. We are not given minds to leave them unused. Things that we take for granted can be denied their place in existence if they seem to threaten how we choose to live. It is well that reality forces us to pay attention to it, that it is not so malleable that it retains no shape of its own. Thus, if we say that the dog is responsible for its barking, on the same basis, we must say that a human being, after his own manner, is responsible for his own speech, for those activities that are unique to his nature.

From these premises, we can conclude that if we are responsible for our speech or our various actions, we can be praised or blamed for what we say or do. That is, we are treated as causes of something that came to exist in the world but need not have existed unless we existed to put it in place. In this sense, we differ from the dog. We do not praise a dog for his capacity to bark, though we may complain if its barking keeps us awake—in which case, we blame the owner of the dog. We do not praise or blame individual human beings for their capacity to speak, but for what it is that they say and why.

If our world contains no place for God as a cause of being, however, we must attribute all action we seem to experience either to our own agency or to accident. Accidents are themselves curious. An accident is what happens when one agent with a purpose crosses another agent with a different purpose in mind. No particular agent caused the accident as such. But purpose was involved nonetheless. The driver of the first car was going to Los Angeles, while the driver that hit him was going to Santa Barbara, when their automobiles collided on the highway intersection. Neither driver "intended" the accident as such, but it was necessary once their paths crossed at the same moment in the same place.

II.

If, however, we do not think that our actions are free—that is, caused by our own agency—then they must be determined to be the way they turn out to be. This view, as is often its purpose, evidently removes any sense of responsibility from our actions. They just happen and could not have been otherwise. The comfort we can derive from this view is that no one can "blame" us for anything that occurs from our apparent agency. A determined world, however, is a world deprived of any drama, of any sign that human agents actually do anything. We become little better than living robots. No one can really think that he has no control over what he does.

Another explanation of the world has all actions, including those attributable to ourselves, directly caused by God. Only God acts. No secondary causes exist in this approach either. This view is often said to exalt God, to give Him proper praise because He causes everything. In this view, God is responsible for both good and evil acts. If He were not, it would indicate a lessening of His power. We would deprive Him of the capacity to do both good and evil acts just because He wills them. Everything that happens is thus caused by God. The most we can do, as we find in Islam, is to submit to God's will, whatever it is. Good and evil have no objective status for anyone to live up to. What is true or good today can be false or evil tomorrow.

We ask ourselves: "Why do these considerations about what causes what come up in the first place?" The most obvious reason is that, in our normal daily affairs, we are praised or blamed for things we do or do not do. Our whole personal and social order is based on this assumption. This experience indicates that it makes a difference what we do. We really are agents. Something is going on here that is more than just watching events unfold. Things happen because free agents make then happen in one way or another.

More importantly, why would God put us in a world wherein we had to make such a momentous choice that involved us in our own transcendent destiny? Isn't there something wrong with God if He created the world in such a way that some people could choose to be lost forever? Would it not have been better for God to have forgotten the whole cosmic mess that He put us in rather than permit some to be lost? It would have been better for God to have created nothing. That would have eliminated any possibility of sin, suffering, uncertainty, or accident. In this view, nothing is better than a something that can act freely.

The best way to think about these considerations is through secondary causes. Is God a great God because He does everything? Is He great because He is responsible for everything? Or is He a greater God because He is able to create beings that have their own relative autonomy and powers? The latter is the much greater world. And this is the world that we are given to live in. It is a world with many flaws and many disorders that have to be dealt with. Since everything is less than God, things can go wrong. But when things that can go wrong do go wrong, is that too surprising or fatal? Is either God or man helpless when things go wrong? Are not some of the greatest things about us the result of something previously having gone wrong?

We must appreciate the risks that occur in a world wherein secondary causality is operative. These risks are ones that even God cannot avoid. And He has not avoided them. *Man is, in fact, the great risk of God.* He is the being that God created with the capacity of going wrong through his own agency, his own secondary causality. This fact means that, in the beginning, the only real choice that God had was either to create a world in which things could go wrong, or to create no world at all out of fear that something would go wrong. Finite beings that are not themselves God could reject Him. The question is, Even if they could reject God, is that a reason to remain with nothingness? And it would make no sense to create a world in which everything was determined. Nothing ever would have happened or have been at stake in such a world.

The reason for this problem lies in the nature of the Godhead itself. The definition and reality of God is the love of oneself and other persons because they are good, worth loving in themselves. The only way anyone who is not God could be invited to participate in this Trinitarian life would be at God's request and with His grace. In this context, the world is created for man. But man is created for God. This invitation to participate in the inner life of the Godhead constitutes the ontological and theological reason for man's existence rather than his nonexistence.

When we read that someone is "invited" to love God, we have to understand that God could not "force" anyone to love Him and still have a being with a genuine free will. Moreover, two identical "gods" cannot exist. In creating anything, what is created is not God. It is other than God, less than God, as it were. But it is not nothing. It is a real being with a will that is free. God created man. All else that is created is subject to his dominion for its own proper order.

By stating that man is made in the "image" of God, this affirmation means that a divine potential is found in man's being that is not due to him by nature. No merely natural man was ever created by God. From the beginning, something more was intended for man. It was indeed possible to create an order of existence in which nothing directly supernatural was included. This alternative never happened. What did happen was the creation of man with, from the beginning, the added potential of being invited to love God face-to-face.

On this hypothesis, God Himself appears to be restricted. He must create a being that really is free to accept or reject Him. The consequence of this decision means that, should man or angel reject this invitation, a whole order of God-rejecting beings is found in existence in this universe. We must add, moreover, that the souls of men are by nature immortal. Reality also contains a "history" or record of this rejection of God, what Augustine called "the city of man" in its final state.

III.

God is often blamed for creating a world in which suffering and evil are possible. Had He created a world in which nothing could go wrong or one in which everything was automatically known without effort on the creature's part, then it is difficult to see why a world was needed at all. Technically, nothing could really happen in such a world that was not caused by the first cause. This is a delicate point. If nothing happened but what God directly caused, why bother with any creation at all if God directly provides for us a world in which there is no need to learn anything or do anything? He would be doing us no favor. He would depriving us of our own efforts to find out what is there in the world and how to deal with it. This effort would include the knowing by finite rational beings what they can from nature about what they are and what God is.

Suffering as such is not itself an evil, though it is generally a sign that something is wrong that needs to be fixed. Nor does the fact that it is not itself an evil mean that it is pleasant or something we should not work to alleviate. As it turns out, suffering becomes a central part of redemption. It is what follows from the Socratic philosophical principle that it is better to suffer evil than to do it. Suffering always points to the locus where something has gone wrong. A toothache does not tell us that something is wrong with our eyes. Once felt, we go to the dentist. Pain is what allows us to find and identify something that is not rightly functioning. But pain does not tell us exactly what to do to alleviate it. We must figure that out by ourselves.

Pain is also information: "Where does it hurt?" Pain, like pleasure, is one way through which we receive information from our bodies. The medical profession is little more than a vast information system that identifies and alleviates pain when it occurs. Its purpose is to restore this patient as much as possible to normalcy. It cannot always manage to achieve its goals. The issue of death is always remotely or closely connected with suffering and pain. Pain does not tell us how to alleviate the thing that has gone wrong. Pain and its alleviation also include what might be called spiritual pain, the pain that comes from the consequences of our evil deeds. All forms of pain point to something that has gone wrong in order to restore the sick person to what goes right. Thus, all pain points to what is good, to what is not in pain.

God did not put us in a world in which everything was done for us. He did put us in a world with other free beings, themselves also subject to pain and evil, whose actions could touch us, help us or harm us. The scientific principles that lie behind the understanding of the nature and workings of the universe are simply there to be discovered. But we must learn to formulate and use them. We do not create them. God did not provide us with a direct knowledge of these things. It was left to rational beings to learn what these principles are.

This learning was a sign of their dignity and connection with the reality that stood behind the world itself. We have learned many things, probably with many left to go. So we have in the universe rational beings that can learn much about how the world works and relates to itself. It seems that one of the purposes of the world was precisely that we have within it people who could understand it, its complexity and its wonder. Human beings want to know what the world is about because it is there to be known.

We also have in the world finite, rational beings who are assigned a transcendent end not finally in this world, an end usually described as "eternal life," something ultimately proper to each created being. This in-built purpose is why no human being is ever fully content in this world, why we seem always to be strangers and pilgrims in this world. In this sense, the world exists as an arena within which these myriads of finite beings destined to eternal life decide, by how they relate to each other and to God, what their eternal life will be. It will be one of either loving God or rejecting Him in the context of the lives they were given in their time in this vale of tears. God does not "cause" the choice we make, though He does give us our freedom and carries out the result of our choice in judgment. Plato had seen much of this drama in his *Republic*.

This eternal life includes the resurrection of the body, the final sign that death is overcome. It is the completion of the human being in his original creation and elevation. It follows the pattern of the Cross. In the logic of creation, justice is achieved only when what was responsible for what went wrong, the whole person, either corrects itself through repentance or accepts the consequences of final rejection of the initial offer of God to spend one's final being within His life. Man thus has a twofold end, one within this world, the other a transcendent end for each person after death. The two are related. It is the same life in both cases. The mortal life of man in time is a real life, but it is not each man's final destiny.

Generally speaking, the rejection of the invitation to eternal life is manifested by an effort to elevate man's inner-worldly life to the center of reality. This effort seeks to supply all the goods that were promised in eternity to man in this life. He comes to identify his ultimate good with what he wants, not with what is given to him. When this effort takes corporate or political form, it usually means that man's inner-worldly good is pitted against his transcendent end.

Indeed, his transcendent end comes to be looked upon as an effort to prevent him from achieving full happiness in this life. Man's mortal life is a relative but real good. An Augustinian outlook on this life would expect a series of very imperfect societies in which the Christian life was either persecuted or most difficult to live. A more Aristotelian view would maintain that a wide variety of regimes exist, some better than others. In both cases, man remains mortal. His personal life in this world ends in his death. He has no "second" chance. As Plato already saw, if he did not do it right the first time, he would not do it right in any number of future times.

No lasting city is found in this world. We have a finite world in which real secondary causes exist. This world exists in order that man's free life might be made manifest. It is within this mortal life—such is its dignity and importance, in no matter what kind of regime, in the best or the worst— that one lives his actual life. Here it is that the central invitation of each person's life is received and worked out in the context of others who live in his same era.

In the end, there is only the kingdom of God and the kingdom of man. The latter kingdom is composed of those who, in their living and freedom, reject God. Either the suffering that occurred brought man back to accepting the good to which it pointed, or it was accepted as the consequence of rejecting the divine invitation to live the life of the Godhead. Neither the world nor man ceases to be finite, but the world itself lives in service to the end for which this race of man was created: to live at a level beyond its natural status, to live an eternal life.

The ultimate meaning of secondary causes is that it is indeed, even though it need not be, good that something exists besides God. We would be less than insightful if we did not understand that in the paradox of secondary causes, we see at the heart of the world the Greek aphorism that man learns by suffering, along with the Christian teaching that we were redeemed when the Man-God accepted suffering as the will of His Father, who took the final risk both to redeem us and to leave us free to love Him in His own life, eternal life. But if we are free to accept this invitation, we are also free to reject it. This is why the two cities, of which Augustine spoke, live together for the time of this life. The final judgment, as Plato saw, finally separates them. Any polity that presumes to take on this final judgment as a political goal ends up as a tyranny. The politics of moderation and the location of man's final destiny relate to each other as means to end. This too is what political philosophy is about.

Chapter 12

Political Philosophy and Bioethics

The modern project . . . was originated by philosophers . . . to satisfy . . . the most powerful of the natural needs of men; nature was to be conquered for the sake of man who himself was supposed to possess . . . an unchangeable nature; the originators of the project took it for granted that philosophy and science were identical. After some time it appeared that the conquest of nature included human nature and hence . . . the questioning of the un-changeability of human nature; an unchangeable human nature might set absolute limits to progress. Accordingly, the natural needs of men could no longer direct the conquest of nature; the direction had to come from reason as distinguished from nature, from the rational Ought as distinguished from the neutral is.

—Leo Strauss, *The City and Man*

Gender theories strip God of his primary creative privileges: assigning indelible features to each individual human being, limiting certain choices, claiming authority over our privacy. . . . The offer of societal or personal gender assignment excises God from our lives so completely that the only way to return to him would be by a total conversion, an earthquake no one has yet anticipated. For now, the drive towards absoluter human autonomy promises to annul the unity of spirit and matter, so characteristic of the Western notion of man.

—Ewa Thompson, "Disenfranchising God"

I.

In his 1922 book *Eugenics and Other Evils*, G. K. Chesterton reached back to once popular discussions on human biological improvement by means of selective breeding. He had begun to write on these issues before World War I. "The wisest thing in the world is to cry out before you are hurt," he began. "It is no good to cry out after you are hurt, especially if you are mor-

* This chapter was previously published in 2018 on the website of the St. John Paul II Bioethics Center as part of their Lecture Series, accessed January 5, 2022, https://liberty4life.org/lecture-series-bioethics-schall-political-philosophy/.

tally hurt. People talk about the impatience of the populace; but sound historians know that most tyrannies have been made possible because men moved too late. It is often necessary to resist a tyranny before it exists. . . . There exists today a school of action, a school of thought; it is called for convenience sake 'Eugenics'; and that it ought to be destroyed I propose to prove in the pages that follow."[1] Reflecting on the nearly one hundred years since these words were published, we can rightly say that Chesterton did prove that the core assumptions of this movement, when spelled out, should have been destroyed.

We can say, likewise, that the general populace, when it did not itself join the movement, again moved too late. We are now confronted with this system of action and thought in its most sophisticated and virulent form. Its premises, now spelled out, have, under the names of "progress" or "modernity," become laws and customs of many civil societies, including our own.[2]

"Eugenics" was the science of "good birth." It held that science, not religion or philosophy, was the agent of man's good through a selective control of human breeding. It turned out to be a science that, in practice, as we see today, almost invariably led to a lack of human births or to births outside of the family manner in which human beings were intended to be born and nurtured. Ecology and bioethics, themselves often legitimate concerns, are the current loci wherein we find quietly simmering the ideas that Chesterton wanted destroyed.

In this context, the pursuit of the human good shifted from a moral endeavor to a medical and genetic one and then to a psychological and political one. In theological terms, what was once considered "original sin" now was to be met with efforts to change and improve the whole human race through gene manipulation and body reconfiguration. The architect of this change is not God but the speculative scientist, himself usually guided by some ideological vision of what man ought to be or can be. Indeed, the principle became that if we can do something, we ought to do it, exactly the reverse of the classical view.

Thinkers, scientists, and technicians still work and experiment, as they maintain, for the most noble of causes—namely, the "improvement of the human estate," as Francis Bacon called it. They will, we are assured, finally eliminate the physical and moral defects of human beings, even the blight

1 G. K. Chesterton, *Eugenics and Other Evils* (London: Cassell, 1922), 3.

2 See Antonio Carlo Pereira-Minaut, "A Letter from Spain, 2050," *Crisis Magazine*, June 8, 2018.

of death. We have scientists working to extend the span of our lives to one, two, or more centuries. Too few ask just why they want to do this and what it would mean if they were to succeed.[3]

II.

Some years ago, I heard a lecture at the Catholic University of America by the late Dr. Edmund Pellegrino, the founder of the bioethics program at George-town University. Today, he said, doctors no longer have a defined concept of what it is on which they exercise the art of medicine.[4] We go to a doctor. He does not tell us what is wrong with us. Rather, we tell him what we want done to us. Some government policy or agency will pay the bill for us to exercise our "right" to be what we want to be. We "plan" our own reconstruction. We implicitly assume something is wrong or missing in the original design from nature. The doctor has become a construction manager hired to carry out our self-designed blue-prints for the remaking of ourselves. We no longer have to carry the burden of sin, disease, and even accident. Our bodies are the raw material of our mental projections about what we choose to look like.

"Human nature," as it once was called, no longer limits our thinking. We are freed of it. It implied an existing order in nature over which we had no control. We have, or think we have, "progressed" beyond nature. The doctor now obliges us. He does not first consult any set standard of what it is to be human. He need not, indeed cannot, ask whether he "ought" to do what it is that his patients seek to have done to them. He tries to make it "work." The doctor, like the state, is at the service of our own concept of what we are or what we think that we want to be. Usually, considerations of cost, order, or democratic theory eventually will see to it that our diverse individual wills themselves become subordinate to the control of the state.

Our bodies are not looked upon as limits or insights into what we ought to be at our best. They are composed of malleable matter waiting to be reshaped in conformity with our ideas of what we want to be. Medical schools become more like art or engineering schools wherein their truth is whether what they do conforms to what the designer wants, not to what ought to be done with given human nature. All "oughts" have ceased. They lack, so it is said, any unchangeable "grounding."

---

3 Benedict XVI's encyclical *Spe Salvi* treats these issues.

4 See Robert Sokolowski, "The Art and Science of Medicine," *Christian Faith and Human Under-standing* (Washington, D.C.: The Catholic University of America Press, 2006), 237–49.

Historically, this latter approach was broadly known as Gnosticism.[5] It held that the human body is either intrinsically evil because it is composed of matter or an impediment to our good because it is ill-designed. We have no choice but to abandon it. We strive to replace the natural body with what Leo Strauss called "the rational Ought"—that is, with our conception of what we would look like if we were all-powerful gods. We have become, to repeat, artists of ourselves. We become selves who willingly deviate from the order that is given in nature. We do not acknowledge how well we were designed and put together in the first place.

This present lecture is entitled precisely "Political Philosophy and Bio-ethics." In classical thought, politics is considered to be the highest of the practical sciences, of the things that can be otherwise, of things not deter-mined by necessity or instinct. It was the arena wherein mortal men worked out, by their free choices under heaven and before their peers, how they finally defined themselves as good or bad men.

In that sense, political things, for their ends, were subject to the theo-retical or contemplative sciences, to things that could not be otherwise. Human nature as such did not change. The world was made for man wherein he strove to achieve his own transcendent and temporal purposes, both of which properly belonged to him. The great drama of the universe was centered on how men with immortal souls lived their passing lives. The universe existed that this drama could exist.

As Aristotle put it, politics did not make man to be man, but, taking him from nature as already man, sought to guide him through his own choices to be good man. It made a difference both to him and to the uni-verse how he turned out. This hypothesis recognized, of course, that man could, by his own choosing and doings, make himself to be bad man, unworthy of anything but himself. That is, man, by his own choices, could fail to become what he ought to be, what he was intended to be by the initial cause of his being *what he is*. Beginning with Plato, the classical discussions of heaven and hell were premised on this hypothesis of moral knowledge, voluntary responsibility, justice, and final judgment. What was mostly wrong in the world arose from the human will, not from the human body, environment, mind, or forces of chance.

---

5 See Thomas Weinandy, OFM Cap., "Gnosticism Today," *The Catholic Thing*, June 7, 2018, https://www.thecatholicthing.org/2018/06/07/gnosticism-today/.

III.

In 1971, I published a book entitled *Human Dignity & Human Numbers.* The book was basically a defense of *what man is* in his given nature. Human beings and this planet were, contrary to much ecological thinking, compatible with each other. With the active engagement of their minds, talents, and numbers, the planet, because of man's mind and hand, had the given capacity to support in a civilized manner the billions of people who sequentially have come to live on this planet.

Indeed the purpose of the planet depended on the proper lives and intelligence of its human inhabitants. The world was given to them, as it were, to see what they would do with it. They were not initially given a perfect world that required nothing of them, as so many paradise stories assume to be the best way for them. This planet was not designed endlessly to circle the Sun unused. Evil and good lives, nonetheless, produced different effects on man's surroundings and especially on himself.

The physical world existed in order to support full human life. But, to accomplish this purpose, man had to work and think about what was to be done in the light of what he was as being. The world itself was finite. It did not exist solely to keep the human race in existence down the ages with no end in sight. It existed as a place in which each of those billions born within it and within his respective city was to achieve his transcendent destiny.

But in the course of the discussion about the relation of man to planet, it was necessary to deal with those proposals that wanted radically to refashion human beings in man's own, not God's, image. At the time, the most articulate proponent of these sundry proposals was the biological scientist Joshua Lederberg. His thesis argued that the notion of what it is to be a good man is no longer, as the Greeks and their successors thought, through self-discipline, virtue, and knowledge. Rather, it was through genetics, through the reconstruction of man's body, especially through control of his begetting capacities.

The fundamental disorder in the universe was not rooted in what Christians called "original sin." Neither was it the ordinary run of human sins as such. These could be repented or ignored. What was once called "sin" could even come to be seen, as in abortion, not as a killing of one of our kind, but as a "virtue" and a "right." The real problem, as postulated, was the human physical configuration itself. "Ethics," as such, was obsolete. The good man, shades of proposals found in book 5 of Plato's *Republic,* even in his physical corpus, could be bred or reconstructed more perfectly according to the designs of a human fabricator.

Religion and philosophy, once thought to discover and explain man's very purpose, would really have nothing to do with this modern endeavor. The elimination of religion and ethics was presupposed to the accomplishment of man's immediate end. This end became a part of what can only be called a replacing of Christian eschatological notions with an inner-worldly project designed to account for man's happiness.[6]

Here, political philosophy and bioethics are to be seen as related to each other in several unsettling ways. "Ethics" usually referred to what Aristotle called the "practical intellect"—that is, to the same intellect when a person, through it, guides himself to the end he has chosen to embody as the purpose of his own happiness. He cannot not seek to be happy, as Aristotle put it.

The four traditional ends that could be chosen were wealth, honors, pleasure, or knowledge. All of these proposed ends had something good about them. That is why they could be chosen. But only a life devoted to the knowing of things, including divine things, could be defended absolutely. Hence, the moral life consisted in ruling our passions and properties in such a way that they could also contribute to the achievement of our natural end.

IV.

The term "bioethics" came into view when, following Strauss's remark, man realized that he could, in the name of science, experiment on his own corporal and psychic being. Was he free to go beyond the normal and moral standards of medicine, which classically were to cure this particular patient of this illness or problem? Could we "reconstruct" our very physical being? If so, why not do so?

"Bioethics" at its best could simply mean new ways of curing and healing after the principles of traditional medicine. But in rapid succession these more perplexing questions followed the given newly proposed premises that man could experiment on himself:

1) Could we lengthen the normal time of life way beyond the four score years and ten?
2) Could we enable great grandmothers to conceive children?
3) Could we enable males to bear children?

6 See James V. Schall, *The Modern Age* (South Bend, Ind.: St. Augustine's Press, 2011).

4) Could two lesbian ladies arrange a conception that included them both plus some male donor, a three-parent child?

5) Could a woman become a man or man become a woman with a few delicate operations?

6) Would it not be better, in the name of equality, if all children had exactly the same genetic parentage?

7) Can homosexuals "marry" to produce children?

8) Could we breed a race of worker drones that were part human and part animal?

9) Could we separate begetting and sex in such a way that all begetting, gestation, and education was in the hands of the state's/scientists' control, while all sex was rendered sterile with no relation to children?

10) Was choosing to inflict death on ourselves whenever we chose to do so a "right" or an obligation?

11) Must we not limit the population of the earth to a few billion?

12) Ought we strive to place our race on some other planet in the solar system?

13) Does not every child have a right to have its own genetic father and mother as responsible for him in a proper home?

Looking back on these questions, we recall that human nature was initially considered to be unchangeable. Aside from Platonic eugenics, no means of more radical changes yet existed. What depended on human, responsible choice was whether each person would live a worthy human life according to the virtues and commandments. It was possible also to choose a life of vice. But vice did not involve a restructuring of man's basic physical configuration. Its consequences were understood as transcendently significant, not to be ultimately resolved in this life.

Thanks to science man was presented, in the course of what was called "progress," with a more basic choice beyond the choice of virtue and vice. He had also to choose to remain what he was by nature. If he did not so choose, what man was could disappear from our midst. He could choose to reject this natural order by changing his parts and purposes. We live in a time when this choice against what we are is not a matter of vice but of biology, politics, and a medicine whose function is to make possible the kind of corporeal life that we propose as an alternative. Once we accept and carry out these proposals, we then have to live with them. Indeed, that is what much of our public life is today, coping with these consequences.

V.

Political philosophy was originally considered to be the effort of the philosopher to teach the politician the value of what is for its own sake, of what is beyond politics, as it were. This theoretic order was the guarantee of a stability of ends not subject to the human will. The first principle of politics is not itself political. That is, it is given to man with his coming to be already man. Once man knows his ultimate end—the knowledge of the truth, the beatific vision—prudence, the intellectual virtue of the practical virtues, guides him to the proper means to achieve it. The account of these choices constituted the drama of the historic existence of each existing person.

The politician, the statesman, does not have time to be also a philosopher. He is a busy man. The closest he can come to philosophy is to sense a hint of transcendence in beauty, in the right order that is found in music, art, literature, and noble action.[7] Yet, he must, at the same time, be aware of the corruption of the personal and social order by unworthy philosophers who themselves reject the order of things. The theme of the "betrayal" of the intellectuals is familiar in Western thought.

The statesman's vocation is to protect his polity and its citizens not only from internal disorder or foreign enemies but also from ideas that can undermine what it is to be human. The really serious disorders in most actual historic societies originated in the souls of the intellectual and clerical dons. In other words, no polity can afford not to know what, in principle, its learned members are saying.

In his remarkable book *Leading a Worthy Life*, Leon Kass, onetime chairman of the president's Commission on Bioethics, was concerned with what he called the most dangerous of modern proposals—that is, "the use of biotechnical powers to pursue 'perfection' both of body and of mind. I do so partly because it is the most neglected topic of public bioethics, yet it is, I believe, the deepest source of public anxiety, represented in the concern about 'men playing God,' or a Brave New World or a 'post-human' future."[8]

In conclusion, we can, without forgetting the things of value in modern society, grant the bleakness of these reflections on what happens when politics and science join to replace the given nature of man with their own

---

7 See Carnes Lord, *Education and Culture in the Thought of Aristotle* (Ithaca, N.Y.: Cornell University Press, 1982).

8 Leon Kass, *Leading a Worthy Life: Finding Meaning in Modern Times* (New York: Encounter Books, 2017), 138.

trans-human concepts. But I would point out that every proposed "improvement" is, at bottom, an attempt to reach goals of human living that were originally Christian teachings. Thus, efforts to prolong life indefinitely or to freeze dead bodies to resuscitate them after death witness to the hope of the resurrection of a particular body. Many earlier utopias concerned themselves with a distant future of a vague collectivity, a classless society. More recent proposals realize that if history means the happiness of some-one down the ages, it leaves most actual people out. This realization is why we now have proposals to keep alive the same individual person, to avoid his death at all costs.

It has long been clear that Marxism was an eschatology that purported to be able to put its finger on the cause of evil in the world and eliminate it. For Marx the elimination of evil was not a moral problem or a medical one, but an economic one. He was not wrong in holding something was wrong with the human condition. He merely mislocated its center in freedom of the will to reject what man was.

When we look at the Christian understanding of sin, love, eternal life, marriage, brotherhood, and virtue, we soon become aware that modern bioethics itself is concerned with these things. In this sense, their secularized versions are not so much a rejection of Christianity but a claim that they can be achieved in a different way. The trouble is that in practice the results of these modern alternatives turn out to be much worse than any classically defined vice. They disorder not only the soul but our very bodies.

The abidingness of the same revelation to be passed down over time means simply that it is not possible to find any more perfect way. The con-clusion to be drawn from modern bioethics and political philosophy is that God and nature made our kind better than we can make ourselves. In reject-ing nature, we do not find happiness, nor do we find God; indeed, we do not find ourselves either. The stability of the world was not put on the shoulders of Atlas. It was put on the minds and wills of individual human beings asked to accept the fact that they were better made from nature than from anything they might propose as an alternative.

Chapter 13

On the Place of Thomas More in Political Philosophy

A Reflection on A Man for All Seasons

Blessed Thomas More is more important at this moment than at any moment since his death, even perhaps the greatest moment of his dying; but he is not quite so important as he will be in about a hundred years' time. He may come to be counted the greatest Englishman, or at least the greatest historical figure in English history. . . . And it will remain a permanent and determining fact, a hinge of history, that he saw, in the first hour of madness, that Rome and Reason are one, He saw at the very beginning, what so many have now only begun to see at the end, that the real hopes of learning and liberty lay in preserving the Roman unity of Europe and the ancient Christian loyalty for which he died.

> —G. K. Chesterton, "A Turning Point of History,"
> in *The Fame of Blessed Thomas More*

May I not come simply to pay my respects to the English Socrates—as I see your angelic friend Erasmus calls you?

> —Chapuys, the Spanish Ambassador, in Robert Bolt,
> *A Man for All Seasons*

As I speak to you in this historic setting [Westminster Hall], I think of the countless men and women down the centuries who have played their part in the momentous events which have taken place within these walls and have shaped the lives of many generations of Britons, and others besides. In particular, I recall the figure of Saint Thomas More, the great English scholar and statesman, who is admired by believers and non-believers alike for the integrity with which he followed his conscience, even at the cost of displeasing his sovereign whose "good servant" he was, because he served to serve God first. . . . The fundamental questions at stake in Thomas More's trial continue to present themselves.

> —Benedict XVI, To Representatives of British Society,
> September 17, 2010

* This chapter was previously published in *Thomas More: Why Patron of Statesmen?*, ed. Travis Curtright (Lanham, Md.: Lexington Books, 2015), 181–96.

I.

Political philosophy as such begins with the deaths of Socrates and Christ in famous trials before the leading cities of their time, cities known for law, justice, and philosophy. The issue was first formulated by Plato: Was it necessary for Socrates to die in Athens? Does a city exist in which the philosopher could live? What is the relation of philosophy, poetry, and politics to each other? Both trials, moreover, had to do with the things that were Caesar's and those that were God's, to use the innovative terms found in the New Testament (Matthew 22:22). The death of Socrates asked whether a philosopher could live in even the best existing city of men, in Athens, the city of philosophers. The death of Christ asked whether the Man-God could live in either the Holy City or the Eternal City, either Jerusalem or Rome. Both deaths implied the existence of a city that was not, as Augustine was to say, an "earthly" city. Though Aristotle did not know of a Church or a purely temporal order, he did distinguish a practical and a theoretical order, a distinction of vast importance when it came both to the "reasonableness" of revelation and to the "practicality" of Machiavelli, the ancients, and the moderns.

In a series of famous executions from Socrates, to Cicero, to Christ, to Seneca, to Justin Martyr, to Boethius, and to Thomas More, we find the same basic issue at sake. It is not a question of how religion or philosophy limits the civil power. Rather, we want to know how the civil power is to understand the place of religion and philosophy relative to the temporal realm for which it is primarily responsible.[1] We seek a balance that does not destroy the existing city, or the things shared by both city and philosophy, or the things beyond Caesar. Political philosophy is nonetheless philosophy. It seeks and is open to the truth that is found in pursuing action to the limits of things political. It is precisely these limits of political things, their inability to explain everything about themselves, that leave us open to what is beyond politics, though, for all that, no less real, no less belonging to the order of being, than the things found in the city.[2]

The central question that More faced—and died for—was whether anything existed beyond the civil power, that power in his time just beginning to be designated, after Machiavelli, as *lo stato*, "the state," something quite differ-

---

1 See Leo Strauss, "What Is Political Philosophy?," *What Is Political Philosophy? And Other Studies* (Glencoe, Ill.: Free Press, 1959), 9–55.

2 See James V. Schall, *At the Limits of Political Philosophy* (Washington, D.C.: The Catholic University of America Press, 1996).

ent from Aristotle's polity of practical virtues. If nothing is beyond the political order, the whole endeavor to limit Caesar seems illusory, hardly worth making the effort to account for it. The return, or, perhaps better, the full establishment, of the absolute or totalitarian state was the work not merely of a line of thought from post-Aristotelian philosophy to nominalism, to Descartes, Hobbes, Locke, Rousseau, Kant, and Hegel, to the French Revolution and the twentieth-century ideologies, but, in a more democratic and graphic form, of the twenty-first century. *The Abolition of Man, 1984,* and *The Brave New World* are much more visible in the twenty-first century than they were in the twentieth century, when they mainly existed in books. Coming together in these considerations, then, are how philosophy, poetry, revelation, and politics are to be related in a coherent, noncontradictory whole.

II.

In this light, I want to reconsider Robert Bolt's most influential play, *A Man for All Seasons*.[3] I will understand this reflection to be an exercise in precisely political philosophy. The subcontext of the play, to be sure, is the classic one from Plato's Thrasymachus and Machiavelli—namely, "Does might make right?" To all outward appearances, in the case of More, "might" did successfully overrule "right," unless what More died for was true. In that case, the violation of justice in More's trial will, if not forgiven, be requited, though not in this life. More was not just a noble man of law and literature, though he was that also. He held that Peter, the "Bishop of Rome," the pope, held authority from God, the origin of all order. This authority covered only what was given to it. But it knew what it was given. It was an active authority. It knew that no temporal power, whose own authority is likewise from God, could replace or overrule divine authority, though many tried—particularly in More's case, the Tudor king.

Authority was given in the Church to the papacy and bishops to uphold and teach what was handed down. That same authority is to be understood. It is to be thought about, and, when reasonable, to be acted upon. Civilization is defined by what is or is not maintained within its confines. The word "barbarian," by contrast, means no law. No formally established procedures are found to requite injustices. In this sense, what More upheld was precisely civilization, the order of human relationships directed to *what is*. He continued—or better, reestablished—at the beginning of modernity the great

---

3 Robert Bolt, *A Man for All Seasons* (New York: Random House, 1960).

Socratic principle that "it is never right to do wrong."[4] Erasmus was right
to see Socrates in More, though More, in his action, saw more than Socrates
but nothing against Socrates. Why this coherence is so is what political philosophy should be about.

In More's death, we see both Socrates and Christ as if one leads to the
other. Athens and Jerusalem came together in the Tower of London. As
Benedict XVI said—also in London, in Westminster Hall where More was
tried—More was the king's "good servant" because he was God's servant
first. In the play itself, More, reacting to Cardinal Wolsey's effort to place
the king first, replied: "When statesmen forsake their own private conscience for the sake of their public duties . . . they lead their country by a
short route to chaos."[5] The public order is basically upheld by the private
conscience of the statesman acknowledging true reason and authority, not
merely whatever it is the prince wants. The contrary is true also; the "chaos"
does follow in the public order when the order of reason is not upheld by
those who are called statesmen.

Bolt wrote an elegant preface to the play in which he tried to explain
More's life as if the specific cause for which he died (that is, the Catholic
understanding of things) was not objectively true. Nor were the transcendent consequences (heaven and hell) true that More, following both Plato
and the Gospels, envisioned and understood to flow from violations of
God's laws. Bolt leaves us with a Camus-type feeling that the "action" of
More's execution must be meaningful even though we do not know why it
makes sense in its own terms. Thus, Bolt writes, "I think the paramount gift
our thinkers, artists, and, for all I know, our men of science, should labor
to get for us is a sense of selfhood without resort to magic. Albert Camus is
a writer I admire in this connection."[6] More's own reasons are passed off as
"magic." More, in Bolt's view, really died for something called "selfhood,"
whatever that might mean. More, however, did not die "true to himself." He
died true to his oath, true to the God he served in serving his king according
to law. In the end, the king was logically forced to use power and not law
against More. Ultimately, this fact is why More is both a philosopher and a
martyr, while Henry is but a tyrant, not a real king.

4 Plato, *Crito*, 49a–b. This and all subsequent quotations from Plato are taken from Plato's *Complete Works* (Indianapolis: Hackett, 1997).

5 Bolt, *A Man for All Seasons*, 22.

6 Bolt, *A Man for All Seasons*, xiv.

Bolt explains himself by making all of us like unto himself. "We (moderns) no longer have, as past societies have had, any picture of individual Man (Stoic Philosopher, Christian Religious, Rational Gentleman) by which to recognize ourselves and against which to measure ourselves; we are anything. But if anything, then nothing; and it is not everyone who can live with that, though it is our true present position. Hence our willingness to locate ourselves from something that is certainly larger than ourselves, the society that contains us."[7] Bolt thinks that More had such an understanding of himself. Bolt wants to preserve More's nobility for us as if More's reasoning is not true, though some other explanation, that of Bolt, makes some sense of him. More is thus pictured as a member of the English polity, which he was, but not primarily a member of the City of God, which was, in Bolt's phrase, "magic." More "hides" in society as a last-resort defense of his "selfhood."

What does Bolt's world look like according to which he tries to make sense of More's murder? It does not look like the world that More saw and in which he explained his actions. "More was an orthodox Catholic and for him an oath was something perfectly specific; it was an invitation to God, an invitation God would not refuse, to act as a witness, and to judge; the consequence of perjury was damnation, for More another perfectly clear concept."[8] Thus Bolt, from the outside, could understand More's position in More's own terms. But since Bolt himself cannot accept this explanation, More's nobility must be explained in other figures—other "magic"?

To illustrate this point, Bolt continues: "But I am not a Catholic, nor even in the meaningful sense of the word a Christian. So by what right do I appropriate a Christian saint to my purposes? Or to put it in the other way, why do I take as my hero a man who brings about his own death because he can't put his hand on an old black book and tell an ordinary lie?"[9] Bolt proceeds to tell us why he finds More worthy even if he (Bolt) does not accept More's theology. This is the explanation. A man takes an oath to establish a relation between his words and his actions. We suspect most men would guarantee their words with "cash" rather than with themselves. "We feel—we know—the self to be an equivocal commodity. There are fewer and fewer things which, as they say, we 'cannot bring ourselves' to do. We can find almost no limits for ourselves other than the physical,

---

7 Bolt, *A Man for All Seasons*, xi.

8 Bolt, *A Man for All Seasons*, xiii.

9 Bolt, *A Man for All Seasons*, xiii.

which, being physical, are not optional."[10] The oath, in Bolt's mind, then, is a self-imposed norm to prevent us from being just anything at all. But this oath is not addressed to "anyone."

For most of the play, as Bolt understands it, More is confident that at some point the law will protect him if he is careful to follow it strictly. In the end, More is broken by Cromwell's perjury, his corruption of the law. Why did More not do as most other English prelates and aristocracy did and go along with Henry? In Bolt's view, More's answer was this:

> The English Kingdom, his immediate society, was subject to the larger society of the Church of Christ, founded by Christ, extending over Past and Future, ruled from Heaven. There are still some for whom that is perfectly simple, but for most it can only be a metaphor for a larger context which we all inhabit, the terrifying cosmos. Terrifying because no laws, no sanctions, no *mores* obtain there; it is either empty or occupied by God and the Devil nakedly at war. The sensible man will seek to live his life without dealings with the larger environment, treating it as a fine spectacle on a clear night.[11]

Bolt passes off any rational foundation of faith as "simple." He sees a universe that more and more reveals order as chaos or as "speculation on a clear night."[12] He concludes that More was his (Bolt's) "sensible man." "He will not try to live in it (the cosmos of God and Devil); he will gratefully accept the shelter of his society. This was certainly More's inclination."[13]

More's "inclination" was certainly to depend on English law and society if he could. But More did not do what his fellow Englishmen did. He did not submit to Henry or renounce the Church's central jurisdiction. He did not approve what was against God's law. More believed for as long as he could that the English would observe their own laws. But when they did not, with Cromwell's perjury under Henry's iron will, More knew that the world he in fact lived in was that of the transcendent order in which the statesman followed his conscience to do God's will and to prevent chaos in his earthly kingdom. For More, to be English was to observe the higher law when the civil law failed, in his case, to be just. Indeed, when he can speak

---

10 Bolt, *A Man for All Seasons*, xiii–xiv.

11 Bolt, *A Man for All Seasons*, xv–xvi.

12 See Robert Spitzer, *New Cosmological Proofs for the Existence of God* (Grand Rapids, Mich.: Eerdmans, 2010).

13 Bolt, *A Man for All Seasons*, xvi.

his mind freely, knowing that he would die, More even cites the Magna Carta and the Coronation Oath.

> To avoid this [condemnation] I have taken every path my winding wits would find. Now that this Court has determined to condemn me, God knows how, I will discharge my mind . . . concerning the indictment and the King's title. The indictment is grounded in an act of Parliament which is directly repugnant to the Law of God. The King in Parliament cannot bestow the Supremacy of the Church because it is a Spiritual Supremacy. And more to this the very immunity of the Church is promised both in Magna Carta and the King's own Coronation Oath.[14]

More understood the nature of both the temporal and the spiritual powers, made even more poignant when we realize that the papacy was governed during his lifetime by some less than stellar men.

I have spent some time on Bolt's efforts to be a modern man and still account for the nobility of Thomas More's action. In the end, More's "magic" is more reasonable than Bolt's "common sense." Bolt does give us, however, a fair understanding of More's own reasoning. It is of some importance, moreover, to recognize that More's "magic" is Plato's (and Aristotle's) kingdom of "prayer." That is, when the practical limits of rule were reached and the question of a better regime still came up, both classic philosophers would say that this best kingdom is something we could "pray for." The same words are striking in More. Wolsey says to More: "You'd like that, wouldn't you? To govern the country by prayers?" More responds: "Yes, I should."[15] More understood the limits of human rule in a way Cardinal Wolsey did not.

Bolt's "common sense," however, is not that of Aquinas, Aristotle, or Chesterton, but that of Machiavelli. The "common sense" to which More is urged to accept in the play by both his friends and those surrounding the king is that of capitulation, of violating both his conscience and the objective order just to stay alive at whatever cost. Thus, early in the play itself, Wolsey says to More: "You're a constant regret to me, Thomas. If you could just see facts flat on, without that horrible moral squint, with just a little common sense, you could have been a statesman."[16] The irony is that More was the

---

14 Bolt, *A Man for All Seasons*, 159.

15 Bolt, *A Man for All Seasons*, 22. See Josef Pieper, *Platonic Myths* (South Bend, Ind.: St. Augustine's Press, 2012).

16 Bolt, *A Man for All Seasons*, 19.

great statesman. Wolsey's own philosophy would not let him admit this with
More standing there before him. This incident again recalls Socrates's "no
evil can come to a good man," that "death is not the worst evil."[17] More's
conscience is freely conformed to an order that governs the universe. He is
not a modern man who first empties the universe of finality and meaning
only then to put his own unrestricted mind, will, and desire in its place.

III.

As I have said, the beginnings and formulations of political philosophy
relate to the trials of Socrates and Christ. More himself refers to Christ's
crucifixion in the light of his own execution. In the end, More is offered a
goblet of wine. He replies: "My Master had easel and gall, not wine, given
him to drink."[18] I conceive the trial of Thomas More to "complete" what
was, as it were, lacking in the earlier trials, however much they established
the basic principle at issue concerning the superiority of the transcendent
order. What the trial of More adds to the trials of Socrates, Christ, Cicero,
Seneca, Justin Martyr, and Boethius is precisely that it is a trial of a statesman about statesmanship and law. The earlier trials, with the possible exception of Cicero, whose death is rather more of a political assassination than
a trial, were of philosophers and prophets before the politicians. These trials
had to do with the limits of the city before the transcendent order. More
himself, when the Erasmus comparison is mentioned, says: "Socrates! I've
no taste for hemlock."[19] More's hemlock was his beheading for treason. He
did have a taste for the integrity of politics.

In More, thus, we have the trial of the politician before the politicians
about the limits of politics within politics. It is true that More was also a
philosopher, but his trial was not about this side of his career, even though,
like Plato, he is known for the "city in speech," for "utopia." More's trial was
about whether politics itself reaches limits within its own order when it
contradicts what it is. To be sure, when it does so contradict itself so that
it acts on power alone, we face the question of the reasonableness of politics
before the transcendent order. That is, we must take a position on whether
revelation itself is addressed to reason and whether reason can remain itself

---

17 Plato, *Crito*. This and all subsequent quotations from Plato are taken from Plato's *Complete
Works* (Indianapolis: Hackett, 1997).

18 Bolt, *A Man for All Seasons*, 161.

19 Bolt, *A Man for All Seasons*, 84.

if it rejects the reasonableness found in revelation. The alternative, as we see all through *A Man for All Seasons*, is Machiavelli, the *raison d'état*, power calculus.

In reading *A Man for All Seasons*, we cannot help but see intimations of the trials of Socrates and Christ reflected in the Westminster trial. Harry Jaffa has remarked that the greatest of the English kings was Lear, a fictional king.[20] And, of course, even Lear, in Jaffa's view, confused the order of politics with the order of love that transcended it. That was the essence of Lear's tragedy even though in the end Lear and Cordelia died together. In the case of More, Alice, More's wife, and Margaret, his daughter, are closer to Xantippe and the potential philosophers present on the last day of Socrates's life. Alice, like Xantippe, simply cannot understand why her husband has to die. In the dramatic scenes near the end, More tells his wife that he does not want to go unless she understands. She replies that she cannot understand, but still she knows that he is "the finest man" she ever knew.[21]

More's love of his daughter did not show any of this confusion between politics and the transcendent order that Lear showed. In their meeting, Henry VIII thought Margaret rather too bookish. Thus, Henry says to Thomas (regarding Margaret): "Take care, Thomas: 'Too much learning is a weariness of the flesh, and there is no end to the making of books.'" The king then asks Margaret if she can dance. "Not well," she replies.[22] But Margaret too wants to understand why More is doing what he does. In this sense, she is analogous to the potential philosophers in the *Phaedo*, who need to be shown why Socrates is not afraid of death, why he is not really abandoning them. More accepts the Christian version of the immortality of the soul.[23] The immortality of the soul is the context of Socrates's reasoning on the topic. Plato wanted to know if the world is created in injustice. It is so created if the crimes in actual cities are not punished or the good deeds occurring in them are not rewarded. More, like Socrates, saw that there was no inner-worldly solution to this problem, only a transcendent one. Hence, we have the last judgment in both the *Republic* and in the Gospels.

20 Allan Bloom and Harry Jaffa, *Shakespeare's Politics* (Chicago: University of Chicago Press, 1981), 113–38.

21 Bolt, *A Man for All Seasons*, 145.

22 Bolt, *A Man for All Seasons*, 49.

23 See James V. Schall, *Reason, Revelation, and the Foundations of Political Philosophy* (Baton Rouge: Louisiana State University Press, 1987).

When Rich is arrested, Margaret says: "Father, that man is bad." More replies: "There is no law against that." Roper intervenes: "There is God's law." More: "Then let God arrest him. . . . The law, Roper, the law. I know what's legal, not what's right. And I'll stick to what's legal."[24] Notice that More does not say whatever is legal is right in the positivist sense. More thinks that English common law is indeed based on reason, to which he clings in the hope that it still is so based even under Henry. This consideration touches our argument that More is using the law against the lawlessness of the king. For most of the trial, More is confident that the law will protect him if he carefully observes it, even in silence.[25] He is in danger only if the king himself, through Cromwell, Rich, and Norfolk, breaks the law of England. He initially does not expect this rejection, but as the play progresses it becomes obvious that breaking it is Henry's only alternative. More is right on the law itself, and he knows it.

More is even accused of giving the Devil the "benefit of the law."[26] But we do not "cut down law to get at evil." More tells Roper: "God or the Devil will find me hiding in the thickets of the law."[27] More informs his daughter that he is safe because he is not "on the wrong side of the law."[28] We see what More is about when he tells Roper: "Will, I'd trust you with my life, but not your principles."[29] It is the law and its consistent principles that More upholds.

In a famous scene near the end of the play, when Alice and Margaret, not unlike Xanthippe and the children visited Socrates, are allowed to visit More in his cell, More continues to teach Margaret: "When a man takes an oath, Meg, he's holding his own self in his own hands."[30] More in other contexts says, rather, his own "soul." Margaret responds, almost in frustration, that her father should be a hero in any just land. This remark brings More to one of the most profound insights in all of political philosophy, one tinged with the Christian understanding of original sin and its scope also in politics. This is the ultimate answer to political utopianism, stated by the author of the *Utopia* himself. More tells Margaret:

24 Bolt, *A Man for All Seasons*, 61.

25 Bolt, *A Man for All Seasons*, 150.

26 Bolt, *A Man for All Seasons*, 66.

27 Bolt, *A Man for All Seasons*, 67.

28 Bolt, *A Man for All Seasons*, 69.

29 Bolt, *A Man for All Seasons*, 43.

30 Bolt, *A Man for All Seasons*, 140.

If we lived in a State where virtue was profitable, common sense would make us good, and greed would make us saints. And we'd live like animals or angels in the happy land that needs no heroes. But since in fact we see that avarice, anger, envy, pride, sloth, lust, and stupidity commonly profit far beyond humility, chastity, fortitude, justice, and thought, and have to choose, to be human at all . . . why then perhaps we must stand fast a little—even at the risk of being heroes.[31]

We have to choose to be human at all. We do not escape death by failing to be heroes. If we do fail, our reward is an ignominious death sooner or later and its eternal consequences. Thus, More tells Margaret: "Death comes to us all, even at our birth."[32] The great question is not whether, but how we live and how we die.

IV.

The trial of More, as I have indicated, clarifies the conflict between ancients and moderns. It does so by exemplifying what Machiavellianism means both in terms of politics itself and in terms of the revelational response to it, the only one that really makes sense of all factors. Constantly, throughout the play, More is chided at being against the "spirit of the times." This emphasis on the "now" is what we have come to call "historicism." Morality is not universal in all times and in all places, but what people of a given time do or do not do. Cromwell at one point tells More that he was once up to date, but now he opposes "the whole movement of the times."[33] Cromwell offers him the highest posts if he recants.

Norfolk, whose own corruption by Cromwell and Henry is part of the tragedy, tries to convince More of the same thing on the grounds of friendship. Norfolk says to More: "Can't you do what I did, and come with us, for fellowship?" More: "And when we stand before God, and you are sent to Paradise for doing according to your conscience and I am damned for not doing according to mine, will you come with me, in fellowship?"[34] Again this passage is a key to understanding More. His integrity as a statesman lies in his loyalty to what he holds to be true. Thus, More says to Norfolk:

---

31 Bolt, *A Man for All Seasons*, 140–41.

32 Bolt, *A Man for All Seasons*, 161.

33 Bolt, *A Man for All Seasons*, 114.

34 Bolt, *A Man for All Seasons*, 132.

"But what matters to me is not whether it's true or not, but that I believe it to be true."[35] More cannot be properly explained outside his understanding of revelation. Thus, the overtones of true friendship are also, as in Aristotle, found in the trial of More. True friendship, friendship in the highest things, includes truth.

Actually, the king understands that this integrity of More is the major obstacle to his achieving the divorce. Thus, More says to Cromwell: "It is not for the Supremacy [of the King over the Church] that you have sought my blood—but because I would not bend to the marriage."[36] This moral witness of More is the real reason why he is killed. Henry pleads his own conscience about the marriage to Catherine. He does not need a pope to tell him that he (Henry) sinned. More asks then: "Why then does Your Grace need my poor support?" Henry replies: "Because you are honest." Others follow for base motives.[37]

So Henry has to corrupt More as precisely an honest man whom people respect. If More yields, Henry's path will be clear. But Henry says that he will "have no opposition."[38] More insists that "I am your Grace's loyal minister."[39] But only in the things that belong to the king. Henry asks More to agree to the divorce. More replies that, if he cannot come along, he will not think about it. More vividly makes clear the distinction between his loyalty to the king and to God: "Take your dagger and saw it [right arm] from my shoulder, and I will laugh and be thankful, if by that means I can come with your Grace with a clear conscience."[40] His conscience he cannot so easily "saw off."

The play shows a constant search for More's weak spot. The view of human nature in those surrounding the king makes it certain that one can be found. Early in the play, the steward observes: "My master Thomas More would give anything to anyone. Some say that's good and some say that's bad, but I say he can't help it—and that's bad . . . because some day someone's going to ask him for something that he wants to keep; and he'll be out of practice. There must be something that he wants to keep.[41] Thus Alice at

35 Bolt, *A Man for All Seasons*, 91.
36 Bolt, *A Man for All Seasons*, 160.
37 Bolt, *A Man for All Seasons*, 55.
38 Bolt, *A Man for All Seasons*, 56.
39 Bolt, *A Man for All Seasons*, 57.
40 Bolt, *A Man for All Seasons*, 53.
41 Bolt, *A Man for All Seasons*, 17.

one point tells her husband: "Be ruled, if you won't rule him, be ruled." More replies: "I neither could nor would rule my King. But there's a little . . . little area . . . where I must rule myself."[42] The play, of course, inevitably takes us to this one thing that More keeps.

We see both the Machiavellian and Christological dimensions of this one thing that More keeps. Rich broaches the issue:

> "But every man has his price!" More: "No-no-no—" Rich: "But yes! In money too. . . . Or pleasure. Titles, women, bricks and mortar, there's always something." More: "Childish." Rich: "Well, in suffering certainly." More: "Buy a man with suffering?" Rich: "Impose suffering, and offer him—escape." More: "Oh, for one moment I thought you were being profound." . . . Rich: "No, not a bit profound; it then became a purely practical question of how to make him suffer sufficiently." More: "And . . . .who recommended you to read Signor Machiavelli? . . ." Rich: "Master Cromwell." More: "He's a very able man."[43]

The real Machiavellian figure in the play is Cromwell. Machiavelli is said to be the founder of specifically "modern" political philosophy. This is the philosophy that rejects Aristotle. *A Man for All Seasons* is a working out of the logic of Machiavelli as it brings about the execution of More. In doing so, it restores the integrity of classical and medieval political philosophy.

At one point, Norfolk says to Rich: "I've never found much use in Aristotle myself, not practically. Great philosopher, of course. Wonderful mind." More responds: "Master Rich is newly converted to the doctrine of Machiavelli." Rich: "The doctrines of Machiavelli have been largely mistaken, I think; indeed, properly apprehended, he has no doctrine. Master Cromwell has the sense of it, I think."[44] Both the politics of Aristotle and that of Machiavelli are called "practical." What makes Aristotle's politics "practical" is its prudent application of the first principles of morality to each particular situation, neither too much or too little. What makes Machiavelli's politics "practical" is whether they "work," no matter what the first principles might imply.

We notice how Cromwell reduces the status of More from that of good man to that of mere man so that he can better deal with him. Cromwell: "When the King wants something done, I do it." Cromwell to Chapuys:

42 Bolt, *A Man for All Seasons*, 59.
43 Bolt, *A Man for All Seasons*, 4–5.
44 Bolt, *A Man for All Seasons*, 12–13.

"Meanwhile, I do prepare myself for higher things. I stock my mind."
Chapuys: "Sir Thomas is a good son of the Church." Cromwell: "Sir Thomas
is a man."[45] For Cromwell, the "highest things" are not metaphysics and the
things of God but precisely practical politics. This passage recalls Aristotle's
seminal statement that "if man were the highest being, politics would be
the highest science."[46] But since man is not the highest being, politics is not
the highest science.

When politics is made to be the highest science, unrelated to any transcendent order, we have "modern" politics where the prince, lo stato, is the
highest law, grounded in nothing but itself. Ironically, Cromwell, who was
himself executed by Henry's orders on July 28, 1540, seems to understand
the fate he himself is caught in by pursuing his own politics. Cromwell: "He
[More] must submit, the alternatives are bad. While More's alive, the King's
conscience breaks into fresh stinking flowers every time he gets from bed.
And if I bring about More's death—I plant my own, I think."[47] "The End of
Machiavellianism," as Maritain once called it, does not exempt the greatest
of the Machiavellians from its logic.[48]

How does this Machiavellianism work? At the end of the first act of the
play, Cromwell tells Rich that after the first betrayal of his own conscience,
he will find the next time "easier."[49] Cromwell explains the logic of dealing
with an honorable man: "But Sir Thomas has plenty of sense; he could be
frightened." Cromwell, to illustrate his point, burns his own finger in the
fire.[50] More, Cromwell is certain, will yield under torture and threat of death.

But can More be "frightened"? Is the theory valid? Cromwell understands why More must be dealt with. Norfolk asks: Why do we not leave
More "silent"? Cromwell replies that More is a man of letters; his silence is
heard throughout Europe. But to try to frame More won't work. "He was
the only judge since Cato who didn't accept bribes."[51] Another way, then?

45 Bolt, A Man for All Seasons, 38–39.

46 Aristotle, Ethics, 1140b20–25. This and all subsequent quotations from Aristotle are taken
from Aristotle's Basic Works (New York: Random House, 1941).

47 Bolt, A Man for All Seasons, 137.

48 Jacques Maritain, "The End of Machiavellianism," The Review of Politics 4, no. 1 (January
1942): 1–33.

49 Bolt, A Man for All Seasons, 76.

50 Bolt, A Man for All Seasons, 77.

51 Bolt, A Man for All Seasons, 98–99.

Cromwell tells a reluctant Norfolk that he has "no choice" but to be part of More's trial. Cromwell threatens to tell the king of Norfolk's tenuous friendship with More.[52] Fear works with Norfolk. How to approach More? Cromwell tells Rich: "It must be done by law. It's just a matter of finding the right law. Or making one."[53]

This passage again explains why the trial of More is a trial of the politician by the politician, but of opposing conceptions of what it is to be political. All tyrants, if they can, want the cover of law even if they have to make it up themselves. This is pretty much what Henry does with the Act of Supremacy whereby he becomes the head of the Church in England. Cromwell sees the alternatives. What is to be done? "Whatever is necessary. The King's a man of conscience and he wants either Sir Thomas More to bless his marriage or Sir Thomas More destroyed."[54]

More does not see himself as a hero itching to be a martyr. "But Man he made to serve him wittily in the tangle of his mind! . . . And no doubt it delights God to see splendor where He only looked for complexity. But it's God's part, not our own, to bring ourselves to that extremity! Our natural business lies in escaping."[55] More sticks to the letter of the law. He knows that silence legally is not guilt. He knows that if he approves the king's divorce, he lies, since he knows that it is not in his power to grant it. More asks: "Can I help my King by giving him lies when he asks for truth? Will you help England by populating her with liars?"[56] These are the words of a statesman in the classic sense.

The point is made even more graphically when Rich finally perjures himself to testify against More as someone who committed treason. More tells him: "In good faith, Rich, I am sorrier for your perjury than for my peril."[57] More denied what Rich said is true. "If what Master Rich has said is true, then I pray I may never see God in the face."[58] More continues by addressing Norfolk and Cromwell: "For first men will disclaim their hearts and presently they will have no hearts. God help the people whose Statesmen

---

52 Bolt, *A Man for All Seasons*, 102–3.

53 Bolt, *A Man for All Seasons*, 104.

54 Bolt, *A Man for All Seasons*, 119.

55 Bolt, *A Man for All Seasons*, 126.

56 Bolt, *A Man for All Seasons*, 154.

57 Bolt, *A Man for All Seasons*, 156.

58 Bolt, *A Man for All Seasons*, 156.

walk your road."[59] This is the teaching of ancient and medieval political philosophy to the moderns who break the bond of reason and power. *God help the people whose statesmen walk your path.* Cromwell threatens "harsher punishments," by implication torture and death, as certain to make More yield.[60] At this, More chides Cromwell. He is talking like a "dockside bully." Cromwell retorts: "How should I threaten?" More replies, in the name of true political philosophy, "Like a Minister of State, with justice." Cromwell: "Oh, justice is what you're threatened with." And to this More simply replies: "Then I am not threatened."[61] The two equivocal meanings of justice, the Aristotelian and the Machiavellian, are contained within this exchange. The true minister of state is responsible for justice, not naked power as if it alone were just. This classical idea of justice is why More sees himself to be secure, even when power comes to be used against him. He understands Socrates's "No evil can come to a just man" and "It is better to suffer evil than to do it."[62]

The point is brought out graphically in the final scene of the play. More goes to the block. He says to the headsman: "Friend, be not afraid of your office. You send me to God." Cranmer, who has accompanied More to his end, says to him, as the notes say, in a manner "envious rather than waspish": "You're very sure of that, Sir Thomas."[63] The headsman, after the deed, then announces to the attendees: "Behold the head—of a traitor." With these ironic words, we also recall the words at the end of the *Phaedo,* after Socrates has drunk the hemlock, words reminiscent of those of Margaret of her father: "And such was the end of our comrade, Echecrates, a man who, we would say, of all those we have known the best, and also the wisest and the most upright."[64] Socrates too was tried for not believing in the gods of the local city and for disobeying its laws. On this scene in the play the Common Man has the final word: "It isn't difficult to keep alive, friends—just don't make trouble—or if you must make trouble, make the sort of trouble that's expected."[65] Sir Thomas More made the sort of trouble that was not expected. This is his place in political philosophy.

59 Bolt, *A Man for All Seasons,* 157.
60 Bolt, *A Man for All Seasons,* 133.
61 Bolt, *A Man for All Seasons,* 134.
62 Plato, *Crito.*
63 Bolt, *A Man for All Seasons,* 162.
64 Plato, *Phaedo,* 118a.
65 Bolt, *A Man for All Seasons,* 162–63.

In conclusion, I would like to return to the remarks of Chesterton in 1929 that I cited in the beginning of this consideration of More. Chesterton began that essay by stating that More was more important at that time than he had been since his death, but that he would be more important still in another hundred years. The hundred years have almost passed. We must ask ourselves what Chesterton had in mind. More, he thought, could become the greatest historical figure in English history in the European civilization crisis continued. This estimate of More follows the line of argument I have presented here. More stood for what England ought to be, but chose not to be. The English are said to be pragmatic. But it was precisely this pragmatism, cut off from a principled end that made the means intelligible, if they were intelligible, that killed More. Modern England exists on the firm foundation of Henry's power, not on the better foundation of More's principles.

But more than England is at issue. More stood for what Europe ought to have known about itself but rejected. In our time, when Europe finally thought to unite itself, it did so by rejecting its connection with its Christian origins. More saw that Rome and reason are one. Modern Europe wanted to make a groundless reason its foundation. The Enlightenment on its political side, as we see more clearly now, was not an elevation of reason but of will to power. Reason has become simply the tool of power, not its judge and justification. The execution of More is in the line of the executions of Socrates and Christ. Jerusalem and Athens need Rome. Rome stands for the transcendent reason that is directed to the human mind wrestling with itself about what it can know and do.

What revelation finds is a reason already in things that itself seeks to explain its own curious existence. It is in this sense that modern science has Christian origins. There really is something there to be discovered, something that reveals intelligibility in its tiniest and most expanded parts, but especially in ourselves. The execution of More justified itself by following that line of thought that elevated will and power to the center of political life. Reason was merely an instrument in its goal. More showed that the reason in politics so understood must contradict itself and proceed as pure will when the law is not consistent with reason based at every step on *what is*. More's place in political philosophy is that, by his execution, he upheld the transcendent order from within politics itself. In the hundred years after Chesterton's observation, we can see clearly that the rationale that executed More has finally turned on man himself. As Chesterton

already said at the end of his 1905 *Heretics*, the day will come when it is
only those who believe who will be able to say that the grass is green. It
will only be those who have made an act of faith who will be able to say of
what is that it *is*, as Plato put it.

Chapter 14

Luther and Political Philosophy
The Rise of Autonomous Man

"Man is by nature unable to want God to be God," Martin Luther wrote in his "Disputations against Scholasticism." "Indeed, he himself wants to be God, and does not want God to be God."[1] The connection between "not wanting God to be God" and political theory may, at first sight, seem strained and tenuous. Yet, there are connections in the strange story of political theory that constantly bring up surprising relationships. This is particularly the case when professional political scientists come to account for the place of Luther in political theory. "We have devoted more attention to an essentially antipolitical figure than might seem appropriate in a study of political thought," Lee Cameron McDonald wrote. "But apolitical thinking can produce some powerful political by-products. In this case, the by-product is something called modern individualism. Modern individualism is, of course, the product of more influences than we can easily catalog or even know. But Luther's radical new confidence in individual conscience is woven into the cultural foundations of Western participant-oriented political systems."[2] Yet, paradoxically, McDonald went on, this same individualism led to a "bias against institutions," both religious and political. This seemed to result in an expansion of political authority as such.[3]

Frederick Herr described the intellectual results of this new theological orientation in this fashion: "Luther's grace had burst all banks and over-run the dikes like a raging torrent. The individual was alone with God, with the spirit of God overshadowing him, summoning him to renew the face of the Earth. Luther had sown the seed and reaped the whirlwind. In his ecstatic experience of God, there was no theology, no metaphysics, no ethics, no cul-

---

* This chapter was previously published in *Faith & Reason* (Summer 1982): 7–31.

1 Martin Luther, "Disputations against Scholasticism," no. 17, *Luther's Works*, 55 vols. (St. Louis: Concordia, 1972), 31:10.

2 L. C. McDonald, *Western Political Theory* (New York: Harcourt, 1968), 238.

3 McDonald, *Western Political Theory*, 238–39.

ture, no state nor church, no history, no mankind seeking salvation and meaning."[4] The overshadowing experience of God had the effect of separating creation from creator. Yet, the autonomy of creation, or political reality, had, as
Johannes Heckel suggested, the eventual effect of subjecting even religion to
the state and its processes.[5] The question arises, then, about the structure of
political theory and the place of Martin Luther within it. This is not so much
the question of just what Luther thought about politics, but whether, in the
metaphysical enterprise that is political theory proper, Luther had any specific
influence such that modern theory is different because of his own orientation.

The use of the term "modern" indicates that classical and medieval
political theory are seen to be, in some basic sense, quite different from
theory after Machiavelli. Does Luther relate directly or indirectly to the
point of this "new" political theory? M. Judd Harmon wrote: "Luther
insisted that men are responsible for their own faith. No one can believe for
anyone else, just as no one can be rewarded or punished for the acts of
another. The beliefs of men are solely a matter of conscience. They cannot
be forced. It follows that secular governments should assume no responsibility in those things that deal with belief. What men believe neither
strengthens nor lessens the secular power."[6] This, of course, is exactly the
"modern" political project, the elimination from politics of any "higher"
norms, something quite alien to classical and earlier Christian theory.

Luther has received considerable attention from theologians interested
in the social and political consequences of his thought. These deserve attention. However, theologians are not usually the best judges of how a given
thinker's position fits into another discipline, especially since a religious
leader like Luther may have been influential in political theory more for
what men *thought* he held than for what in fact he held. Good students of
Luther are aware of this difficulty. Heinrich Bornkamm, for example, wrote
that "Luther was neither a statesman nor a political philosopher but a
preacher of the Gospel. For this reason, it is not easy to fit him into political
history and to label him and his views."[7] Indeed, Gordon Rupp has tried to

4 Frederick Herr, *The Intellectual History of Europe* (London: Weidenfeld, 1953), 229.

5 Johannes Heckel, *Lex Caritatis. Einejuristische Untersuchung uber das Recht in der Theologie Martin Luthers* (Koln: Bohlau, 1973), 291–92.

6 M. Judd Harmon, *Political Thought* (New York: McGraw-Hill, 1964), 180.

7 Heinrich Bornkamm, *Luther's World of Thought*, trans. M. Bertram (St. Louis: Concordia, 1958), 237.

preclude the thesis I will argue here: "So far from leaving politics to itself and free to make its own laws, Luther would have regarded the attempt to establish a secular state apart from the laws of God as the summit of human folly and pride."[8] This may well be true of Luther's own intentions, but another kind of question can be asked—namely, How was Luther's effort understood and interpreted? Did he, knowingly or unknowingly, contribute to something else quite at variance with his own orientations, when his ideas were taken up in other modes of thought? The question here is not so much of assigning praise or blame, but of understanding the elements of an intellectual tradition and its content. The world, it seems, is often as much changed by misinterpretations as by accurate analyses, particularly, one might add, in political theory. On the other hand, there is always some basis, some benefit, in observing how great thinkers may have redirected whole areas of thought and action while, in their own minds, they were busy attending to what they thought to be their major contribution.

Doubtless, many historians of political philosophy have seen in Luther an impetus to freeing politics from natural or theological restrictions, so that it could make "its own laws." This sounds neutral enough, at first sight, until we realize that there is a modern metaphysical content to such a question, which asks: Does the absolute autonomy of politics, as a modern intellectual project, have some kind of theological roots? In this sense, a figure as important as Martin Luther may well have had certain emphases and priorities that have contributed a vital link in the formation of the structure of political philosophy itself. This essay, then, must recognize the unity of intellectual experience, even misinterpreted intellectual experience, in considering how men have arrived at certain basic understandings of their being.[9] Some sense of the importance of this issue, I think, can be derived from the following observations of Eric Voegelin and Jacques Maritain, both of whom have been general philosophers with a special interest in political philosophy. Furthermore, they have both been especially interested in the place of Christianity within rational philosophy, so that they do not, like so many contemporary academic political philosophers, exclude in principle the question of faith from intellectual analysis.

8 Gordon Rupp, *The Righteousness of God: Luther Studies* (London: Hodder & Stoughton, 1963), 297. Cf. also Heinrich Bornkamm, *Luther's Doctrine of the Two Kingdoms*, trans. K. Hertz (Philadelphia: Fortress, 1966), 37.

9 Etienne Gilson, *The Unity of Philosophic Experience* (New York: Scribner's, 1937).

The well-known thesis of Eric Voegelin about the gnostic structure of modern political philosophy is pertinent here, since he has seen modern political philosophy as precisely "autonomous," without any dependence on natural or divine reason.[10] In his analysis of "The Genesis of Gnostic Socialism," Voegelin stated his view of why Luther was of particular importance in one line of modern political philosophy. Voegelin's view shows not so much how Lutheran scholars interpret Luther, but how political philosophers have seen his influence within their own traditions.

> This faith in the translation of philosophy into reality through the German proletariat is supported by a historical reflection on the German Reformation. The faith in a revolution that starts with speculation makes sense in the light of the German past. "Germany's revolutionary past is theoretical, it is the Reformation. At that time it was the *monk*, now it is the *philosopher*, in whose brain the revolution begins." Luther's Reformation was the first step of a German revolution. He broke the faith in authority, but he put in its place the authority of faith. He liberated man from external religiousness but he made religiousness the substance of man. Protestantism, thus, has not brought the true solution, but it has revealed the true task, that is: the struggle against the priest.
>
> The struggle of the layman with the priest outside himself had been won; now the struggle was to be continued against the priest within man, against the priestly substance of man. "The most radical fact of German history [Marx]," the Peasant War, broke against the wall of the new Protestant theology. Today, when this theology itself has broken down, the anachronistic, political state will be broken by the new philosophy. These passages show that Marx was perfectly aware of the connection between his own thought and German Protestantism. There is, indeed, an intelligible line of meaning running from Luther's destruction of ecclesiastical authority, through the destruction of dogmatic symbols in the generation of Strauss, Bruno Bauer, and Feuerbach, to the destruction of "all the gods," that is of all authoritative order, in Marx. While it would be incorrect to say that the way of Protestantism leads with any inner necessity from Luther to Hegel and Marx, it is true that Marxism is the final product of disintegration in one branch of German, liberal Protestantism.[11]

10 Eric Voegelin, *The New Science of Politics* (Chicago: University of Chicago Press, 1952).
11 Eric Voegelin, "The Genesis of Gnostic Socialism," in *From Enlightenment to Revolution* (Durham, N.C.: Duke University Press, 1975), 283.

It is precisely this "intelligible line of meaning," of which Voegelin spoke, that deserves attention. It is important to see its origins. Political philosophers of the stature of Eric Voegelin have understood that from "the destruction of ecclesiastical authority" to the destruction "of all authoritative order," there were the first steps in establishing the political order that presupposed no gods. That is, politics were considered to be totally man-created. This was the of the "modern political project," as it was called.[12]

"But it was reserved for modern times to seek the deification of man by doing away with wisdom and by breaking with God," Jacques Maritain wrote in his essay "The Conquest of Freedom."

> Historically, in my opinion, the two principal sources of this false deification are: 1) the immanentist conception of conscience which, since the Lutheran revolution, has little by little prevailed, and which asks of what is in man, of "my interior freedom," that it alone construct morality for itself, without any indebtedness to law; 2) the idealist conception of knowledge which, since the Cartesian revolution, has little by little prevailed, and which asks of what is in man, of "my self or my spirit," that it alone construct truth for itself, without any indebtedness to things.[13]

The last thing Martin Luther set out to do, of course, was to "deify" man. On the other hand, the notion of an interior freedom is a fertile one in political philosophy, particularly in the line of its development toward the extremes of thought in which such philosophy finds itself involved, once the "practical sciences," as Aristotle called them, have broken all links with religion and metaphysics. The suspicion of historians of political philosophy is not that Martin Luther broke the most important link between man and God, but that, in the actual workings of his system, all other links were broken so that the remaining one became vulnerable to a radical revolution in "the brain" of some "philosopher," as Voegelin put it.

---

12 Leo Strauss, *What Is Political Philosophy?* (Westport, Conn.: Greenwood Press, 1959).

13 Jacques Maritain, "The Conquest of Freedom," *The Social and Political Philosophy of Jacques Maritain* (Notre Dame, Ind.: University of Notre Dame Press, 1955), 23. Cf. Maritain's much controverted thesis about how Luther concentrated on an interiority somehow freed from being and thereby open to political manipulation. Jacques Maritain, *Trois Reformateurs* (Paris: Pion, 1925), 69–70.

THE CONTEXT OF WESTERN POLITICAL THEORY

Before looking more closely at the way Luther is understood in the analysis of recent political theorists, particularly those of Sheldon Wolin and Quentin Skinner, it is well to reflect on the structure of political thought itself, since it is this context that serves to explain why Luther is so often looked upon as a link *and* a break between classical and medieval theory on the one hand, and the program of specifically modern political theory on the other. The specific subject matter of political theory, indeed, has always been somewhat obscure in Western thought, even though reflection about the particular nature of politics as an intellectual category is itself of Greek origin. The difficulty arises, however, because politics has the tendency to become a kind of metaphysics whenever, as Aristotle said, man is held to be the absolutely highest being in the universe.[14] For politics to be a metaphysics means that everything, including man himself, attains reality through the human self-making project. The political process for a Rousseau, then, became that of making man specifically *human*, an idea taken up later in Marx.[15] For Aristotle, on the contrary, man was already "by nature" man, as he said in the beginning of *The Politics*. Politics could not be a metaphysics because man was not the highest being in the universe.[16] This is why Aristotle had two books, *The Politics* and *The Metaphysics*, both legitimate and both necessary for a complete explanation of reality. Both had proper subject matters and their own methods of treating them. Metaphysics was the highest theoretical science, while politics remained the highest "practical" science.[17]

To recognize the validity of a theoretic science higher than politics, moreover, required a certain moderation, a kind of humility. Man was indeed by nature "political." This was what was most natural and most human about him. Nevertheless, he might be related to something higher. This moderation, characteristic of classical political thought, would require the primacy of the contemplative over the active virtues. These latter were

---

14 Aristotle, *Ethics*, 1141a20–23.

15 Jean-Jacques Rousseau, *The Social Contract*, bk. I, chap. 8; Karl Marx, "Economic and Philosophical Manuscripts," in *Marx's Concept of Man*, ed. E. Fromm (New York: Ungar, 1961), 93–196.

16 Aristotle, *Ethics*, 1141a20–23.

17 Aristotle, *Ethics*, chap. 6; *Metaphysics*, bk. 1, chaps. 1–2. Cf. James V. Schall's "The Recovery of Metaphysics," *Divinitas* 23, no. 2 (1979): 200–217; "The Reality of Society in St. Thomas," *Divus Thomas* 1 (1980): 13–23.

the ones that found their perfection in the *polis*.[18] There would be something more noble in *receiving* the truth on the part of men, especially the truth about human nature and the order of the universe, than in properly ordering the city in justice, even though this latter too was a worthy, a true human, worldly endeavor. This moderation, when it came to Christian theory, meant the letting of "God be God," as the Reformation put it with Luther. But if this be permitted—man has a tendency to rebel from his very condition, Aristotle held in *The Metaphysics*, a desire to not want God to be God, as Luther put it[19]—if, on the contrary, we rather rejoice in God being God, nothing in whom is properly of our making, where does that leave our politics, the highest of the practical sciences?

Hannah Arendt, one of the greatest of contemporary political theorists, in the *Willing* part of her *Life of the Mind*, begins her discussion of will and intellect by recalling Gilson's Gifford Lectures on medieval philosophy.[20] She recalled the "fides quaerens intellectum" tradition, the idea that reason is a "handmaiden" of faith. Then she added: "There has always been a danger that the handmaiden become the 'mistress,' as Pope Gregory IX warned the University of Paris, anticipating Luther's fulminant attacks on the *stultitia*, this folly, by more than two hundred years."[21] Luther's ultimate mentor, Paul of Tarsus, of course, had likewise warned that the wisdom of the Cross would seem folly to the Greeks, to the philosophers. And Luther himself, we know, had some harsh things to say about Aristotle and reason, because he saw in them human "works," Pelagianism, the belief that man could save himself, whereas man was so depraved he could only be justified by a faith that accepted as such his deeply fallen, sinful nature.[22] "Virtually the entire *Ethics* of Aristotle is the worst enemy to grace," was Luther's Forty-First Proposition against Scholastic Theology, while, "briefly, the whole of Aristotle is to theology as darkness to light," his Fiftieth.[23] The Third Thesis at Leipzig was: "He who maintains that a good work and penance begin with the hatred of

---

18 See Strauss, *What Is Political Philosophy?* Cf. also the author's "Political Theory and Political Theology," *Laval Theologique et Philosophique* 31, no. 1 (1975): 25–48.

19 Aristotle, *Metaphysics*, 982b28–30; Luther, "Disputation against Scholasticism," *Luther's Works*, 31:10.

20 Hannah Arendt, *The Life of the Mind*, vol. 2, *Willing* (New York: Harcourt, 1978), 113.

21 Arendt, *Willing*, 113.

22 Martin Luther, "Lectures on Romans," *Luther's Works*, 25:109–12; "The Argument of St. Paul's Epistle to the Galatians," *Luther's Works*, 26:4–12.

23 *Luther's Works*, 31:12.

sins and prior to the love of righteousness and that one no longer sins in doing good works, him we number among the Pelagian heretics; but we also prove that this is a silly interpretation of his holy Aristotle."[24]

No doubt, in the history of political theory, it has been difficult to locate Catholicism in relation to classical and modern theory.[25] Yet in this context, it is perhaps even more difficult to locate Protestantism. The momentous event of the Reformation as a political phenomenon will be readily acknowledged, of course.[26] Belloc's affirmation may have been exaggerated, but it is still probably much closer to the truth than any attempt to ignore the impact of the Reformation: "The break-up of united western Christendom with the coming of the Reformation was by far the most important thing in history since the foundation of the Catholic Church fifteen centuries before."[27] But when it comes to understanding this event in terms of political thought as such, we are confronted with a certain hesitation and perplexity. We are generally wont to treat the Reformation as a total movement. Luther and Calvin are often treated together, however great their differences.[28] There is reason for this, no doubt. But it is somewhat different from Max Weber's famous thesis about the greater importance of Calvinism in terms of economic development.[29] What is suggested here is that Luther was more significant in terms of the foundations of *modern* political theory as such. I argue this from the background of a Straussian emphasis on the primary importance of classical theory over modern theory. Contemporary political theorists, to be sure, often try to give a completely "secular" account of the terms and development of political theory from Machiavelli, Hobbes, Locke,

---

24 *Luther's Works*, 31:317.

25 Frederick Wilhelmsen, *Christianity and Political Philosophy* (Athens, Ga.: University of Georgia Press, 1978); cf. also James V. Schall's "The Death of Christ and Political Theory," *Worldview* 21, no. 3 (March 1978): 18–22; "Political Theory: The Place of Christianity," *Modern Age* 25 (Winter 1981): 26–33.

26 R. H. Murray, *The Political Consequences of the Reformation* (York: Russell and Russell, 1960), chap. 2; F. Edward Cranz, *An Essay on the Development of Luther's Thought on Justice, Law, and Society* (Cambridge, Mass.: Harvard University Press, 1959); Hajo Holbrun, "Luther and the Princes," in *Luther, Erasmus, and the Reformation*, ed. J. Olin (New York: Fordham, 1969); *Zur Zwei-Reiche-Lehre Luthers*, ed. Gerhard Sauter (München, Kaiswer, 1973); Luther Waring, *Political Theories of Luther* (Port Washington, N.Y.: Kennikat Press, 1968); Jon Plamenatz, *Man and Society* (New York, McGraw-Hill, 1963), 1:52–57.

27 Hilaire Belloc, *Characters of the Reformation* (Garden City, N.Y: Doubleday Image, 1961), 1.

28 Cf. Duncan Forrester's excellent essay, "Martin Luther and Calvin," in *History of Political Philosophy*, ed. Leo Strauss and Joseph Cropsey (Chicago: Rand McNally, 1963).

29 Cf. Max Weber, *The Protestant Ethic and the Spirit of Capitalism* (New York: Scribner's, 1958).

Rousseau, Hegel, to Marx and the twentieth century. But there are many Christian overtones in even these writers and the reverberations originating in them. To attempt to eliminate the changes in theology from political philosophy renders the latter almost unintelligible, even in its own terms.

VIEWS ABOUT LUTHER

To argue the importance of Luther, however, goes against much of the contemporary literature on the subject, though most competent scholars do grant a place for Luther in political theory, as we have suggested earlier. This problem can, perhaps, be best approached by returning to the earlier writers on the history of political thought. The Carlyles, for example, in their *Medieval Political Theory in the West*, remarked, evidently to their own astonishment: "As far as we have been able to discover, the first writer of the sixteenth century of whom we can say that he, at one time, held and affirmed the conception that the temporal ruler was in such a sense representative of God that under no circumstances could he be resisted, was Luther."[30] This is, of course, startling because it reverses the medieval political traditions affirming that all political authority as such was limited.[31] Suddenly, we discover that a revolt from the medieval tradition on religious grounds ended up in the direction of political absolutism, the justification of which was the burden of early modern theory.[32] Somehow, attention to faith alone and to Scripture, along with the denigration of reason, has the paradoxical result of exalting the state, even though Luther himself never gave the state jurisdiction over the internal forum, nor did he deny that the two kingdoms of community and church both have God as ultimate ruler.[33]

---

[30] R. W. and A. J. Carlyle, *Medieval Political Theory in the West* (Edinburgh: Blackwood, 1926), 6:272. Raymond Gettell's estimate was similar: "By applying these doctrines in practical politics, the Reformation substituted once for all in men's minds the authority of the state for the authority of the Church. The supremacy of the law of the land over every one within its borders, including the clergy, now triumphed universally. . . . To Luther, the state was essentially holy. Accordingly, he paved the way for the exalted theory of the state held later by Hegel and by recent German theorists. The purely secular theory of the state came down through the followers of Calvin and through the utilitarian doctrines of the Jesuits." *History of Political Thought* (New York: Appleton, 1924), 151.

[31] Ernest Barker, "Medieval Political Thought," in *The Social and Political Ideas of Some Great Medieval Thinkers*, ed. F. Hearnshaw (New York: Barnes and Noble, 1923), 9–33.

[32] Joel Lefebvre, *Luther et l'authorite temporelle* (Paris: Aubier, 1973), 21–22.

[33] "The result of Lutheranism was on the whole quite different from what Luther intended. Religiously more liberal, at least by inclination, than Calvin, he instituted the Lutheran state churches, dominated by political forces and almost, it might be said, branches of the state. The

Here, I do not propose to argue the famous question of Lutheran political quietism, the idea that Luther's concern for God left him unconcerned
about the means a state might take to keep the peace, means which in the
modern era turned out to be considerable.[34] There is much of Augustine in
Luther, and perhaps even an anticipation of Hobbes.[35] Mulford Sibley wrote
of Luther:

> There was little in Luther's theories that might give his followers hope that
> the world of politics could be redeemed for positive purposes: for he
> always tended to think of law and government as primarily negative: they
> existed to suppress the wicked, punish blasphemers, and guard the faith
> against its enemies. He appeared to doubt that the Kingdom of this world
> could ever be transformed into the Kingdom of Christ by human effort,
> for his sense of the corruption of human reason was so strong that he at
> least appeared to see all efforts to eliminate the violence of human affairs
> as fruitless.[36]

Sibley's implied criticism, that somehow the kingdom of this world in Christianity ought to be transformed into the kingdom of Christ, is itself a basic
misunderstanding of Christianity. This would be but another version of the
Enlightenment project, which secularized Christian eschatology.[37] On the
other hand, Luther's elevation of his interior relation to God apart from any
worldly relationship did, in an odd way, cut the world off as an avenue of

---

disruption of the universal church, the suppression of the monastic institutions and ecclesiastical corporations, and the abrogation of the Canon Law, removed the strongest checks upon
secular power that had existed in the Middle ages. Luther's stress upon the pure inwardness of
religious experience inculcated an attitude of quietism and acquiescence toward worldly power.
Religion perhaps gained in spirituality but the state certainly gained in power." George Sabine,
A History of Political Theory (New York: Holt, 1937), 362. Luther's principal political works are
found in vols. 44–48 of *Luther's Works*. Probably the most complete and scholarly analysis of
Luther's political views is found in *Luther und die Obrigkeit*, ed. Günther Wolf (Darmstadt: Wis-
senschaftliche Buchgesellschaft, 1972).

34 John Dillenberger, "Introduction," *Martin Luther* (Garden City, N.Y.: Anchor, 1961). Cf. also
"Luther's View of the State," *Encyclopedia of the Lutheran Church*, ed. Julius Bodensieck (Min-
neapolis: Augsburg Publishing House, 1965), 3:2258ff.

35 Heckel, *Lex Caritatis*, 32.

36 Mulford Sibley, *Political Ideas and Ideologies* (New York: Harper & Row, 1970), 320.

37 Cf. the thesis of J. B. Bury in *Idea of Progress: An Inquiry into Its Origins and Growth* (London:
Macmillan, 1920); Carl Becker, *The Heavenly City of the Eighteenth-Century Philosophers* (New
Haven, Conn.: Yale University Press, 1932); Robert Nisbet, *History of the Idea of Progress* (New
York: Basic Books, 1980).

reason and grace. The "corrupted" world thus became a kind of plastic noth-ingness potentially controllable by the ablest political powers. What was important for man in this approach was not what politics was historically about—forms of regime, citizenship, war, civil peace, or choice of political ends. Rather, the inner workings of man became the locus from which plans for the order of the world might come, since the world itself provided no norms worthy of human reflection or action.[38]

This uncertainty about how Luther related his primary inner life to the exterior world caused some earlier writers like J. W. Allen to doubt if there was such a thing as Lutheran political thought: "I find that Luther is spoken of as a great political thinker; whereas I do not myself find that he was, in any strict sense, a political thinker at all. . . . Except by unavoid-able implication, Luther never dealt at all with any problems of political thought save so far as circumstances forced him to do so. He never thought in terms of the state at all."[39] And yet, as Robert Nozick empha-sized in his *Anarchy, State, and Utopia*, political philosophy must be about the state first of all if it is to be a viable category of thought.[40] But perhaps Luther's emphasis on personal justification, apart from works or reason, was the key to a separation of the world from intelligence. This would enable subsequent political philosophy to think independently of either natural reason or revelation. This latter result, of course, need not be thought of independently of other influences, particularly those from Machiavelli, Descartes, or Hobbes, all tending in the same direction.[41] From this point of view, touching the roots of the ideas forming modern political theory, it may be possible to suggest, contrary to any direct impact, that Luther did have a major influence on the development of modern political theory.

The question arises, then, whether we ought to treat Luther as apolitical philosopher, or at least as an influence in political philosophy, when his thought on the state and politics is so variable and when much of it seems to be merely an elaboration of scriptural attitudes or of Augustine's Two

---

38 Cf. John Hallowell, *Main Currents in Modern Political Thought* (New York: Holt, 1950), 60–67.

39 J. W. Allen, "Martin Luther," in *Social and Political Thinkers of the Renaissance and Reforma-tion*, ed. F. Hearnshaw (New York: Barnes and Noble, 1923), 171, 174.

40 Robert Nozick, *Anarchy, State, and Utopia* (New York: Basic Books, 1974).

41 Cf. James V. Schall's "Cartesianism and Political Theory," *The Review of Politics* 24, no. 2 (April 1962): 260–82.

Cities.[42] Luther's outer and inner man seems to abandon the state, leaving it devoid of any connection with any kind of positive moral purpose.[43] He followed the medieval idea that good Christians cannot properly be themselves subjects of the coercive state.[44] Luther thought almost exclusively in terms of Paul's Epistle to the Romans, of punishing wrongdoers.[45] His own experiences with the pope, the emperor, local princes, the peasants, and the Turks were the context in which he came to consider the state's coercive power.[46]

POLITICAL THEORISTS AND LUTHER

Writers in Lutheran thought have tried to emphasize that Luther did not totally abandon the older natural law tradition.[47] Luther's two "regiments" did have a single unity in one God, so that the Christian found an ultimate unity in spite of the seeming divergence between politics and faith. W. D. J. Cargill Thompson has put it this way:

> Underlying Luther's political thought are two concepts which are central to his theology as a whole-the doctrine of the "Two Kingdoms" or "Regiments" (*die zwei Reiche* or *zwei Regimente*) through which God governs the world; and the doctrine, which is closely related to it, of the eternal conflict between the Kingdom of God and the Kingdom of the Devil. Luther's doctrine of the Two Kingdoms or Regiments is one of the most important and one of the most complex elements in his theology, for it runs through all his thinking not only about politics and society, and the relation of Church and State, but also about justification and good works, the nature of man and the way in which God operates in the world. At the centre of the doctrine is the idea that God has established two different orders in the world, through which he governs mankind—the spiritual order (*das geistliche Reiche* or *Regiment*) through which he brings men to

42 Cf. Christopher Dawson, "The Religious Origins of European Unity," *The Judgment of the Nations* (New York: Sheed and Ward, 1942), 33–56. Cf. also Cranz, *An Essay on the Development of Luther's Thought*, xv.

43 Cf. Martin Luther, "The Freedom of the Christian," *Luther's Works*, 31:327–78.

44 Cf. Martin Luther, "Temporal Authority," *Luther's Works*, 45:75–130. Cf. also Thomas Aquinas, *Summa Theologiae*, I-II, 96, 5.

45 Cf. Martin Luther, "Lectures on Romans," *Luther's Works*, 25:109–12.

46 The essays in *Luther's Works*, vol. 46: "Admonition to Peace," "Against the Robbing and Murdering Hordes of Peasants," "Whether Soldiers, Too, Can be Saved," and "On War Against the Turks."

47 Cf. Heckel, *Lex Caritatis*, 68–167; F. Arnold, *Zur Frage des Naturrechts bei Martin Luther* (München: Heuber, 1937).

salvation, and the temporal order (*das weltliche Reich* or *Regiment*) through which he provides for man's natural life.[48]

In so far as these two kingdoms find unity in God, Luther is not seen to be too much different from earlier thinkers, though the unity no longer seems to have a "worldly basis." Gilson said that we cannot hold writers responsible for what later thinkers make of their works. On the other hand, thinkers do enable others subsequently to proceed differently, often on the basis of a change they did not themselves fully see. Luther held, certainly, that faith plus works were necessary and the normal results of Christian life. Yet, recent political philosophers have seen problems here pertinent to political thought.

Professor Quentin Skinner, for example, in his *Foundation of Modern Political Thought*, has written:

> Luther certainly never seeks to deny the value of natural reason, in the sense of man's reasoning powers, nor does he condemn the use of "regenerate reason" when it is "serving humbly in the household of faith." He even makes a residual use of the concept of natural law, although he usually equates this source of moral knowledge simply with the promptings of man's conscience. . . . The true situation . . . is that our wills remain at all times in total bondage to sin. . . .
>
> This vision of man's bondage to sin commits Luther to a despairing analysis of the relationship between man and God. He is forced to acknowledge that since we cannot hope to fathom the nature and will of God, His commands are bound to appear entirely inscrutable. It is at this point that he most clearly reveals his debt to the Ockhamists: he insists that the commands of God must be obeyed not because they seem to us just but simply because they are God's commands. This attack on the Thomist and humanist accounts of God as a rational lawgiver is then developed into the distinctive Lutheran doctrine of the twofold nature of God. There is the God who has chosen to reveal Himself in the Word, whose will can in consequence be "preached, revealed, offered, and worshipped." But here is also the hidden God, the *Deus Absconditus*, whose "immutable, eternal and infallible will" is incapable of being comprehended by men at all. The will of the hidden God is omnipotent, ordaining everything that happens in the world. But it is also beyond our understanding.[49]

48 W. D. J. Cargill Thompson, "Martin Luther and the 'Two Kingdoms,'" *Political Ideas*, ed. D. Thompson (Harmondsworth: Penguin, 1966), 40.

49 Quentin Skinner, *The Foundations of Modern Political Thought*, vol. 2, *The Age of Reformation* (Cambridge: Cambridge University Press, 1978), 5.

Professor Skinner went on to indicate that Luther's notions of justification by faith, of the Church as a congregation of the faithful, and of Christology serve to concentrate thought on the individual and God in such a way as to reduce the real content of any presumed natural order. "But [Luther's] main concern is clearly to reiterate his belief in the ability of every faithful individual soul to relate without any intermediary to God."[50]

What is of interest here are "the political implications" that Professor Skinner draws from this background. He points out that this thesis eliminates the older canon law notion of ecclesiastical jurisdiction, so that the Church is ruled by Christ directly. But also left a vacuum filled by the secular authorities: "He first of all sanctioned an unparalleled extension of the range of their powers. If the Church is nothing more than a *congregatio fidelium*, it follows that the secular authorities must have the sole right to exercise all coercive powers, including powers over the Church. This of course does not impinge on the true Church, since it consists of a purely spiritual realm, but it definitely places the visible Church under the control of the godly prince."[51] Luther did not deny that the duty to obey God does place some limit the prince, but his notion of the powers ordained by God, particularly the civil power, seemed to make this limitation much less effective or even intelligible.[52] This is Professor Skinner's conclusion:

> Luther's major political tracts may thus be said to embody two guiding principles, both of which were destined to exercise an immense historical influence. He treats the New Testament, and especially the injunctions of St. Paul, as the final authority on all fundamental questions about the proper conduct of social and political life. And he claims that the political stance which is actually prescribed in the New Testament is one of complete submission to the secular authorities, the range of whose powers he crucially extends, grounding them in such a way that their rule can never in any circumstances be legitimately resisted. The articulation of these principles involved no appeal to the scholastic concept of a universe ruled by law, and scarcely any appeal even to the concept of an intuited law of nature: Luther's final word is always based on the Word of God.[53]

50 Skinner, *Foundations*, 11.
51 Skinner, *Foundations*, 15.
52 Skinner, *Foundations*, 17.
53 Skinner, *Foundations*, 19.

Professor Skinner's analysis gives some suggestion of how the changes in ideas rooted in Luther came in a very different way to be taken into political philosophy.

Professor Sheldon Wolin's analysis, I believe, is most perceptive in further grasping the exact point of Luther's relation to the evolution and structure of political philosophy. He writes:

> Luther's political authoritarianism was the product of anti-political, anti-authoritarian tendencies in his religious thought. The shape of his political thought was determined in large measure by the basic aim of reconstructing theological doctrine. But . . . one consequence of the critical destructiveness which accompanies this effort was to depoliticize religious categories. Not only did this have a profound effect on theology, but it had important political repercussions as well. The political elements which had been rejected in matters of dogma and ecclesiology could now be more wholly identified with the concerns of political thought.
>
> The effect of this was to be far-reaching, even though Luther had not intended it; for the necessary precondition for the autonomy of political thought was that it become more truly "political." That the independence of political thought involved more than a matter of theoretical interest is evidenced by the fact that these developments were accompanied by practical actions on Luther's part which pointed in the same direction. The autonomy of political thought, now rid of the enclosing framework of medieval theology and philosophy, went hand in hand with the autonomy of national political powers, now unembarrassed by the restraints of medieval ecclesiastical institutions.[54]

Modern political philosophy, in practically all its forms, has been rooted in this notion of the "autonomy of political thought," so that Luther's relation to this concept becomes crucial. If law is essentially will and institutions have no salvific effect, then of course there is no real restraint to be found in the civil order itself. Thus, "if we are to look for the fundamental weakness in Luther's thinking, it is to be sought in his failure to appreciate the importance of institutions."[55] This failure, no doubt, is itself rooted in the notion that revelation cannot itself be directed to intelligence, so that the accumulated wisdom of human reflection and experience offers some-

---

54 Sheldon Wolin, *Politics and Vision* (Boston: Little, Brown, 1960), 144.

55 Wolin, *Politics and Vision*, 162.

thing more than mere arbitrariness.[56] "The problem presented by Luther was not one arising from the divorce between politics and religious values," Professor Wolin concludes, "but from the political irrelevancy of the christian ethic."[57] And if this ethic is irrelevant to politics, then politics either is fully autonomous or else it must find within itself some cause for self-limitation. It is the latter position, as we shall see, which was taken by Professor Leo Strauss.

Thus, it would seem that from the viewpoint of political philosophers themselves, Luther lacked any rational theory of the state which might have bridged the gap between faith and what could be expected of men. The evaporation of content from the natural order was the result of trusting nothing but God. This position, within a voluntarist and nominalist background, tended, as I have suggested elsewhere, to leave the world itself open to a kind of atheism, since it became in this context a world with no authentic "signs," no "vestigia" of God within its internal structure.[58] If then there is no link between God and the world, except through the internalization of scriptural faith, any philosophical or political denial of God as a proper object of intellect in some fashion would leave the world an open field for man's practical intellect to refashion as it chose. Such refashioning is then dependent on no prior objective norms of man or cosmos. Politics would then be the self-contained metaphysics that Aristotle denied it to be. It would possess its own "autonomy," as Professor Wolin suggested. Does Luther, with this background, then, have any particular place in Western political theory other than his Reformation attack on the external structure of the Church, which resulted primarily in the elevation of the local prince over the emperor and pope? Does he have, at least in the logic of an intellectual evolution, any place comparable to Machiavelli, or Locke, or even to Hobbes, with whose pessimism the great Reformer's views are often compared? And if so, how are we to understand it?

Such a question, as I have indicated, can only be answered in the broader context of the development of Western political philosophy, in which the overall enterprise in the modern era has been to place "autonomous man" at the center of a project whereby man creates himself to be "human,"

56 Wolin, *Politics and Vision*, 51.

57 Wolin, *Politics and Vision*, 163.

58 Cf. James V. Schall's "Protestantism and Atheism," *Redeeming the Time* (New York: Sheed and Ward, 1968), 121–74.

whereby he proposes to himself no natural or divine law.[59] This means logically the elimination of the metaphysical tradition of Aristotle on the rational side so that there is no norm in particular that would prevent man from being "God"—that is, from being his own self-creation capable of explaining all reality, including man himself, in his own terms.[60] The modern political project, from Machiavelli's proposal to make the prince indifferent to the distinction of good and evil to Hume's negation of the connection between mind and nature, has moved primarily in this direction.[61]

LOCATING LUTHER'S PLACE IN POLITICAL THEORY

The problem, it seems, is clarified by some remarks of Professor Leo Strauss in his *The City and Man*, wherein he argued precisely for the validity of political philosophy as such. Strauss wrote:

> It is not sufficient for everyone to obey and to listen to the Divine message of the City of Righteousness, the Faithful City. In order to understand it as clearly and as fully as possible, one must consider to what extent man could discern the outlines of that city if left to himself, to the proper exercise of his own powers. But in our age, it is much less urgent to show that political philosophy is the indispensable handmaid of theology than to show that political philosophy is the rightful queen of the social sciences, the science of man and human affairs.[62]

These remarks reflect Strauss's concern to leave a place open for revelation, but to leave this place open only by stressing the legitimacy of reason.[63] Nevertheless, these are also reflections, almost literally, of the traditions of Augustine and Luther, which seem to play down, if not eliminate, the

---

59 Cf. Charles N. R. McCoy, *The Structure of Political Thought* (New York: McGraw-Hill, 1963).

60 Cf. A. P. D'Entrèves's analysis of the two natural law traditions in Western thought, the modern one especially, which has eliminated a metaphysical background. *The Natural Law* (New York: Hutchinson's, 1951).

61 Cf. John Finnis, *Natural Law and Natural Right* (Oxford: Clarendon Press, 1980), chap. 1.

62 Leo Strauss, *The City and Man* (Chicago: University of Chicago, 1964), 1. Cf. also Strauss's *Natural Right and History* (Chicago: University of Chicago Press, 1953); Ernest Cassirer, "Nature and Grace in Medieval Philosophy," *The Myth of the State* (New Haven, Conn.: Yale, 1946). The later chapters of Josef Pieper's *Scholasticism* (New York: McGraw-Hill, 1972) are well worth attention here.

63 Cf. Leo Strauss, "The Mutual Influence of Theology and Philosophy," *Independent Journal of Philosophy* 3 (1979): 110–18. Cf. also James Steintrager, "Political Philosophy, Political Theology, and Morality," *The Thomist* 32, no. 3 (July 1968): 307–32; E. B. F. Midgley, "Concerning the Modernist Subversion of Political Philosophy," *The New Scholasticism* 53, no. 2 (Spring 1979): 168–90.

"handmaiden" relation of reason to faith. Strauss was not wrong in sensing the critical need for rational philosophy to locate politics within its own limits. Politics is not a mere adjunct to theology, though Strauss's major problem seems to have been just how the two were related.[64]

Frederick Wilhelmsen, however, in a recent essay, has pointed out that the tradition of philosophy as the handmaiden of theology has another more positive aspect—namely, that questions raised by theology enable philosophy to ask questions of itself that would never otherwise arise, questions indeed that keep philosophy to its main task.

> Christian philosophy is marked by conclusions whose spring-board has been Christian convictions: The Faith. There is nothing in pagan antiquity that is remotely comparable to the sophisticated body of philosophical doctrines that grew up around the Christian belief in the intrinsic dignity of the person; the providence of God over each man; creation out of nothing by a God whose name is "I am"; the basic dignity of the family; the distinction between nature and person; natural and international law. . . . Christians have asked superior questions because those questions have been quickened by faith in the word of God.[65]

This would suggest that political philosophy, "the queen of the social sciences," might well be more itself *because* of revelation. The questions that arise to be asked because of revelation might be closer to the heart of the human given, the heart of politics, and therefore more capable of bringing forth what reason "knows."[66] Moreover, it may well be that the most crucial questions for "the queen of social sciences" are those, in the empirical order, which find focus and precision because of revelation. The "life" question, the value of human life in all its forms, certainly seems to be one of these in our era. Likewise does the question of the precise meaning of "human right"

---

64 Strauss's ability to east [*sic*] the relation of nature and grace is much less clear in *Natural Right and History*, 163–64. Steintrager felt that Strauss was practicing his own "secret writing" theory in view of the hostility of modern thought to any revelation. Charles N. R. McCoy was rather of the opinion that there was a more theoretical error in Strauss. Cf. McCoy, "On the Revival of Classical Political Philosophy," *The Review of Politics* 35, no. 2 (April 1973): 161–79. Cf. also James V. Schall's "Revelation, Reason, and Politics; Catholic Reflections on Strauss," *Gregorianum* 62, no. 2 (1981): 349–66 (part 1) and no. 3: 467–98 (part 2).

65 Frederick D. Wilhelmsen, "Faith and Reason," *Modern Age* (Winter 1979): 31–32. See also Finnis, *Natural Law and Natural Right*, chap. 13; Etienne Gilson, *Reason and Revelation in the Middle Ages* (New York: Scribner's, 1938).

66 Cf. Etienne Gilson, "Greek Philosophy and Christianity," *The History of Christian Philosophy in the Middle Ages* (New York: Random House, 1955), 540–48.

in a period when its current content and emphasis have often been set against the structure of classic natural law.[67]

The thrust of Luther's deep broodings, his inner doubts, *angst*, and fear, was to evolve a theory of justification that rendered him independent of all worldly certitudes and contacts of either church or state. To be sure, Luther never denied that justification ought to produce good works, but the project of discerning what men could do if left to themselves could only have resulted in an antihuman city. It would be this latter sort of a city that men would be most tempted to make for themselves, "not wanting God to be God." This is perhaps the significance of Arnold Brecht's cryptic passage on Luther:

> As regards imposters, there are stories in the Bible in which the voice was that of Satan or where Moloch imitated the voice of God. Luther was once asked by some more radical religious reformers the—"Zwickauers"— whether he would allow them to prove their divine mission by telling him what he was just then thinking in his mind; and when he gave permission, they stated correctly that he felt inclined toward them in spite of the objections he had raised. Luther, however, at once exclaimed that this was a sign of Satan's and not one coming from God. There is obviously no scientific proof possible that Luther's interpretation was correct or that there was a transcendent sign at all. If there was one, however, then it mattered whether it came from God or from Satan.[68]

The Straussian project, in any case, became the very antithesis of this worry about what would happen if man were to be left to himself taken in a diabolic or antihuman sense. The Straussian "reason" is Aristotelian and objective, whereas for Luther there were no signs of God in the world as such. The break of faith and reason thus resulted in a twofold infinite project. On the one hand, there was a project of inner spirit, wherein salvation was strictly spiritual apart from the world, and on the other, a worldly project, a la Hobbes, to improve man, grounded precisely on the corrupt being of man in the world, the war of all against all, a side that eventually led to the Enlightenment in a roundabout way.[69]

---

67 Cf. Strauss, *Natural Right and History*, 163ff. Cf. also John Paul II's Address on the Philosophy of Aquinas, November 11, 1979. Cf. also James V. Schall's "Second Thoughts on Natural Rights," *Faith and Reason* 1, no. 3 (Winter 1975): 44–59.

68 Arnold Brecht, *Political Theory* (Princeton, N.J.: Princeton University Press, 1959), 370–71.

69 Hallowell, *Main Currents*, 65. Cf. also Leo Strauss, *The Political Philosophy of Hobbes* (Chicago: University of Chicago Press, 1952).

"You must know that since the beginning of the world," wrote in an oft-cited passage from his *Temporal Authority*, "a wise prince is a mighty rare bird, and an upright prince even rarer. They are generally the biggest fools or the worst scoundrels on Earth; therefore, one must constantly expect the worst from them and look for little good, especially in divine matters which concern the salvation of souls."[70] With Hobbes, political theory saw these very rare birds and big fools enter into an intellectual project to give man the only kind of "humanity" supposedly open to him.[71] Salvation and things divine had little to do with such things. The proper exercise of man's own powers, the affairs of "the queen of the social sciences," could, in this sense, yield little. On the other hand, the world would yield nothing for salvation, not even with the Incarnation, so that the classic insistence on the continuity and distinction of all being was undermined. Christology, as it were, came to be seen without creation, and eventually anthropology replaced theology. "Luther taught that original sin had so utterly destroyed the goodness of human nature," Professor Heinrich Rommen wrote,

> that even grace did not reform its inner-most malignity, but simply covered it. He denied that reason is able to recognize natural law and that will can strive for it. The universe is broken up: the realm of nature is evil, separated from the realm of supernature. There is no bridge between religion as grace and the world as the field of reason and natural ethics. The Thomist principle that grace presupposes nature and perfects it, has no validity, even though upon this principle is based the participation in the redemption of the world of politics and social order. For Luther, there is only one morality, the supernatural one.[72]

Precisely this conclusion seems to join Strauss's remark about political philosophy without the theological "handmaiden." The Catholic tradition, for

---

70 *Luther's Works*, 45:133; cf. 120ff.

71 In this context, Strauss said of Hobbes: "Modern and classical political philosophy are fundamentally distinguished in that modern political philosophy takes 'right' as its starting-point, whereas classical political philosophy has 'law.' . . . If modern and classical political philosophy stand in this relation to one another, there is no possible doubt that Hobbes, and no other, is the father of modern political philosophy. For it is he who, with a clarity never previously and never subsequently attained, made the 'right of nature,' i.e., the justified claims (of the Individual), the basis of political philosophy, without any inconsistent borrowing from natural or divine law. Strauss, *The Political Philosophy of Hobbes*, 156. Strauss later reassessed the importance of Hobbes in relation to Machiavelli, without changing the point at issue. Cf. Strauss, *Thoughts on Machiavelli* (Chicago: Free Press, 1958).

72 Heinrich Rommen, *The State in Catholic Thought* (Saint Louis: B. Herder, 1945), 63.

its part, has been historically directed to reason from the view that a higher, though not "unreasonable," realm existed, one that did not address human-kind in rationally contradictory terms. Revelation was meant among other things to cause men to think, perhaps first of all. The Lutheran tradition, while rightly emphasizing the transcendence of God, seemed in the history of political theory to separate reason and revelation, in the name of the pri-macy of God. And when it did refer to reason or natural law, these were often to be understood within the context of late scholastic voluntarism.

The Straussian reproposal of classical thought as a contemporary enter-prise of intellect recognized the existence of revelation as an historical fact, incapable of being excluded by means of philosophy alone.[73] Strauss was not dogmatically opposed to the possibility of any fact, even that of revelation. That modern "autonomous political theory" *must* be opposed to revelation in principle is the reason why Professor Strauss represents such a challenge to the very basis of modern theory. In this, no doubt, as Professor Wilhelm-sen noted, there is still some problem with precisely Christian revelation.[74] In any case, Strauss did not want revelation to be used in politics in order that politics, finally learning what it is about, can accept its own limits. This is an especially difficult project since the whole historical project of the state, learning that it is not absolute, was hammered out primarily by the Christian tradition of some things not belonging to Caesar. As Heinrich Rommen held, the intelligence of the state itself was precisely *not* revealed. It was a proper task of the human intellect, even though questions addressed by faith may have better enabled it to understand what this meant.[75]

The significance of this can perhaps be further seen from Professor Jacobson's recent *Pride and Solace: The Functions and Limits of Political Theory*, itself a contemporary restatement of skeptical political tradition as an argument for "limits" over against the classical tradition of moderation as it arose out of metaphysics. Jacobson wrote:

> Despite the "heretical" nature of the teachings of Thomas Aquinas when viewed from the vantage point of our own time . . . they usher in the great Age of Solace. From the vastness of the firmament to the minutest of God's creations, there is structure in the Universe, and Law both Natural and Divine.

---

73 Strauss, "On the Mutual."

74 Cf. Wilhelmsen, *Christianity and Political Philosophy*, chap. 8.

75 Rommen, *The State in Catholic Thought*, 11ff.

> But the human animal is restless, alternately bored and excited, an unmaker as well as a maker. The manifestations of these alternate states we call history. The structure of Christian solace is shattered by a Reformation in religion and a Renaissance in learning.[76]

The shattering of Christian solace by the Reformation is in the name of man as both "maker and unmaker," a rejection of the total order of the universe itself.

CONCLUSION

What are we to conclude from this? It would seem that Luther stands, in a paradoxical way, at the heart of contemporary theory because he was the major source—there were significant others, notably Descartes[77]—for the separation of reason and faith, which has resulted in a twofold endeavor to reconstruct the human city independently of the mutual requirements of both.[78] Professor Porter argues that Luther was a bulwark against political utopias, while Professor Heer felt he was the primary cause of utopias reaching the European underground, albeit Luther himself was afraid to go where his principles led.[79] In either case, however, Luther stood at the origin of a separation that is now being rethought in other terms in political theory—namely, How are we to establish a valid theoretical limit to politics if we do not admit the truth of that introduced also by revelation? The Thomist tradition had found limits in *both* reason and revelation, not to mention in the experience of history itself given content by both. Strauss seemed rather to stress reason independently, but in such a fashion that revelation would not be intrinsically denied to political theory, however difficult it might be to find a place for it.

Luther's suspicion, then, was that man by himself wanted to be God, that his inner self was cut off from all metaphysics, theology, ecclesial jurisdiction, and culture because of the primacy of God. But this turned out to

---

76 Norman Jacobson, *Pride and Solace: The Functions and Limits of Political Theory* (Berkeley: University of California Press, 1978), 17. Cf. James V. Schall's review of this book in the *New Oxford Review* 46 (April 1979): 22–23.

77 Cf. Schall, "Cartesianism and Political Theory."

78 Cf. James V. Schall's "The Best Form of Government," *The Review of Politics* 40 (Jan 1979): 97–123.

79 Cf. J. M. Porter, "The Political Thought of Martin Luther," in *Luther: Selected Political Writings* (Philadelphia: Fortress Press, 1974), 2–21. Cf. Herr, *Intellectual History of Europe*, 231–32.

be the other side of the modern enterprise that wanted to refashion completely the world and man as part of it, to eradicate its "evil," while presupposing no dependence on history or nature or God, so that all evil would be removed by man's political project.[80] Luther himself sought to exalt God by his meditations on justification through faith. Yet, ironically, it was but a small step, intellectually, however monstrous in another sense, from Luther's exaltation of God to the modern projects of a completely autonomous man, in the "genus" of man, in whom this exaltation came to reside when early modern individualism eventually led to a collectivism that sought to command all the "human." "Man is by nature unable to want God to be God." By taking this Lutheran aphorism seriously, modern political theory has come to be a covert metaphysics, as it were, wherein God was not God.[81] Strauss was right to see that "it was not sufficient to listen to the Divine message of the City of Righteousness." The question remains, however, whether the greater urgency of showing "political philosophy to be the rightful queen of the social sciences" will itself leave room for the Reformation's basic cry, "Let God be God." The "heretical" structure of Aquinas's solace is not easily dismantled even by specifically "modern" autonomous political philosophy.

---

80 Cf. James V. Schall's "On the Scientific Eradication of Evil," *Communio: International Catholic Review* (Summer 1979): 157–72.

81 Cf. Schall, "The Recovery of Metaphysics."

Commentaries

The last part of this book, as I mentioned above in the "Studies" section, is devoted to four commentaries on one or another significant issue that is pertinent in its own way to political philosophy. These commentaries flow from books that I have read, enjoyed, and reflected on.

Each of these books will provide much insight. Political philosophy needs to be aware of more than political things, if only to let them be what they are from nature. These four commentaries show why political men need to know more about reality than about themselves.

Commentary 1

On Appreciating Aristotle

The power of symbolic signification is possible only because the human mind has an unlimited openness to the entirety of reality, and can thus create a connection between any two entities. Aristotle expresses this openness in the *De Anima* when he states: "The soul is, in a sense, all things." The mind has the ability to intentionally receive any reality in mental form and intentionally fabricate countless modalities of meaning. The mind, he states, can become everything and make everything.

—Fran O'Rourke, *Aristotelian Interpretations*

To accept that we have a genetic propensity to behave morally does not yet explain why we are obliged to act morally. Applying Aquinas's comment on the individual nature of knowledge (*hic homo intelligit*), we may affirm: *hic homo deliberat et agit*. Moral action is a matter of personal motivation, resolve, action, responsibility, and consequence. It requires a sense of personal identity and continued moral commitment over time. The center of moral behavior is the individual person, consciously aware of herself or himself as motivated for individual reasons, and aware of the responsibilities and consequences attending on one's actions.

—Fran O'Rourke, *Aristotelian Interpretations*

I.

Liberal education means insight into *what things are*, into the truth of things, and into how they fit together, how and why they act. The word "liberal" in "liberal education" means freedom from ignorance, coercion, and vice in order to discover the whole of reality. It never properly means doing or thinking as we please with no relation to reality, including our own nature. The best way to acquire a "liberal education" today might well be simply to imitate James Joyce's early 1900s sojourns in Paris. There, as Fran O'Rourke recounts, Joyce set himself down in the *Bibliothèque de Sainte-Geneviève* to read a French translation of most of the works of Aris-

* This commentary was previous published online, *University Bookman*, May 25, 2018, https://kirkcenter.org/schall/on-aristotle-impressive-interpretations/.

totle. He had already begun reading Aristotle in his earlier academic life in Ireland.

Of course, today nothing more countercultural could be imagined than a "liberal education" consisting of a careful reading and rereading of Aristotle to understand both present and past times and minds. And yet, when we come across a writer like Fran O'Rourke, who does know his Aristotle, we begin to suspect that, just maybe, we best begin here with Aristotle whose ostentatious rejection is often held to be the foundation of the modern world. But, as Henry Veatch wrote in his incisive 1974 book on Aristotle, when this same modern world has exhausted itself in following the consequences of what happens when we reject Aristotle, it may be best to return to the sanity that always prevails when reading Aristotle.[1] This view was also that of Leo Strauss, who understood that the recovery of our souls involved recovering the sanities that we find in Aristotle.[2]

But doesn't the main problem in Paris today revolve around Muslim terror, not the condition of European philosophy? Yet, if we recall Avicenna, Averroes, Al-Ghazali, and other Muslim philosophers, we will soon see that Aristotle was very much pertinent to most of the issues that we have with Islam today. I recall hearing the famous Lebanese philosopher and politician Charles Malik once remarking in conversation that the main intellectual link between Islam and the West was precisely Aristotle. To understand why Islam did not, in the end, follow Aristotle is to understand why the terror can be and is claimed to be a good.[3] The main problem with Islam does not concern its terror, but its ideas about truth and terror.

Aristotle is himself a liberal education. He is the one who best explains to us why we seek to know things "for their own sake," why we need to know the order of things. No one, even to this day, works his way as carefully though the whole range of reality as carefully and clearly as does Aristotle. And when other thinkers come close, it is usually because they are themselves first readers of Aristotle. To read Aristotle is to begin to know how things are. And to know how and why things are is to be educated liberally.

1 Henry Veatch, *Aristotle: A Contemporary Appreciation* (Indianapolis: Indiana University Press, 1974). See also Robert Sokolowski, *The Phenomenology of the Human Person* (New York: Cambridge University Press, 2008).

2 Leo Strauss, *The City and Man* (Chicago: University of Chicago Press, 1964).

3 See Robert Reilly, *The Closing of the Muslim Mind* (Wilmington, Del.: ISI Books, 2010).

We cannot deal with Muslim voluntarism, itself a rejection of Aristotle, if the root of our own philosophy, as it has mostly been since the fifteenth century, is basically but another form of the same voluntarism. The initial problem with Islam is, in fact, the rejection of the central teaching of Aristotle that man is a rational animal in which will follows intellect. The will cannot create its own contents. It must first receive them from reason open to what already is. Man cannot define what is real or good apart from his knowledge of *what is*. Aristotle and Islam do not come up in O'Rourke's book as Aristotle and Ireland and Europe do.[4] But still, we would not be wrong to suspect that the present problems of the souls both of Europe and of Islam are linked to each other by the rejection of what is central in Aristotle, who, more than anyone, stood at the origin of the mind of our civilization.

II.

Fran O'Rourke is a man of many parts, even a singer of Irish folk music. He retired in 2014, after thirty-five years teaching in the philosophy department of University College, Dublin. He studied in Cologne and Vienna. His doctorate is from Leuven in Belgium. He has written on Pseudo-Dionysius, Aquinas, and James Joyce. His *Aristotelian Interpretations*, in fact, ends with a chapter on the influence of Aristotle on Joyce. The chapter serves as a summary of the work of both men. "True genius discerns both the singularity of the grand unity and the minutiae of multiplicity; for that reason it is exceedingly rare," O'Rourke wrote. "The brilliance of [Joyce's] *Ulysses* is that of a universal panorama woven from the torn threads and broken shards of multifarious living; its success derives from the writer's mastery of creative analogy. Joyce is himself proof of Aristotle's conviction that analogy is a sign of unique genius, a natural gift that cannot be acquired. Joyce effected in art a fundamental insight gained from his study of Aristotle."[5] One of the most remarkable themes in this book is how analogy and metaphor can bind all things together, even the most disparate ones. This capacity is due in large part to the mind's ability to abstract the forms of concrete, individual things and in that spiritual form to see the relations that exist between even the most remote or unsuspected things.

For an academic book, it begins unexpectedly with a nostalgic account of the author's family experience on the farms and lands of Ireland. At first,

4 See Joshua Mitchell, *Tocqueville in Arabia* (Chicago: University of Chicago Press, 2013).

5 Fran O'Rourke, *Aristotelian Interpretations* (Dublin: Irish Academic Press, 2017), 238.

this introduction seems out of place. Yet, it is a very poetic chapter. "I loved the wonderful landscapes of the west of Ireland, especially the mutual proximity of land and sea," O'Rourke wrote. "Coming from the flat Irish midlands, I was immediately attracted to the mountains of Connemara. Martin Heidegger once remarked that the philosopher should also be a good mountain climber. This is true not only in a vague metaphorical sense; there is a keen affinity between mountaineering and philosophy, a parallel between the physical of one and the spiritual activity of the other."[6] In this passage, we already glimpse at work that analogous relation of things that enables us to understand one thing by its similarity to another.

When we come to the end of this introduction to O'Rourke's childhood memories of what he saw and did in Ireland, we begin to realize that what he is really doing is to introduce us to the world that Aristotle saw, not in Ireland, of course, but in Macedonia or any place where nature, human and otherwise, presents itself for us to observe it, to behold it, to think about it, *what it is*. All the way through this book, we are conscious of the fact that to understand *what is* we cannot bypass our own individual seeing, hearing, smelling, tasting, and touching things with the faculties that are given to us by the mere and wondrous fact that we exist and exist as human beings, body and soul, our own body and our own soul. And yet, we constitute one being, one substance, one person. We may be tempted to think we are pure spirits, but we are not and it is best that we are not. O'Rourke wisely repeats the passage in Aristotle's *Ethics* that reminds us that, given a choice, no one would want to be someone else.

III.

Aristotle covers so much. O'Rourke systematically goes through how Aristotle looks on being, the causes, our final destiny, how we know, what "mind" means, what "soul" means, why there is a "First Mover" who moves by thought thinking itself. "Existence is naturally desirable; to be happy is to actualize human existence in the best possible manner."[7] We "actualize" our existence by living it. But as human beings it is not just brought to its perfection automatically or by some outside agent, however much we depend on the cosmos and its origins for what we are initially. I was particularly struck by O'Rourke's awareness that the drama of existence itself

6 O'Rourke, *Aristotelian Interpretations*, 10.

7 O'Rourke, *Aristotelian Interpretations*, 86.

is what is played out in each of our human lives. The existence of millions and billions of human beings on this planet is not actualized in some collective form or ideal. It is actualized in each existing human being.

"We do not have simply a vague desire for the fact of being," O'Rourke wrote. "Our happiness derives from the awareness of our own life as good; each man's existence is desirable for himself. . . . Self-awareness is a certainty; it is concomitant self-awareness of ourselves in our knowing the world and as agents within the world."[8] Though we exist as individual persons, because of our knowledge and our power to act on account of it, we are not deprived of the rest of the world. Through knowing, we can become what is not ourselves without changing what is not ourselves. This fact is basically why it is all right to be a single, relatively insignificant human being. We desire our own existence, but this existence opens out on to *all that is* wherein we self-actualize ourselves in terms of our chosen relation to the good that is there and that we come to know, to accept or reject.

The chapters on the ethics and politics of Aristotle are very good. But in reading them, we are conscious of the fact that, without that to which Aristotle has argued in his metaphysics, physics, *De Anima*, and logic, we will not catch just how ethics and politics fit into the whole, why man is such a unique being in the universe. Aristotle says that "if man were the highest being, politics would be the highest science."[9] But since he is not the highest being, his own highest practical science is politics. But this politics, at its best, is itself ordered to what is higher than man. He is ordered to what is higher through his own soul as it exists in his own personal being.

This ordering is the ultimate source of his dignity and why politics is ultimately limited by the good, by the Socratic principle that it is never right, for anyone, including the statesman, to do wrong. "The city came into being that man might be *able* to live, but continues to exist that he may live well."[10] The living well includes all the practical and theoretical things that can manifest what it means to be mortal in this world. The common good means the effort to actualize all the goods man in his variety can bring forth in this world.

When politics has come to be what it ought to be, it turns us finally not to the practical life of this world but indirectly to the contemplative life, to

8 O'Rourke, *Aristotelian Interpretations*, 86.

9 Aristotle, *Ethics*, 1140b20–25. This and all subsequent quotations from Aristotle are taken from Aristotle's *Basic Works* (New York: Random House, 1941).

10 O'Rourke, *Aristotelian Interpretations*, 124.

our wonder about what it is all about and how to articulate what we can know about the highest things, even if, as Aristotle also said in the last book of the *Ethics*, it is small in comparison to other, more visible practical things. "There is ambivalence at the heart of wonder. It is not simply the absence of knowledge, but a knowledge that there is something beyond its reach. This finds its explanation in Aristotle's distinction between what is intelligible in itself and what is evident to us."[11] We realize that we are limited beings with a power of mind that is *capax omnium*, capable of knowing *all that is*. Thus we must grant that "the intelligibility of the real far exceeds our understanding." It is this realization that is no doubt the primary natural reason why something like a divine revelation might just be both possible and even actual.[12] It also explains the "restless hearts" that we so readily associate with Augustine.

IV.

"Truth is the affirmation of reality as it is; in so far as something is, it necessarily is; in so far as a judgment is true, it is necessarily true. Truth has an absolute and necessary quality deriving from the unconditional character of existence itself. Once being is, it cannot not be: in so far as an assertion is true, it is true for all time."[13] The contemplative order beyond politics but not bypassing it and its relation to the virtues is the proper locus of the truth to which the mind is open. Truth is concerned with the things *that are*, with their affirmation. The practical world is filled with things made, spoken, sung, tasted, with the things that result from our capacity to imitate things, to find out how they work, what they are. The things that are and the things made need not be antagonistic to each other, though they can be when used by men out of their proper order.

O'Rourke, again, is fascinated with the relation of things to each other. He even catches Aristotle's oft-quoted remark about the relation of humor to intelligence. "Most witty sayings, according to Aristotle, derive from metaphor and beguile the listener in advance: expecting something else, his surprise is all the greater. His mind seems to say, according to Aristotle, 'How true, but I missed it.' Such discovery provides the pleasure of easy and

---

11 O'Rourke, *Aristotelian Interpretations*, 32.

12 See James V. Schall, *Political Philosophy and Revelation: A Catholic Reading* (Washington, D.C.: The Catholic University of America Press, 2014).

13 O'Rourke, *Aristotelian Interpretations*, 91.

rapid learning."[14] We learn by distinguishing one thing from another, by recognizing that this thing is not that thing. We name things; sometimes very different things have the same name. There are many languages that name the same thing differently. Laughter is a sign, a hint that the universe reveals ultimately a joy that is both expected and unexpected. This truth was the marvelous point on which Chesterton ended his *Orthodoxy*. The possibility of wit, of humor, relates to the fact that we can hold in our spiritual souls at the same time words with different meanings, experiences with different understandings about what they are. The simultaneous seeing of all these possibilities makes us laugh.

The subject of wit and laughter again brings up a refrain in O'Rourke's understanding of Aristotle that gets to the core of things. Aristotle's view of the cosmos is that ultimately it is coherent. "Nature is inherently coherent; it is not, as he expresses it, a 'series of episodes like a badly constructed tragedy.' The perception of the world as an interrelated wickerwork of substances and causes gives foundation to the conviction that the cosmos is essentially and integrally united."[15] When we read these words, we are not reading the words of an astronaut or an astronomer. What we are reading are the words that flow out of Aristotle, who already sensed and understood how and why things fit together. What follows in light of our true knowledge is not something that Aristotle would not have recognized, but something that he argued to be the case all along.

In conclusion, let me return to the two initial citations that are found at the beginning of these reflections. The first concerns the mind that is found in each member of our kind. It is because we have minds that we can worry about, wonder about, what is out there, what is not ourselves. And we can not only pay attention to it, but we can see its diversity and its unities. But we know with our mind not only what is not ourselves, but also the possibility that we can change or reshape many things. We even suspect that we can and should use things that are just there through no contribution of our own. Indeed, it suggests that the uninhabited world was in fact meant to be inhabited. It was meant to provide a place for a being that knew and acted. In so doing, it revealed his soul.

The second citation concerns the fact that it is not the species man that thinks and acts, but its individual members, Socrates, Mary, and Henry.

---

14 O'Rourke, *Aristotelian Interpretations*, 116.

15 O'Rourke, *Aristotelian Interpretations*, 110, citing *Metaphysics* bk. 3, 1090b19–20.

Human life exists in the form of lives of individual persons in given times and places, four score years and ten. All such beings have talents and capacities that might differ somewhat. At bottom they know that what they do with their given span of time defines what they shall be. O'Rourke is consistent in his insistence that for Aristotle man has a soul; he is not just a soul. His senses and his mind work together to provide him with knowledge of what is not himself. "Responsibilities and consequences" do follow on our actions. These actions in turn are based on knowledge that we initially acquire from our beholding what is out there, what is not ourselves, whether it be in the Ireland of Joyce or in the Macedonia of Aristotle.

When we reread Aristotle in the light of Fran O'Rourke's "interpretations," we quickly become aware that the most secure path we can find to a "liberal education" still begins with Plato and leads through the works of Aristotle, whether we read him in French, Greek, or Irish. Most of the reasons given about why Aristotle is out-of-date either are themselves now also "out-of-date" or were never understood with the clarity that Fran O'Rourke saw in the natural things in Ireland that led him to the wondrous things seen and recorded by Aristotle. Finally, this is where we need to begin reevaluating what we mean by a "liberal education."

Commentary 2

On Being and Politics

The moral life is the nexus for our involvement in the drama of good and evil that is greater than ourselves.
>—David Walsh, *Politics of the Person as the Politics of Being*

The only way the transcendent can be present within time is through the person who is transcendent, Jesus Christ. Only a person can access the transcendent for only a person is beyond all that is, but to be the transcendent in history the person must be identical with the transcendent as such. He must be God. This is the uniqueness of Christ that makes unmistakably clear the impossibility of anything else representing the transcendent. History cannot reach its end within time and therefore must point to an end beyond it.
>—David Walsh, *Politics of Person as the Politics of Being*

I.

Though I had an online copy of David Walsh's new book, *Politics of Person as the Politics of Being*, I did not carefully read the full text till I had a hard-copy of the book. It has taken me over a month to read this remarkable book. It is not that Walsh is not a good and memorable writer. It is that he is precisely both. Almost every page contains passages and considerations that took me back to almost everything I had ever read before—to wit, three random examples:

1) "We are called upon to give without asking why and, in that, is brought to light the extent to which all giving is made possible by such self-forgetfulness."[1]
2) "A Creator who discloses himself completely to his creatures would overwhelm them, depriving them of their freedom and absorbing them

---

* This commentary was previously published in the *New Oxford Review* 83 (July–August 2016): 36–40.

1 David Walsh, *Politics of the Person as the Politics of Being* (Notre Dame, Ind.: University of Notre Dame Press, 2015), 59.

again into himself. It would betoken a deficiency of love within the Creator, which is impossible."[2]

3) "Persons are united through sacrifice, which is the only means by which they can hold on to one another as persons."[3]

From such examples alone, we are aware of the extraordinary scope of Walsh's thinking. I found myself "delayed," as it were, by each page. I did not want to "hurry." Continually I found understandings that so struck me that I simply had to let them sink in. This was a book that I did not want to end, even though somehow I was in a hurry to finish it to see if its conclusion would be what I suspected all along that it might be.

David Walsh's previous books are the following: *The Growth of the Liberal Soul*, *Guarded by Mystery*, *The Third Millennium*, *After Ideology*, and *The Modern Philosophical Revolution*. I wrote an appreciation of this latter book when it came out in 2008.[4] I used *After Ideology* with a class at Georgetown. The thesis of that latter book was that we could finally grasp the terrible consequences of modern ideologies. We saw this in the lives of those great and small individuals who suffered under the carrying out of ideology's deranged tenets. These tenets were always proposed as cures for the ills of our kind in this world. They ended in the gulags and concentration camps. Likewise, it was clear, on finishing the more recent *The Modern Philosophical Revolution*, that Walsh had one more book to go to complete his four-book "quartet," the book on liberalism, the book on ideology, the book on philosophy, and finally the book on being and politics. That final book is the one that I should like to reflect on here. It is a book, I think, of unsurpassed genius. Let me see if I can give some indication why this judgment is correct.

David Walsh is an Irishman, a long-time student of Eric Voegelin, and a much-beloved professor of politics at the Catholic University of America. In his own quiet way, Walsh has thought his way through the whole tradition of philosophy, politics, and revelation from its Greek, Roman, and scriptural origins to modern efforts to explain it all by its own methods. Along with Msgrs. Sokolowski and Wippel and many others in the distinguished School of Philosophy at Catholic University, Walsh represents the

---

2 Walsh, *The Politics of the Person*, 146.

3 Walsh, *The Politics of the Person*, 244.

4 See James V. Schall, "The World We Think In and the Drama of Existence," *Ignatius Insight*, October 29, 2008, http://ignatiusinsight.com/features2008/schall_davidwalsh_octo8.asp.

mind and intellectual tradition that takes everything into account, including revelation, history, art, literature, and science. Walsh thinks his way through things that few others thought could ever be thought through.

On finishing Walsh's *Modern Philosophical Revolution*, I recall being struck by how utterly "Thomist" Walsh is. He had, as far as I could judge, literally taken account of modern philosophy not to "refute" it but to understand whither, intellectually, it was going. He strove to see how each thinker did have some glimmer if not glow of truth that caused him dissatisfaction with what went before in modern thought. In reading Walsh, we have the sense that, in its logic, thought is going somewhere, whether it likes it or not. What Walsh has spent his life seeking to accomplish is a coherent, thorough, and valid understanding of the relation of God, man, nature, and politics in the light of what it is to be a person.

II.

Here, I do not wish to "review" this book. It is too good simply to be "reviewed." David Walsh is a friend. When a friend does something worthy, something that makes our own living ever more "luminous," to use one of Walsh's favorite words, we have a debt of gratitude to those who give us the light to see so much that we might otherwise have missed. The topic of what it is to be a friend is indeed one of the major themes of this book, the abiding paradox we receive from both Aristotle and Scripture, that we are admonished to love everyone, but also that "he who is a friend of everyone is a friend of no one." Walsh deftly works his way through this realization that friendship, especially the friendship of marriage, is exclusive and cannot exist in plurality. The effort to see the truth in all of these insights brings us to ultimate things about what we are, who God is, how we relate to all other human persons who exist, whether it be in our time and place or in any time and place.

The core of this book can best be seen from Walsh's understanding of a phrase from Maritain, that the human person is a "whole" within the "whole" that is God's transcendent order, whereby it stands outside of nothingness. The city is made up of citizens, each of whom is a "whole." Each transcends the city, indeed the cosmos. This relationship between the wholes is where the person and being in the title of the book arises. All through this study we are reminded that the person that each human being is and the persons that God is are the realities of the universe. The universe follows from them, not vice versa.

What Walsh wants to know is this: Why do we each also need to transcend the world that we need for our very existence? What Walsh seeks to explain—this is the root of his whole thought—is why the world, and our individual lives in it, rise or fall according to what we do to the least of our brethren. While the origin of this phrase is scriptural, it is already in Socrates's "It is never right to do wrong," a phrase that I have often called the foundation of civilized life.[5] This dignity of the person is not merely an abstraction or an "ideal" or a "form." So much modern thought has ended up with a willingness to sacrifice an existing person, be it an unborn child, an old woman, a desperately sick youth, or a class of this or that variety. This dire result is but the carrying out of the principle that "it is better to sacrifice one innocent man to save the people," now universalized as public policy. The wrongness of this principle is best seen in a fuller understanding of what the person is, an understanding that Walsh provides.

In order to show this truth, Walsh has argued that what modern philosophy and politics have been looking for is a language to describe this uniqueness of each person. Walsh here takes up the modern notion of "rights" as that for which modern philosophy has been trying to articulate a proper understanding. We find this same "rights" language in many other sources, in the documents of the Church, in the American founding, in John Finnis, in Maritain. Basically, I think Walsh proves his point, but the dangers of "rights" language remain.

Indeed, I have often argued that the modern language and concept of "rights" is the main avenue by which the overturning of natural law, reason, and human life has entered modern society. Almost all of the aberrations we know are justified by the language of "rights." We have seen the principles of human nature overturned one by one in the name of someone's "rights." We cannot ignore this fact. We have "rights" enforced by one state or another to do almost anything that we do not have a real "right" to do—abortion, euthanasia, single-sex marriage, fetal experimentation, cloning, almost every one of the aberrations found in *The Brave New World*, already foreshadowed in Plato.

The modern origin of "rights" talk is basically Hobbes, for whom a "right" is whatever we need or want to keep ourselves going against death, the worst evil. The state exists to enforce or provide us these "rights." So there is a whole

5 Plato, *Crito*, 49a–b. This and all subsequent quotations from Plato are taken from Plato's *Complete Works* (Indianapolis: Hackett, 1997).

language of "rights"—I would say the dominant language—that undermines almost everything that Walsh holds. The same word, "rights," is used to indicate almost the exact opposite of each element said to be a "right." Why then do Walsh and others persist in using the term? They are perfectly aware of the intrinsically contradictory phrase "a right to abortion," or "a right to choose" with no object to indicate what is chosen. The same problem exists with regard to the words "duty" and "human dignity" and even "person." Walsh is careful to go through all this history and the thought behind it.

Why Walsh insists on keeping the language of rights to present his overall understanding is—as I think is also the case with Finnis, Maritain, and others—that a better word cannot be found. Walsh is perfectly well aware of the aberrations of the "rights" usages. He is not out to defend a "right to abortion." Quite the contrary, he knows why such an understanding is contrary to the whole meaning and order of reality. It is precisely because we do not have a "right to abortion" that makes him want to keep the word but reject a meaning of "right" that has no grounding in *what is*. As he understands it, the whole drift of modern thought is to discover a way in which we could express the truth of the transcendent reality of the human person. All morality ultimately depends on how we take a stand on this issue of whether rights themselves are limited by what a person is in a reality that we did not create or determine.

While I am inclined to think that the word "rights" is always going to be corrosive, the fact is that this problem exists more in English, the home of Hobbes and Locke, than in other languages. In Latin the word *justum* always had an objective basis in reality and was not simply something attached to a person to enable him to do whatever he wanted. Rather, it was used to define what he was, whether he liked it or not. It was from this grounding in being, not will, that Walsh's position arose. The human person was created free to choose to be what he was in being. His freedom was given to him precisely that what he finally would be was his own choice. He could remain what he was, a finite human person, even in eternity. This end was why he was created, but even God could not "make" him choose what was offered to him as his end.

III.

What exactly does this book have to do with politics? No person is complete by himself, as Aristotle said. His origins are in others as are the exercises of his perfections. Indeed, his whole existence is ordered to his own origin, which is identical with the origin of being itself. But the polity is not a "thing." It is not a "person." We can speak of a nation or polity lasting down the ages so that it has a certain "immortality" about it. Its order outlasts the individuals who brought it into ordered being. The "being" of any corporate thing, including the civil state, is in the category of relation, not substance. Aristotle can say that man's end is to live in relation to others as ordered in a civil society. In that sense, the "state" is prior to this or that individual person. What it is to be a complete human being is the "end" to which existing human beings are ordered. But no state can exist by itself. In the order of time, it is grounded in the substantial being of the many and changing human persons that compose it. Each of these "mortals" passes away in some allotted time. The language of eternal life and resurrection applies to the individual person, not to the polity

What, then, is the polity? Walsh, I think, understands quite well that God, not wishing to overwhelm us, leaves us time to decide what we are before Him. For this purpose, we need a place or an arena in which to "disclose" in public what kind of person we make ourselves to be in the light of what we are. In this sense, the polity is the arena or stage in which many separate personal dramas take place. These dramas have to do with our relation to others and through them to our origin as images of the persons in the Godhead. Any polity is a reflection of the souls of its citizens, as Plato said. This fact is the origin of the differing kinds of polity—good ones that follow law, bad ones that follow the wills of the citizens.

The greatness of Walsh's book, following on his previous ones, is that it sees that persons bear reality and give it its meaning and purpose. Their ultimate status in reality transcends the city but includes it. Nonetheless, this completing of each individual person is played out in how each lives in the time and place in which he found himself existing among other persons. In this sense, we can say that no polity is closer or more distant from its final purpose than any other polity. Generations and nations are not there simply as "means" to something further down the path of time, the mistake of much modernity. But this stress on the importance of the actual person in his own time and place, the very condition of being human in the first place, does not mean that what we do makes no difference to other times and places. Our deeds and words do affect one another. Walsh sees that man is a political animal, that his being needs the life in the city to be what it was intended to be. In so being, it is connected with each person's final end, which transcends the city, any city, but does not bypass it. This transcendence finds expression in Augustine's *City of God*, which teaches us the ultimate seriousness of lives intended for eternal happiness.

The origin of the human adventure was in the Godhead itself, in the communication of the divine Persons, in the choice to associate other free beings to participate in their own way in this inner life. This end was higher than their natural being. Man began as supernatural, not natural. This end is something requiring the personal relation of all things to the God who sees and loves us as persons. This relationship is necessarily suffused with the freedom required for any communication of love and knowledge to take place. The seeing of this relationship as one whole is the contribution of this most insightful book both to political philosophy and to metaphysics, both to ethics and to physics.

Walsh is persistent in seeing that many philosophers who, in fact, seemed to cause much of the chaos in modern political life were first seeking to see the reality that the human and divine Persons imply. In the end, it is no accident that Walsh sees the universe and our place in it as "luminous," as shining with light and intelligence, for, when we finally see *what is*, we see it as members of that city in which only what is finally personal exists. Even the cosmos itself is finally seen through its fulfillment in being known for what it is in truth by persons, both divine and human.

Commentary 3

The Shadow over All Politics

> The Athenian Stranger (in Plato's *Laws*) seems to think that adults retain (or at least should retain) the same wonder toward fellow human beings that children have for wonders. In fact, an authentic beholding of other human beings necessitates such wonder. As a child knows that a puppet is inanimate, yet lets herself believe it is animate for the sake of participating in the greater story, so too does an adult know that another human being is mortal, yet divines that human beings have a connection to immortality.
>
> —John von Heyking, *The Form of Politics*

I.

Anyone who has taught college students, especially if this teaching included Plato and Aristotle, as it should for it to be properly called an "education," can be certain of one thing. The single most riveting and perplexing issue that personally concerns students of early adulthood is not justice or pleasure, but friendship. This topic is, as Aristotle also intimated, a most unsettling question about a god who is only a "First Mover." When sorted out, friendship is ultimately grounded in the Trinity, in the fact that God is not lonely or in need of something besides this inner Trinitarian life. Though our culture is almost totally politicized in all areas, much to its own self-inflicted harm, friendship is the one issue that gives most everyone pause. The lack of or the betrayal of friends is what loneliness and sin are about. Friendship implies more than most of our philosophies allow us to consider about the fullness of reality. It is the one sure path out of ourselves to the rightness of the human order of virtue and the completion of our conversations with others about the truth of things.

Aristotle himself told the legislators of Greece, and thereby all of us, his readers, that the lawmaker is more concerned with friendship than he is with justice. This insight is ever an astonishing yet intuitively true affirma-

* This commentary was previously published in the *New Oxford Review* 84 (January–February 2017): 43–47.

tion. Modern polity is suffused with slogans such as "faith and justice," diversity, relativism, rights, fluidity, feelings, social justice, and other such issues that really, when uncritically carried out, impede us from understanding why friendship exists in the first place. A reconsideration of the relation of friendship and politics is most welcome. It is what John von Heyking has given us in *The Form of Politics*, a moving, learned, yet experiential explication of friendship.[1] The primary interest of this book is political friendship, the kind of friendship that Aquinas called "concord." It consists in an explicit or tacit agreement to live peacefully together in a given polity according to its laws and customs, which can themselves be seen to conform to the norms of truth, of reason.

Nonetheless, von Heyking recognizes that without the understanding of virtue or mutually willed friendship, political friendship will not be likely. He has no problem with Aristotle when he distinguishes between friendships based on utility, those on pleasure, and the highest sort based on truth. All types of friendship are good and play significant roles in our lives. Without them, we would only know the "just" life, which does not look to the other person as other but to the righting what is owed to another. Pure justice is a dangerous and harsh virtue if it is not mitigated by friendships of various sorts. Justice is a virtue and a necessity amid large groups of interrelated and potentially interrelated people not necessarily of the same polity. It makes economics, with the production and distribution of goods, possible. But justice is not directly interested in the other person's irreducible uniqueness. It does not deny it, but its purpose is limited to the objective "rightness" in exchanges and controversies.

Not a few of our contemporaries consider life in this world and its preservation at any cost to be the highest human good. Death, especially violent death, is, as Hobbes told us, the greatest evil, beyond which no hope or judgment is found. In both the classical and Christian traditions, however, the greatest love is shown by laying down one's life for his friends, an act necessarily rooted in hope. We cannot sacrifice our life if we insist that this world is all there is. The most heart-rending act we witness in our lives, as Belloc wrote in *The Four Men*, is the breaking of human companionship. Divorce in marriage, in its essence, is long considered the collapse of the most intimate form of true friendships that our kind knows. Its con-

---

1 John von Heyking, *The Form of Politics: Aristotle and Plato on Friendship* (Montreal: McGill-Queen's University Press, 2016), 162.

sequences remain one of the often-unacknowledged scourges of our culture not just for the children but for the individuals involved. In reading this insightful book, one has the impression that it is written by a happily married man. But friendship does not come about nor is it preserved or broken solely by chance, even if an element of chance is always found in it.

Von Heyking is a professor at the University of Lethbridge in Canada. He has spent much time in thinking and writing about Augustine as well as about the classical authors. Friendship, as he tells us, has long been a topic to which he wanted to turn in a more careful way. And no one can turn to this topic without attending to Plato and Aristotle, which is exactly what von Heyking does in this remarkably insightful book. The first part of the book is devoted to Aristotle's several discussions on friendship in the *Ethics*, *Politics*, and *Poetics*. The second part deals with Plato's *Lysis*, *Laws*, *Republic*, and other dialogues in which this topic arises. The overall attention of the book, as I mentioned, is devoted to political friendship. Most people, when they travel overseas, chance to meet someone from their own country. Aristotle said that, when we encounter someone of our own country in foreign parts, we immediately see our common values and ways of doing things at home. We greet him as a friend even if we do not know him. We see that people in the land we visit do not do things quite the same way that we do at home. This is a sign of the civic friendship that von Heyking seeks to clarify and reconsider as "the form of politics."

II.

Readers of the fifth book of Plato's *Republic* are already alert to the dangers of universalizing friendship so that we make everyone else without distinction our sisters or brothers, our mothers or fathers. Much political philosophy has seen this line of thought that von Heyking also notes, to be paradoxically the doorstep to ideology and the totalitarian state. Much in modern culture, including the gay agenda and much of the sexual revolution, is, in its spiritual roots, a failure to understand the nature and condition of true friendship. Nature, however much denied or positively rejected, is always present as a measure and standard of the virtue that friendship requires.

Aristotle's critique of many of Plato's proposals was based on the principle "friends of everybody, friends of nobody." Christians find themselves involved in the same paradox, that the command to love everyone without

distinction can, as Samuel Johnson once pointed out, result in the love of
no one in particular. The human race does not exist in time as an abstract
universal, but as a series of individual persons, each a whole, each with a
destiny that is not wholly subsumed by the temporal polity in which they
dwell. The point is pertinent today especially because that is precisely the
kind of polity we now face in most modern political societies, a polity that
denies any law superior to its own positive laws and an individual destiny
beyond this world.

The abiding value of von Heyking's book is his ability to see that friendship is something that relates individual persons to each other, to will the
good of another. Thus, the world is filled at any given time with people who
relate themselves to each other. The quality of this relation indicates what
they are. Von Heyking insists that we understand individual lives in terms
of actual stories, accounts of particular lives, and not generalities or genders,
classes, races, religions, or nationalities. "Storytelling is not philosophizing
but it shares a similar relationship to action that contemplation does," von
Heyking writes. "In the context of friendship, storytelling with friends 'completes' the 'events of our days' by capturing or illuminating the meaning of
those events. Without that meaning, the events would not register in the
choice-making activity that constitutes our ethical lives. . . . Storytelling is
the narration of a life lived together, created by that life and by friends'
reflection upon it."[2] This stress on storytelling is not a rejection of philosophy but a reminder of how it best exists among us, in conversation, both
serious and lighthearted. We cannot forget Chesterton's remark that simply
because something is funny does not mean that it is either untrue or not
philosophical.

III.

Through his comments on Lincoln, Churchill, the Duke of Marlborough,
and even the Calgary Stampede, von Heyking seeks to show that the notion
of festivity and the deep, personal friendship of individual politicians are
still needed concepts and relationships in the modern world. The careful
reading of Plato's *Laws* provides a way to discuss the importance of public
life and its relation to the gods, to other polities, and among a country's own
citizens. Von Heyking intimates that both Lincoln and Churchill, even if

2 Von Heyking, *The Form of Politics*, 26.

they were not exactly believers, still stood for objective virtue and honor as the basis of civil society. These qualities are not imagined or arbitrary realities. The strength of this book, I think, is its careful awareness that political societies are made up of persons who are citizens but whose final ends and purposes are not political. Still, the polity exists as the place where the days of our lives are lived out. We live in and work out our destinies in the polities we live in, however they are classified by the philosophers. Here is where the choices and events of individual lives are made manifest not only to fellow citizens but likewise to God.

Von Heyking is very good in his recognition that the best forms of friendship involve conversations about the highest things, about truth, the truth *that is*. If we cannot or will not have truth, we cannot be friends together in anything more than a passing sense, something that is contrary to the nature of friendship itself. Friendships at their best and deepest are lifetime occupations, though we outlast many of our friends or they outlive us. The lives of the elderly are filled with memories of lost friends who remain alive in their memories and hopes. Death seems an end but not a completion. Our lives are not just ephemeral discussion groups. They are made manifest in stories that have a beginning, middle, and end. They must finally be judged to be complete, a truth that is likely the most important thing we can know about ourselves.

Plato understood this fact. "Our capacity to behold the moral character of our friend is based on a life shared together," von Heyking writes. "Paradoxically, we are most complete, most alive, when we live for another, and when we tell each other stories about our lives together. Thinking is a shared activity. My insight does not preclude you from having that insight."[3] That is very well said. We do not "own" truth. We find it. We affirm what is there not of our making. The world we behold is not filled with "nothings" or chaos. It is willed along with an abundance of things that we encounter in our travels. We want to know and name them. Once we know and name, we wish to tell someone else about what we see and know, to have him see also. The world was created not just to be known in the Godhead but also to be known in the minds of men and acclaimed by them as good. The connection between things and their origins explains why we can never fully exhaust the wonder that is in the smallest thing that stands outside of nothingness.

3 Von Heyking, *The Form of Politics*, 17.

IV.

The title of this essay, "The Shadow over All Politics," could come from the shadows on the walls in Plato's cave. It might come from an eclipse of the Sun by the Moon, or, more ominously, from the title of Owen Francis Dudley's novel *The Shadow on the Earth*. In this essay, I use it to stress something von Heyking notes about friendship. In it, we always encounter more than ourselves, always a "beyond politics" element. Why is this? At the end of the *Apology*, Socrates tells the jury solemnly that he goes to die but they remain to live. Who has the better part is known only to the gods. Either death is a reduction to nothing or our souls are immortal. If immortal, we shall continue our many already begun conversations and initiate new ones in the Isles of the Blessed. Christians have practically no trouble understanding this view of Socrates. They add that souls talking to one another is not exactly what they mean by human conversation, which includes the body. The resurrection is a remarkable revelational response to what appears to be a philosophical perplexity, that of souls conversing with one another with no incarnational hope.

The same issue comes up in another way when we speak of friends. Anyone with self-reflection can see that he cannot fully explain his own existence, as if somehow he caused himself to be and to be what he is. Yet he exists. The experience of friendship heightens this awareness both of his own existence and that of another person not himself. It is not an exercise in complete futility to wonder about the lastingness of any particular friendships. Rather, as in all good conversations, friendships of the highest sort seem to reach things that cannot be otherwise, things that exist for their own sakes, truths that simply are. A comment I once read said that civilization is two or three men in a room conversing with one another. We are at our best when we are in act, when we are actually knowing. This possibility is what friends make available to each other. We are in act when we exercise our highest faculties. And we cannot know one another unless we choose to be known, unless we want to be known. This too is what friendship is about. Hell for us, I suspect, is nothing less than our not wanting to be known by God.

The shadow on human friendships at this other level, at the level of its betrayal, recalls original sin and the choice of our first parents to be like gods. Yet, friendship as such seems more like a light that does not fully shine for us. For if the full light of divine being were upon us, finite creatures that we are, something von Heyking notes, we would be blinded and over-whelmed in intelligible and lovely light. There is a reason why revelation took place slowly over time, a divine "plan" that gradually works its way out. Revelation thus does not meet us full force. If it did, we could not carry out the lives for which we have been created wherein we are to manifest our own souls in our deeds and words. For it is on these deeds and words, what they bring about, on which the real story of our lives will be dependent and will be made manifest. The world is not complete until, on the side of the world itself, some few beings know or at least understand the importance of the good and the true as the purpose of our lives to discover.

The most lasting and countercultural reminder in this good book, in conclusion, is found in the following passage: "As it is with the judgment of the dead at the end of the *Republic*, this judgment (of our deeds) occurs not simply in the afterlife but at every moment and at every second. It is now. We stand eternally in responsibility under the light of judgment."[4] The "serious play" for which we are made, to recall Plato's words, is itself based on our virtue and the objects of our friendships, on our delight in the same truths that we did not make but only, after much conversation, discover in the cities of this world. These cities exist for many reasons, but most nobly, they exists so that we can be friends together and, in so being, realize that the city of man points, at its best, to the City of God. Von Heyking's book *The Form of Politics* reveals to us with great perception how our pursuit of *what is* leads us through existing polities to that contemplative life that lies in the shadows beyond the things we know in this life. When we know these things with our friends, we have reached the threshold of the reason for our own existence.

---

4 Von Heyking, *The Form of Politics*, 188.

Commentary 4

On the Catholic Appreciation of Leo Strauss

Strauss embraced classical philosophy over religious faith, not as a system of set doctrines, but as a "way of life" following the model of Socrates, featuring a Socratic ignorance and a searching (*zetetic*) or erotic skepticism. In this view, the philosopher lives happily with merely human wisdom, not because he has refuted divine wisdom, but because he simply does not understand it or experience it; he treats religion like a band of light beyond the visible spectrum and suspends judgment about biblical revelation.

—Robert Kraynak, "Reason, Faith, and Law: Catholic Encounters with Strauss," in *Leo Strauss and His Catholic Readers*

Strauss, however, judges that it is best to preserve philosophy from getting too mixed up with the articulation of personal love or with the hopes of universal salvation associated with love; instead he prefers to keep sacred law separate from the nobility of philosophy, Jerusalem (i.e., Judaism) separate from Athens; proud reason on the one hand and divine law on the other. . . . But the decisive point that has not been appreciated in interpretations of Strauss is that his insistence on the separation of Athens and Jerusalem is intended as a means of preserving the sense of the eternal order and natural limits that they share.

—Ralph Hancock, "Leo Strauss's Profound and Fragile Critique of Christianity," in *Leo Strauss and His Catholic Readers*

I.

The publication of *Leo Strauss and His Catholic Readers* on Leo Strauss and political philosophy by the Catholic University of America Press is a manifestation of the Catholic Mind at its best. In dealing with Leo Strauss, a man of formidable insight and thorough scholarship, we need to know the Hebrew Bible and the various schools of Jewish thought. We need to know

---

* This commentary was previously published online, *Crisis Magazine*, August 31, 2018, https://www.crisismagazine.com/2018/on-the-catholic-appreciation-of-leo-strauss.

how Islam with its thinkers is related to Jerusalem. We also need to know modern philosophy—Machiavelli, Hobbes, Locke, Spinoza, Kant, Hegel, Marx, Nietzsche, Husserl, Heidegger, and Kojève, as well as St. Thomas and the dimensions of Christian revelation in both its Catholic and Protestant traditions.

Above all, Strauss takes us back to Plato and Aristotle as well as to the Epicurean post-Aristotelians. These latter—the Stoics, the Epicureans, the Cynics—are often neglected. Father Charles N. R. McCoy, one of the most penetrating commentators on Strauss, taught us much about the relation of modern thought, not just to Plato and Aristotle, but to the post-Aristotelians. Bradley Lewis's chapter on McCoy, sometime chairman of the politics department at Catholic University, is most insightful. Of all the Catholic commentators on Strauss, McCoy is the one that is most respectful of Strauss, while, at the same time, the one that is most critical of the completeness of Strauss's political philosophy.

"Strauss's methods are those of a great humanist scholar," Lewis observed.

> He was far more than an intellectual historian in the usual sense because he took so seriously the claims of the thinkers he studied to be the truth and put those claims through their paces in a way that few scholars have ever done. However, his methods were always akin to Socrates's turn to logic; his philosophical quest was always a search for the truth of things in, as his students used to like to say, old books. McCoy's interest in the history of political philosophy was rather different. Philosophy for McCoy was a systematic enterprise aimed at stating with increasing precision the truths of things. His history of political philosophy is not aimed at discovering the permanent horizon of fundamental problems, but at stating how the structure of political thought was discovered and explicated only to be progressively repudiated with the direst practical consequences.[1]

McCoy always seemed to me, as one of his students, to be the one thinker most conscious of the negative effect on Strauss's thinking caused by his respect for but hands-off attitude to particularly the Catholic view of revelation.

Leo Strauss (d. 1973) was a German Jewish scholar who came to the United States—as did many others, including Catholics like Jacques Mari-

1 Bradley Lewis, "'Wine with Plato and Hemlock with Socrates': Charles McCoy's Dialogue with Strauss and the Character of Thomistic Political Philosophy," in *Leo Strauss and His Catholic Readers*, ed. Geoffrey Vaughan (Washington, D.C.: The Catholic University of America Press, 2018), 73.

tain and Heinrich Rommen—because of the turmoil of World War II Europe. He became a professor of political philosophy at the University of Chicago. In that capacity, through a series of some fifteen dense, tightly argued books, Strauss took the measure of what he called "the modern project" and found it lacking. Strauss is sometimes, at a stretch, said to be the father of neo-conservatism. He is certainly, along with Eric Voegelin, responsible for the revival of study of the whole Western tradition, especially its beginnings and their pertinence to today's political and moral problems. Strauss's books such as *The City and Man, What Is Political Philosophy?, Thoughts on Machiavelli*, and *Natural Right and History* need to be read and reread.

Readers of Strauss know of the East Coast and the West Coast Straussians. These schools, as it were, follow the path of the many students who were students of Strauss. Perhaps the most famous are Allan Bloom, whose commentary on Plato's *Republic* and *Closing of the American Mind* are rightly held in high esteem, and Harry Jaffa, himself a man of remarkable energy. Jaffa represented, at the Claremont Graduate School, a Strauss more concerned with statesmanship than metaphysics. Lincoln and Churchill were often studied in the light of Thucydides and Plato.

II.

This book was edited by Geoffrey Vaughan at Assumption College. Assumption was the original home of Father Ernest Fortin, AA. Fortin later became the chairman of the theology department at Boston College. Fortin was certainly the most well-known Catholic commentator on Strauss. Some thought him "too Straussian"; others thought him just about on target. The chapter on Fortin and Strauss, written by Douglas Kries at Gonzaga University, is most valuable. Fortin was very critical of what came to be known as "Catholic social thought" with its often uncritical acceptance of modern "human rights" as if that phrase had no ideological overtones. One can say, without too much exaggeration, that, except for Benedict XVI, Catholic social thought had little idea of what political philosophy was really about. It seemed to accept value-free sociology as if that too were a neutral discipline in lieu of a serious understanding of political philosophy and its relation to revelation and philosophy itself. Reading Pope Francis's encyclical and exhortation is almost like reading everything that Fortin worried about.

"Fortin's concern was rather to engage a number of medievalist scholars, especially Catholic ones, who were arguing and had been arguing for some decades that the transition from the natural law of Thomas Aquinas and his followers to modern natural rights or human rights was one of continuity rather than discontinuity," Kries wrote. "These scholars, according to Fortin, had run together premodern thinking with modern thought, teleological thinking with non-teleological thinking, natural law with natural rights."[2] The obvious result of this confusion was to find that upholding the natural rights of the unborn ran smack up against the claim and practice of the civil law in many countries that abortion was a "human right." A careful reading of Hobbes would explain why this confusion was possible.

III.

The book is divided into three general parts: (1) the issue of natural rights, (2) Strauss's relation to Catholic concerns, and (3) Strauss's understanding of Christianity, politics, and philosophy. In the first section, in addition to Kraynak, Lewis, and Kries, Geoffrey Vaughan writes on Strauss and the natural law, while Marc Guerra relates Strauss to the thought of Benedict XVI especially on the relation of modernity and our understanding of creation. "To believe in the primacy of *Logos*, Benedict explains, is to believe in 'the primacy of the particular', rather than the universal. Yet it is also to believe in the 'primacy of freedom as against the primacy of cosmic necessity,'" Guerra writes. "Catholicism argues that we live in a world that is created, sustained, and governed by a God who both stands outside the world and enters into the world he created. Such a God revealed himself both as 'I am' and as 'the god of Abraham, Isaac, and Jacob, and he freely acts out of love for his creation."[3] Anyone who has read Joseph Ratzinger's *Eschatology: Death and Eternal Life* will realize that the issues brought up by Strauss often find their clearest Catholic response in this book.

Gladden Pappin's essay comes to grips with three thinkers—d'Entrèves, McCoy, and Yves Simon—who considered the issues of classical thought in a way that found Strauss helpful but not definitive. "D'Entrèves, McCoy, and Simon highlight the same changed relationships between philosophy

---

2 Douglas Kries, "Leo Strauss's Critique of Modern Political Philosophy and Ernest Fortin's Critique of 'Modern Catholic Social Teaching," in *Leo Strauss and His Catholic Readers*, 127.

3 Marc Guerra, "Modernity, Creation, and Catholicism: Leo Strauss and Benedict XVI," in *Leo Strauss and His Catholic Readers*, 114–15.

and society that Strauss noticed, but with a greater focus on the effects of that change on the ordinary citizen of modern politics."[4] Like the classical authors, Strauss was often accused of elitism. But the question of what to do with the aristocrats was already found in Aristotle and in the American founders. The whole hypothesis of the mixed regime centered on the rightful place of experience and knowledge in any polity.

Carson Holloway's chapter on how to reconcile Strauss and Catholicism, along with Gary Glenn's fascinating chapter on what Catholics might learn about Catholicism from reading Strauss, deserves much attention. Brian Benestad's analysis of historicism serves the vital function of spelling out the implications of this most widespread issue, one that Strauss treated with great care. The three essays on Strauss and Christianity by Giulio De Ligio, James Stoner, and Ralph Hancock respectively take us to the theoretical roots that separate Strauss from Catholic thinkers but which, at the same time, show how what they have in common represents a great area for future studies in political philosophy.

I was especially struck by the following comment of De Ligio about the difference between what belongs to politics and what belongs to philosophy. "The understanding of politics would then prefigure nothing less than the 'deeper meaning' of political philosophy. *Political* philosophy refers not so much to a subject matter—political life—but to a manner of treatment that in the praise of the philosophical life, or in the examination of the alternatives which lead to absolute truth and which are the only things which are truly worthy of study: 'We have to choose between philosophy and the Bible.'"[5] The main difference between Strauss and a Catholic Mind is that the choice is not "between" philosophy and the Bible, but includes both.

The well-known French philosopher Philippe Bénéton relates Strauss to Pascal and his wager. Reflecting on Strauss's choice of philosophy rather than the Bible, itself a kind of elitism, Bénéton writes: "It is surprising that Strauss presents his alternative as the drama of the human soul. True philosophers, he says, are extremely rare. What then about mankind in general? The difference between Strauss and Pascal is related to the fact that the first

4 Gladden Pappin, "The Mutual Concerns of Strauss and His Catholic Contemporaries: D'Entrèves, McCoy, and Simon," in *Leo Strauss and His Catholic Readers*, 165.

5 Giulio De Ligio, "The City and the Whole: Remarks on the Limits and the Seriousness of the Political in Strauss's Thought," in *Leo Strauss and His Catholic Readers*, 275.

gives primacy to the mind and the second to the heart."[6] It is perhaps not surprising that the purpose of revelation is to save all men, while the object of philosophy is to know the truth.

To this latter concern, sensed by both Bénéton and De Ligio, James Stoner's brief comment on why Strauss sticks to political philosophy rather than philosophy itself seems illuminating: "If one cannot know the whole of nature, but only the longing in the soul of man for wisdom, then it is the ordering of the soul that commands our attention."[7]

This well-presented book brings us to the central issue that the work of Strauss leaves Catholics with—namely, How are classical thought and revelation, both Jewish and Christian, able to exist together in a coherent, noncontradictory whole that, in its truth, illuminates modern thought and politics in terms of ultimate things? This is, as I say, scholarship at its best.

6 Philippe Bénéton, "Strauss and Pascal: Is Discussion Possible?," in *Leo Strauss and His Catholic Readers*, 298.

7 James Stoner, "Aristotelian Metaphysics and Modern Science: Leo Strauss on What Nature Is," in *Leo Strauss and His Catholic Readers*, 279.

Conclusion

n the beginning of this book, I cited six passages, two from Leo Strauss, one from Aristotle, one from Rémi Brague, one from Joseph Ratzinger, and one from Plato. Strauss pointed out that the great antagonist to that version of modernity that based itself on nothing but a voluntarist humanism was the Catholic Church. We observed in these pages signs of the weakening of the antagonism to which Strauss referred. Strauss also noted that it was a manly thing not to resort to dreams and myths instead of reality, a view that went back to the critique of Epicureanism in the ancient world. Safranek had pretty much the same idea about modern ideology. When revelation is often made out to be a myth, on careful examination, it is, as Tolkien once said, the one myth that is true.

Brague added that when we take into consideration everything we can know, we still need to know what God knows or what He wants us to know. The studies on political philosophy in this book have often revolved around this issue. Do we need to know what is revealed to us to know ourselves? Ratzinger again refers to what Strauss called the "modern project" to remove suffering by man's own powers rather than to face the fact that much suffering, to recall Spitzer's reflections, had a transcendent purpose as manifested in the death of Christ. And finally, Plato tells us that if anyone has been saved in our present condition or constitution, it is not by his own powers.

Political philosophy is one way through which we can open ourselves to what is not ourselves. The answer to the question of "What do we do when all else is done?" is not "nothing," but rather most everything. This view does not mean we politicize all aspects of human life but rather that we allow the potential capacities, given in nature to each of us, to develop and flourish. This possibility requires a political order that itself realizes its own limits. The purpose of each human life transcends the civil society. This does not deny that the purpose of a human city is to provide an arena wherein the finite and transcendent ends of human life manifest themselves and work themselves out. What is true for both the best and the worst actual political regimes is that the salvation of each citizen is worked out within its confines.

The incompleteness of political philosophy, along with the notion that the world is not itself perfect, reminds us of a fuller explanation of human life. Salvation and politics are not the same things, but both belong within the whole of reality. The Roman Catholic contribution to political philosophy is its ability to show why man, having actively reached the limits of his own reasoning powers, can see that the revelational truths are addressed to his own active intellect.

The adventure of political philosophy, at its highest point, consists, as Walsh rightly argued, in relating the citizen to *what is*. However, when the revelational tradition, as its end, identifies itself as the political tradition, we know that neither tradition is true. When they are distinguished, kept for what they are, we can conclude that political philosophy, at its best, has become what it ought to be, not a dream, not an ideology, not a metaphysics, not a theology, not a history, and not a novel, but a relation to all of them by dealing with concrete citizens in real cities on this earth in its existing cosmos. To gain some sense of this project is the purpose of this book. Reason, revelation, and political philosophy all deal with the same unified human person whose end is and was from its beginning one that transcends both the city and the cosmos without denying the reality of either.

Appendix

In this appendix, I wish to at least call to the reader's attention a number of my other commentaries on books related to political philosophy that were not included in this collection. Information concerning the book being commented upon is in parentheses.

"Is Scholasticism Making a Comeback?," *Crisis Magazine*, January 19, 2015 (Edward Feser, *Scholastic Metaphysics*, 2015)

"What "Social Justice" Really Means," *Crisis Magazine*, December 17, 2015 (Michael Novak and Paul Adams, *Social Justice Isn't What You Think It Is*, 2015)

"Islam and French Politics: A Reflection," *Homiletic & Pastoral Review*, May 14, 2016 (Pierre Manent, *Beyond Radical Secularism*, 2016)

"The End of Time," *Homiletic & Pastoral Review*, December 20, 2016 (David Horowitz, *The End of Time*, 2005)

"What We Know About Evil, Hell, and Final Damnation," *Crisis Magazine*, May 3, 2017 (Adrian Reimers, *Hell and the Mercy of God*, 2017)

"Liberal Myths Have Consequences," *Crisis Magazine*, May 25, 2017 (John Safranek, *The Myth of Liberalism*, 2015)

"Under Eden's Spell," *Homiletic & Pastoral Review*, September 27, 2017 (Joshua Mitchell, *Tocqueville in Arabia*, 2013)

"On the 'Creases in Being,'" *Catholic World Report*, November 25, 2017 (Robert Sokolowski, *Moral Action*, 2017)

"Suffering, Salvation, and the Mystery of Our Imperfect World," *Catholic World Report*, February 17, 2018 (Fr. Robert Spitzer, SJ, *The Light Shines on in the Darkness*, 2017)

"The Plain Truth: Leon Kass on Just about Everything," *Catholic World Report*, May 31, 2018 (Leon Kass, *Leading a Worthy Life*, 2017)

"Is Francis Doing What Jesus Did? On 'Going Beyond Jesus,'" *New Oxford Review*, September 2018 (Ross Douthat, *To Change the Church*, 2018)

"On the Purpose of Islam," *Catholic World Report*, October 24, 2018 (Raymond Ibrahim, *Sword and Scimitar*, 2018)

"'With the Help of the State,'" *Crisis Magazine*, November 2, 2018 (Jennifer Roback Morse, *The Sexual State*, 2018)

"What Is & What Ought to Be: On Humanism and Being Human," *New Oxford Review*, November 2018 (Rémi Brague, *The Legitimacy of the Human*, 2017).

"Social Justice, Judaism, and the Primacy of the Sacred,'" *Catholic World Report*, November 23, 2018 (David Goldman, "When Social Justice Replaces Judaism," *Torah Musings*, June 27, 2018)

Selected Bibliography

Aristotle. *Basic Works*. New York: Random House, 1941.

Boswell, James. *The Life of Johnson*. London: Oxford University Press, 1931. 2 vols.

Brague, Rémi. *On the God of Christians (And on One or Two Others)*. South Bend, Ind.: St. Augustine's Press, 2013.

————. *The Legitimacy of the Human*. South Bend, Ind.: St. Augustine's Press, 2018.

Brown, Rachel Fulton. *Mary in The Art of Prayer: The Hours of the Virgin in Medieval Christian Life and Thought*. New York: Columbia University Press, 2018.

Butterfield, Herbert. *Christianity and History*. London: Fontana, 1964.

Chaberei, Michael. *Catholicism and Evolution*. Kettering, Ohio: Angelico Press, 2012.

Chesterton, G. K. *Orthodoxy*. San Francisco: Ignatius Press, (1908) 1995.

————. *What's Wrong with the World*. San Francisco: Ignatius Press, (1910) 1994.

————. *Saint Thomas Aquinas*. San Francisco: Ignatius Press, (1923) 1986.

————. *Everlasting Man*. Garden City, N.Y.: Doubleday Image, (1925) 1955.

————. *The Fame of Blessed Thomas More*. London: Sheed and Ward, 1929.

Cicero. *Selected Works*. Harmondsworth: Penguin, 1971.

Curtright, Travis, ed. *Thomas More: Why Patron of Statesmen?* Lanham, Md.: Lexington Books, 2015.

Deane, Herbert. *The Political and Social Ideas of St. Augustine*. New York: Columbia University Press, 1966.

Douthat, Ross. *To Change a Church*. New York: Simon & Schuster, 2018.

Feser, Edward. *Scholastic Metaphysics: A Contemporary Introduction*. N.P.: Editiones Scholasticae, 2014.

Gilson, Etienne. *The Unity of Philosophical Experience*. San Francisco: Ignatius Press, (1937) 1999.

Guerra, Marc. *Christians as Political Animals*. Wilmington, Del.: ISI Books, 2010.

Horowitz, David. *The End of Time*. San Francisco: Encounter Books, 2005.

Ibrahim, Raymond. *Sword and Scimitar*. New York: Da Capo Press, 2018.

Kass, Leon. *Leading a Worthy Life*. New York: Encounter Books, 2017.

Kirwan, John. *An Avant-garde Theological Generation: The Nouvelle Théologie and the French Crisis of Modernity*. Oxford: Oxford University Press, 2018.

Lawler, Peter Augustine. *American Heresies and Higher Education*. South Bend, Ind.: St. Augustine's Press, 2016.

Little, Derya. *From Islam to Christ*. San Francisco: Ignatius Press, 2017.

Lord, Carnes. *Education and Culture in the Thought of Aristotle*. Ithaca, N.Y.: Cornell University Press, 1982.

Machiavelli, Niccolò. *The Prince*. London: Penguin, 1999.

Mahoney, Daniel. *The Other Solzhenitsyn*. South Bend, Ind.: St. Augustine's Press, 2016.

————. *The Idol of Our Age: How the Religion of Humanity Subverts Christianity*. New York: Encounter, 2018.

Manent, Pierre. *Seeing Things Politically*. Translated by Ralph C. Hancock. South Bend, Ind.: St. Augustine's Press, 2015.

————. *Beyond Radical Secularism*. South Bend, Ind.: St. Augustine's Press, 2016.

————. *La loi naturelle et les droits de l'homme*. Paris: Presses Universitaires de France, 2018.

Maritain, Jacques. *Being in the World: A Quotable Maritain Reader,* edited by Mario d'Souza and Jonathan Seiling. Notre Dame, Ind.: University of Notre Dame Press, 2016.

McCoy, Charles N. R. *The Structure of Political Thought*. New York: McGraw-Hill, 1963.

McNerney, John. *The Wealth of Persons*. Eugene, Ore.: Cascade Books, 2016.

Mitchell, Joshua. *Tocqueville in Arabia*. Chicago: University of Chicago Press, 2013.

Morse, Jennifer Roback. *The Sexual State*. Charlotte, N.C.: TAN Books, 2018.

Mueller, John. *Redeeming Economics*. Wilmington, Del.: ISI Books, 2010.

Novak, Michael, and Paul Adams. *Social Justice Isn't What You Think It Is*. New York: Encounter Books, 2015.

O'Rourke, Fran. *Aristotelian Interpretations*. Dublin: Irish Academic Press, 2017.

Orr, Susan. *Jerusalem and Athens: Reason and Revelation in the Works of Leo Strauss*. Lanham, Md.: Rowman & Littlefield, 1995.

Pieper, Josef. *Scholasticism: Personalities and Problems of Medieval Philosophy*. New York: Pantheon, 1960.

_____. *Josef Pieper: An Anthology*. San Francisco: Ignatius Press, 1989.

_____. *Living the Truth (The Reality of All Things* and *Reality and the Good)*. San Francisco: Ignatius Press, 1989.

_____. *A Guide to Thomas Aquinas*. San Francisco: Ignatius Press, 1992.

_____. *For the Love of Wisdom: Essays on the Nature of Philosophy*. San Francisco: Ignatius Press, 2006.

_____. *Leisure: The Basis of Culture*. San Francisco: Ignatius Press, 2009.

Plato. *Complete Works*. Indianapolis: Hackett, 1997.

Ratzinger, Joseph (Benedict XVI). *Introduction to Christianity*. New York: Herder and Herder, 1973.

_____. *Eschatology: Death and Eternal Life*. Washington, D.C.: The Catholic University of America Press, 1988.

_____. *Co-Workers of the Truth*. San Francisco: Ignatius Press, 1992.

_____. *Truth and Tolerance*. San Francisco: Ignatius Press, 2003.

_____. *Christianity and the Crisis of Cultures*. San Francisco: Ignatius Press, 2006.

_____. *Last Testament in His Own Words*, with Peter Seewald. London: Bloomsbury, 2016.

_____. *Faith and Politics*. San Francisco: Ignatius Press, 2018.

Ratzinger, Joseph, and Jürgen Habermas. *The Dialectics of Secularization*. San Francisco: Ignatius Press, 2006.

Redpath, Peter. *A Not-So-Elementary Christian Metaphysics*. Manitou Springs, Colo.: Socratic Press, 2012.

Reilly, Robert. *Making Gay Okay*. San Francisco: Ignatius Press, 2014.

_____. *Surprised by Beauty*. San Francisco: Ignatius Press, 2016.

Reimers, Adrian. *Hell and the Mercy of God*. Washington, D.C.: The Catholic University of America Press, 2018.

Rommen, Heinrich. *The Natural Law*. Indianapolis: Liberty Fund, 1998.

Rowland, Tracey. *Catholic Theology*. London: Bloomsbury T&T Clark, 2017.

Royal, Robert. *A Deeper Vision: The Catholic Intellectual Tradition in the Twentieth Century*. San Francisco: Ignatius Press, 2015.

Safranek, John P. *The Myth of Liberalism*. Washington, D.C.: The Catholic University of America Press, 2015.

Sayers, Dorothy. *The Lost Tools of Learning*. London: Methuen, 1948.

Schall, James V. *The Politics of Heaven and Hell: Christian Themes from Classical, Medieval, and Modern Political Philosophy*. Lanham, Md.: University Press of America, 1984.

_____. *Another Sort of Learning*. San Francisco: Ignatius Press, 1987.

_____. *Reason, Revelation, and the Foundations of Political Philosophy*. Baton Rouge: Louisiana State University Press, 1987.

_____. *At the Limits of Political Philosophy*. Washington, D.C.: The Catholic University of America Press, 1996.

_____. *Jacques Maritain: The Philosopher in the City*. Lanham, Md.: Rowman & Littlefield, 1998.

_____. *On the Unseriousness of Human Affairs*. Wilmington, Del.: ISI Books, 2001.

_____. *Roman Catholic Political Philosophy*. Lanham, Md.: Lexington Books, 2004.

_____. *The Order of Things*. San Francisco: Ignatius Press, 2007.

_____. *The Regensburg Lecture*. South Bend, Ind.: St. Augustine's Press, 2007.

_____. *The Mind That Is Catholic*. Washington, D.C.: The Catholic University of America Press, 2008.

_____. *The Modern Age*. South Bend, Ind.: St. Augustine's Press, 2011.

_____. *Reasonable Pleasures: The Strange Coherences of Catholicism*. San Francisco: Ignatius Press, 2013.

_____. *Political Philosophy and Revelation: A Catholic Reading*. Washington, D.C.: The Catholic University of America Press, 2013.

_____. *A Line Through the Human Heart: On Sinning & Being Forgiven*. Kettering, Ohio: Angelico Press, 2016.

_____. *On Islam: A Chronological Record, 202–2018*. San Francisco: Ignatius Press, 2018.

_____. *The Universe We Think In*. Washington, D.C.: The Catholic University of America Press, 2018.

Sokolowski, Robert. *Moral Action: A Phenomenological Study*. Washington, D.C.: The Catholic University of America Press, (1985) 2017.

_____. *The God of Faith and Reason*. Washington, D.C.: The Catholic University of America Press, 1995.

_____. *Christian Faith and Human Understanding*. Washington, D.C.: The Catholic University of America Press, 2006.

_____. *The Phenomenology of the Human Person*. Cambridge: Cambridge University Press, 2008.

Spaemann, Robert. *A Spaemann Reader*. Edited by D. C. Schindler and Jeanne Heffernon. Schindler. Oxford: Oxford University Press, 2015.

Spitzer, Robert. *New Cosmological Proofs for the Existence of God: Contributions of Contemporary Physics and Philosophy*. Grand Rapids, Mich.: Eerdmans, 2010.

_____. *Finding True Happiness*. San Francisco: Ignatius Press, 2015.

_____. *The Soul's Upward Yeaning*. San Francisco: Ignatius Press, 2015.

_____. *The Light That Shines in the Darkness: Transforming Suffering through Faith*. San Francisco: Ignatius Press, 2017.

Strauss, Leo. *What Is Political Philosophy? And Other Studies*. Glencoe, Ill.: Free Press, 1959.

_____. *The City and Man*. Chicago: University of Chicago Press, 1964.

Thompson, Ewa. "Disenfranchising God." *The American Thinker*, April 3, 2018.

Vaughan, Geoffrey, ed. *Leo Strauss and His Catholic Readers*. Washington, D.C.: The Catholic University of America Press, 2018.

Voegelin, Eric. *The New Science of Politics*. Chicago: University of Chicago Press, 1952.

_____. *Order and History*. 4 vols. Baton Rouge: Louisiana State University Press, 1974.

_____. *The Collected Works of Eric Voegelin*, ed. Michael Franz. Columbia: University of Missouri Press, 2000.

von Heyking, John. *The Form of Politics*. Montreal: McGill/Queens University Press, 2016.

Walsh, David. *The End of Ideology*. San Francisco: Harper's, 1990.

_____. *The Modern Philosophical Revolution*. Cambridge: Cambridge University Press, 2008.

_____. *Politics of the Person as the Politics of Being*. Notre Dame, Ind.: University of Notre Dame Press, 2015.

Weigel, George. *The End and the Beginning. Pope John Paul II*. New York: Doubleday, 2010.

Index